Exponential

Better life, better performance:
from Formula 1 to Fortune 500

JAMES HEWITT & AKI HINTSA

Exponential

Better life, better performance: From Formula 1 to Fortune 500

Authors: James Hewitt & Aki Hintsa

Graphic design and layout: Mari Huhtanen and Jyri Öhman

Published 2016

Hintsa Performance, Lapinlahdenkatu 1 C, 00180 Helsinki, Finland

ISBN-13: 978-1539538486

ISBN-10: 1539538486

Exponential

Better life, better performance:
from Formula 1 to Fortune 500

JAMES HEWITT & AKI HINTSA

Contents

Exponential is dedicated to my friend and mentor,
Aki Hintsa.

1958 - 2016

1.
THE STORY BEHIND THE STORY

Aki's office is the centrepiece of Hintsa's Geneva clinic. It's a bright, spacious room, with one wall dominated by a large window. I'm staring out at an expansive view of the office buildings, homes and beyond, to the mountainous ridge that flanks Geneva's west side.

It's my first day at work. I've recently been appointed 'Science & Development Director' for the Hintsa company. The design of Aki's office is as minimalist as my job description. It's more vision than substance at this point. A few weeks earlier, I sat in this same room for three hours telling my story, and Aki and I shared our passion for exploring science, technology and helping people improve their life and performance.

The weather outside is dreary, but my eyes are drawn to the light from an embedded wall cabinet at the end of the room, where a collection of sport memorabilia and awards shine out from under the unit's subtle, integrated lighting. A high-backed leather swivel-chair faces the cabinet, rotated away from a large white-gloss desk, featuring a distinctive curved design.

I step around the desk and take the opportunity to get a closer look behind the cabinet's spotless glass. I recognise one thing immediately: Mika Hakkinen's helmet, from his last season in Formula One. I inspect the surface; it's shiny but retains the patina that comes from being exposed to wind speeds of over 300 kilometres an hour for countless laps. I'm overtaken by a sudden and irrational desire to try it on, but I resist.

Framed certificates hang on the wall next to the desk. They detail Aki's right to practice medicine in Switzerland and his specialisms in trauma and orthopaedic surgery.

A second cabinet stands at the other end of the office. It houses an eclectic mix of items: Haile Gebrselassie's biography, Mihaly Csiksgentmihalyi's influential publication, 'Flow' complex medical texts, a picture of Aki with his family in Africa, another of him with his youngest daughter on a ski slope; a robust polycarbonate case, enclosing a rare aviator's chronograph-watch. The case is marked with a handwritten note of thanks to Aki, in white permanent-marker, and is signed by a well-known professional sportsman. I notice a trophy, in the form of an upward spiral, engraved with the words "We did it!!" from a famous F1 driver. In the centre of this diverse arrangement, two 'Kuksa', Finnish carved wooden cups, take pride of place.

I'm expecting Aki soon, and keen to avoid being caught with my nose pressed up against his carefully curated collection, I take a seat at the large table in the centre of the room.

Just in time, the door swings open. Aki greets me with a broad smile and a big "Hello." I stand to shake his hand then we sit opposite each other. He's smiling, with the same lively curiosity in his eyes that I noticed during my interview with him just a few weeks before.

Aki begins.

"What are we here for?"

Aki is relaxed. Straight to the point. Typically Finnish. I'm hoping that he'll tell me a bit more about my new role as Science and Development Director, but I guess he's looking for a more abstract response.

"To help people improve their performance?" I reply, a little sheepishly.

His face suggests it's not the right answer, but he leaves me hanging.

"To help people have a better life?" I suggest.

"Exact!" says Aki.

"It's important that you know something about me." Aki continues.

"Sometimes I will give you very clear instructions about what I want you to do. Mostly, I will just mention something. In a few weeks, I might ask you what you have found out. You may not have even realised that I was asking you to look for it. This is just the way I work, but you will learn to figure it out."

Aki smiles, picks up a marker pen, and walks to the flip chart in the corner of the room. He begins to draw a circle that looks something like a wheel. It has seven sections: physical activity, nutrition, recovery, biomechanics, mental energy, general health and core. He fills the centre with the words 'identity', 'purpose' and 'control'.

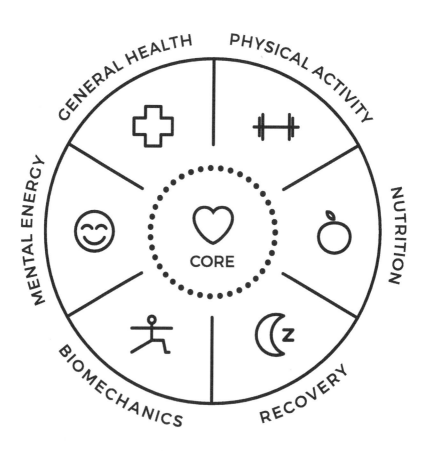

THE CIRCLE OF A BETTER LIFE

Aki explains how the elements are discrete, but interconnected, that we need to keep building our knowledge about how to improve all of them, and that every component needs to function well, for the 'wheel' to keep spinning. I scribble notes as fast as I can. He's telling me stories about the drivers he's worked with, the executives, the world-leading scientists, his framework, his thoughts about the future, the things he's not convinced by, the trends he's noticed, the ideas about what's coming next. The list of things to look into is growing by the second.

"We are scientific and evidence-based," he reminds me. "We are not a typical wellbeing company."

Aki's assistant knocks on the door. A Formula One driver is here for his pre-season check-up, so the meeting draws quickly to a close. Aki stops me briefly, as I move to leave the room. "We'll continue this conversation," he says.

During that first conversation, Aki mentioned at least 10 specialisms and areas: neuroscience and physiology, what we could learn from sport and apply to business, philosophy and psychology, science, technology and economics; and he suggested that they all had interesting perspectives, which could help us to improve people's lives.

I couldn't wait to get going. It was the start of an ongoing exchange with Aki and an exciting journey of discovery, the learning from which I'll share with you in this book. But as I scanned through my notes and actions, I paused wondering where to start. My eyes settled on the words in the centre of the scribbled circle I'd copied from the flip-chart. 'Core' and 'Identity'. "The journey," Aki had said, "starts with knowing yourself."

2.
TELL ME ABOUT YOURSELF

I drive home after my meeting with Aki. There is very little traffic, and I let my mind drift, reflecting on how I ended up here. The story we tell about our self plays a fundamental role in shaping our identity.

Six weeks earlier I was still living in London, running a coaching business. I worked with endurance athletes, mainly cyclists. Some were at the elite level; but many were busy executives, 'knowledge workers' trying to combine demanding careers with fitness and sporting ambitions.

Before I began working with athletes, I invested a number of years in pursuing my own sporting career, as a racing cyclist. As I watch the tarmac surface unfold before me, driving South, in the direction of our new home in the Rhône-Alpes, I reflect on the countless hours I spent training and racing on the roads of France.

I was with an Elite 'Espoir' cycling team, set up to develop riders under the age of 23. Scenes from those races are forever burned into my memory. Sprinting up short climbs with small groups of riders, desperately determined to keep up. With stinging legs and lungs I remember pushing the pedals as hard and as fast as I could, the desire to prove myself against my competitors, the urgent need to get results.

I'm fascinated with human performance. In particular, how the human body and mind can adapt in the face of demanding physical and mental challenges. I've often asked: "What does it take to be the best we can be?"

That was more than 10 years ago. Since then I've been helping others explore the limits of their potential.

EXPLORING HUMAN POTENTIAL

I also have an enduring passion for technology and how we can use it to explore and make ourselves better. As a child, I spent a few years living in the United States during the 'glory years' of the Space Shuttle Programme, and read everything I could about the astronauts' training and equipment: the simulators, the spacesuits and life-support systems.

I was never a particularly talented athlete, but found that if a sport had a significant technological component, I could perform better than most. I enjoyed learning how man and machine could work as a system and I also liked challenging the status quo when it came to using new equipment. This led me first to an obscure sport called 'inline speed-skating', where I represented Great Britain on a number of occasions, then to road cycling.

I started racing at a young age, but my cycling career truly began at the age of 19 when I moved to France, to train and race full time. I crossed the Channel from my home in England with a suitcase, a contract with a small regional French team and a vision of becoming a top professional rider.

AERODYNAMICS

The cyclist's greatest enemy is actually their own body. The human form has the aero-dynamic qualities of a brick, so the majority of a cyclist's effort goes into pushing this mass through our planet's thick atmosphere. Aerodynamic drag, sometimes known as wind-resistance, increases exponentially with speed. The faster you ride, the harder it

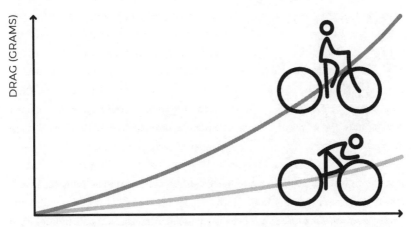

gets. Consequently, cyclists are obsessed with finding ways to reduce wind-resistance. The flip side of aerodynamic drag is that finding ways to reduce it can have an exponential impact on your performance. You can go faster, for the same effort.

There are two principle methods for reducing aerodynamic drag in cycling. The first is very objective and quantifiable: choose the design of your equipment carefully and set it up to minimise the drag created by your body. This could involve spending time in a wind tunnel, trying various equipment options and body positions until you discover the optimal combination.

FOCUS AND ATTENTION

The second method is more subjective and nuanced; it involves responding to the changing conditions around you and making decisions about where you position yourself in a race, relative to other riders.

When you begin to race, the experience is overwhelming, but in time, patterns begin to emerge. It's impossible to comprehend everything in the colourful, fast moving stream of riders, dodging bollards and weaving between buildings, but you do develop the capacity to narrow your attention and focus on what is really important.

THE PELOTON

The main group of riders in a bike race is known as the peloton. This group could represent 150 riders or more and behaves like a fluid. Riders move around each other like molecules in a stream, often only millimetres apart. The peloton's shape shifts continuously as it flows through the roads that make up the course of each race.

If you don't learn to position yourself appropriately in this stream, it doesn't matter how fit or strong you are, or how aerodynamic your bike is, you'll work significantly harder than you need to, become exhausted more quickly and struggle to respond to the changing rhythm of the race.

THE SWEET-SPOT

A low air pressure region pulls riders along. Positioned close to the front, they are also well-placed to respond to unexpected events. As the route twists and turns, you have more control over the line you take, rather than being dragged around at the end of an erratic thread of cyclists.

There is a sweet-spot towards the front of the peloton where the power required to keep up with the speed of the group is reduced by 40% or more.

Everyone wants to be in this sweet-spot, but it's a moving target. You have to work hard to get there and stay there. It requires preparation, effort and active decisions to make your way up, and to return if you slip back. It also requires experience and courage. It's a skill that develops over time and is difficult to quantify objectively. To be successful and reach their full potential, a cyclist needs to be comfortable blending these objective and subjective factors.

MOVING UP

Every season, the composition of the peloton changes. A constant stream of riders enter and leave the sport, so each year of a cyclist's career, especially in the early stages, they need to show improvement. I knew if I wanted to secure my place, I'd need to get better results, more results and move upwards to bigger and better teams.

When we stopped for espresso in the middle of long outings waiters would ask if we were 'riding the Tour?' "Not this year," I'd reply, secretly delighted by the case of mistaken identity.

That's why the move from regional to elite level cycling, when I secured a contract with an Elite Espoir team, marked a significant step up in my career. The Espoir team was associated with a professional senior team, receiving some of their bikes from the previous season. We wore the same design of shorts as the real 'pros' and our kit included their distinctive sponsor's logo.

We were promised the chance of securing a contract with the full-professional team, if we demonstrated that we deserved it. Because my new team raced internationally and provided a credible path to a professional career, it attracted a more diverse range of riders from Europe and beyond. One such rider was my Eastern European teammate. We'll call him Aleksy for the purposes of this story.

MOTORPACING

Aleksy was an older rider, but we started riding for the team at the same time. We were placed in an ex-pat team-house in the small French town we eventually called home. I lived there with another English rider and a Canadian.

Aleksy fit all the stereotypes of an athlete from the ex-Soviet Bloc. He was tall, strong, stern and introverted to the point that some riders nicknamed him 'Terminator' behind his back.

I was delighted that he was our housemate. I'd always been fascinated with the Eastern European sport systems and Aleksy was the closest I'd got to it in real life. He was the product of a dilapidated sports school – one of the few that remained – and had been nurtured in its traditions of hard work, sacrifice and the suppression of emotion. I did my best to tease the stories out of him.

When we were training out on the road, Aleksy always insisted that I ride on his right side. I wondered why, but was too shy to ask. However, one day, about two hours into a six-hour winter ride, I summoned up the courage to ask him. Aleksy began by explaining how important 'motor-pacing' was to the training of an aspiring professional rider. This practice involves riding at speed, close behind a motorized vehicle. This could be a car, other times a scooter or motorbike. The sessions are designed to simulate riding in the peloton, as you are pulled in the vehicle's slipstream, enabling you to adapt to the rhythm and gear selection associated with a fast race. Often, two cyclists ride side-by-side with their front wheels millimetres from the rear bumper to maximize the slipstream effect. If you get the chance to visit a bike race, look closely at the rear bumpers of the team cars. You will likely find a spectrum of black, vertical lines, created as the riders' front wheels rub against the surface.

In one such training session with a previous team, Aleksy had been riding next to a teammate behind their team-car, at high-speed. Suddenly, the drop-handlebars of their road bikes became locked together. Aleksy and his teammate battled to uncouple their machines but Aleksy's front wheel turned and he hit the road at over 80 km/hr. Aleksy wasn't wearing a helmet and the side of his head smashed into the tarmac. His team manager heard the shouts, tangle of tubes and glanced into his rear-view mirror just in time to see the two riders drop out of the reflected image. He screeched to a halt, jumped out of the car and ran back to the stricken riders.

Aleksy's teammate sat on the side of the road, covered in grazes and nursing his potentially broken arm. Aleksy lay unconscious, with blood trickling from one ear. His manager stabilized his head and neck, and called an ambulance. Thankfully, Aleksy regained consciousness before the ambulance arrived. Nevertheless, he was rushed to hospital and spent a couple of days under observation.

It turned out that Aleksy had fractured his skull in the crash, damaging some of the fragile bones in his inner-ear on the left side, which resulted in permanent hearing loss. That's why Aleksy always asked me to ride on his right side, so he could hear me.

Even after the accident, Aleksy still did not wear a helmet in training. He was a real hard-man. Aleksy was a robot.

MAN AS MACHINE

I had idealized the notion of man as machine in athletic performance and in life, and my robotic, un-smiling teammate epitomized this. Training continued to go well and in January we began to think about racing. Well, that's not technically true. If I'm honest, all I ever thought about was racing, training, eating and sleeping. There wasn't a life outside of cycling, but I didn't care. I loved it and, for the time being with few commitments and things going well, I felt fulfilled.

I was living with a clear sense of identity as a racing cyclist. Shaved legs, emaciated upper body and 't-shirt' tan-lines from my jersey. We actually wore these tan-lines with a sense of pride, even if they didn't do much to help us attract girls at the beach. I had a strong sense of purpose: I wanted to explore the limits of my performance potential and I was getting regular, objective feedback about my progress. I felt in control of my destiny. I was going to be a great professional cyclist and all it required was consistent hard work and patience.

USING SCIENCE AND TECHNOLOGY

Measurement has always been important in cycling. Races are won and lost based on how hard you can ride at key moments and for how long. Riders and coaches aim to define the demands of these moments as objectively as possible. They use this data to design training programmes to prepare riders to perform.

The more precise and objective you can be in your measurement, the more specific, efficiently and effectively you can prepare. You begin by measuring where you are now, describe where you need to be to achieve your aims and plan the steps needed to get there.

As a form of physical exertion, cycling is relatively easy to quantify and control. A rider's productivity can be measured by recording how hard and for how long they can push the pedals. This quantifiable nature makes cycling a popular form of exercise in research environments. Scientists can precisely control the intensity of an effort, so all participants in a study receive the same exercise 'dose' during a study. It also makes it relatively easy to see how much a subject has improved.

In the early 1980s, a German engineer called Ulrich Schoberer developed a technology that could measure the power-output of a cyclist in a zero-gravity environment. Cosmonauts needed to use exercise bikes for fitness and health during their long-stays aboard the MIR space station, and Ulrich Schoberer created a system to monitor the specific training 'dose' they were receiving and how their performance changed over time.

Schoberer realised that the technology could help many scientists, coaches and cyclists, which led to him founding a company called 'SRM' ('Schoberer Rad Messtechnik', literally translated as Schoberer bike measuring technology) in 1986.

Most power meters, including SRM, use strain gauges to measure the forces being imposed by the rider as they pedal. They can provide a deep insight into a cyclist's performance, but they didn't appear in the relatively conservative world of professional cycling, with the exception of one or two pioneers, until the early 2000s.

SRM power meters became the 'gold standard' from laboratories to the road and have been used by many of the world's best riders – and by me. I'm an early adopter of technology. I began training with a power meter not long after my arrival in France, when my forward-thinking coach purchased a system. I enjoyed the romanticism of the technology's connection with a space programme, but it was the objective simplicity of the numbers that really attracted me. I could describe the demands of my events and I knew what power numbers were required to compete as a successful professional cyclist. It reinforced my objective worldview.

It took time to learn how to make best use of the technology. I love gadgets but, if their use is not applied judiciously, they can easily distract, rather than augment performance.

My coach and I applied a logical approach to experimenting with power-based training. This was in stark contrast to the traditional approach based on 'feel' and received wisdom, which most of my teammates followed. At that time, the advice from most French riders was simply to 'ride your bike', without paying too much attention to intensity or distribution of effort.

Many of them were sceptical of my scientific methods, but I enjoyed the notoriety. It's much easier to ride in an unstructured way, spending most of your time at a moderate intensity that's neither too hard, nor too easy. It's more challenging to be proactive; planning structured training sessions, disciplining yourself to ride slow and long, even when others around you want to race up every climb; and building your tolerance to the painful, repeated high-intensity efforts that are required to develop your full aerobic capacity.

As I trained consistently, ate well, rested and recovered, I saw my power numbers increase on a curve I plotted using a simple spreadsheet. Other riders and coaches noticed my progress and methods, and I began to teach and share my findings with them in person as well as on a rudimentary website, which I set up during my free time.

However, my focus was still my own riding. Aleksy and I rode on parallel paths as we pushed ourselves to higher levels of fitness and endurance on the roads of the Midi-Pyrénées. I'd idolised Aleksy's robotic discipline, and now I was a machine too, one that could be described in watts, joules and statistical trends.

PREPARATION

In many ways, it was one of the happiest times of my life. In the off-season, each week followed a rhythm, the non-cycling highlight of which was the Wednesday night dinner with my coach and his wife. He's a hospitable character and often gathered an assorted group that could include other young riders who were based in the town, local artists or visiting friends. The dinner took place at my coach's house, a beautiful restored monastery that was inconspicuously located on a side street among a row of buildings. The house was full of exposed stone and antique furniture juxtaposed with clean and modern design.

Aleksy was coached by someone else, an older guy associated with a very successful professional team. He occasionally came to stay at our house and Aleksy spent long hours speaking to him on the phone. Aleksy first introduced him to us at one of the Wednesday night meals, when he was passing through town.

THE 'STUPS'

One Wednesday evening, early in the year before the racing season had begun, Aleksy and I had been invited to my coach's house for dinner. It was around 9:00pm, we'd finished two-courses, and had moved onto a huge tin of sugary meringues: essential recovery food from the day's training exertions, or so we told ourselves.

Unusually, there was a knock at the front door. My coach asked me to go and see who it was. I pushed my chair back from the table and stood up, but not before I grabbed a final meringue to take with me.

I walked through the hall, across the monastery's ancient stone slabs towards the front door and glanced up at the grand double-height ceiling. It was an impressive building, but like many in small, French towns it had an unassuming appearance when viewed from outside on the street. I shoved the meringue into my mouth, whole, so I had both hands free. The front door was large, wooden and very heavy, requiring two hands to open – one to hold the iron latch mechanism and the other to pull the door.

I released the latch but the door suddenly swung open seemingly of its own volition. It moved with such speed and force towards my meringue stuffed-face that I was forced to leap backwards against the wall. A tall man in a bomber jacket confronted me. I noticed he had one hand on a gun, which hung on a holster at his waist, but his most noticeable feature was his large, almost comedy-sized moustache. "Reste où tu es" he said, or something to that effect. At this point, I spoke little French, but I knew I should stay where I was. His furious eyes sent the message clearly. The whole experience was so surreal it could have been funny, except for the procession of men, all with guns, who proceeded to file past me into my coach's house. I looked back into the hallway and saw Aleksy's face poking around the corner, his eyes wide with fright. I'd never seen him look so emotional before.

Their moustached leader attached a patch to a Velcro square on his shoulder. It had a unique design. The men were from the 'Brigade de stupéfiants', commonly known as the 'Stups', France's anti-drug trafficking police.

After the procession of mean-looking agents passed by into the house, I had no intention of hanging around. I snuck out of the front door and walked in the direction of my home, as quickly as possible. I'd taken no more than 10 steps down the street when a car screeched to a stop beside me. The rear passenger-door swung open, pushed from the inside. The driver leapt out of the car, grabbed me by the scruff of the neck and practically launched my 62kg body into the backseat of the vehicle, which he promptly slammed shut. "Où vas-tu?!" He demanded to know where I was going. "Home," I replied in English. They'd clearly been watching the monastery, in case anyone decided to leave. "Take us there, then!"

The car sped off as I directed them over the bridge to the other side of our small town. The driver accelerated down our narrow street and pulled to a halt outside our three-story corner-house. All the lights were on. I could see bodies moving behind every window, but the most unusual scene was presented in the entry hall. Two of my housemates stood handcuffed together in the doorway. My irreverent English friend had a huge grin on his face and clearly found the whole scenario hilarious. My Canadian teammate was not so amused. As the driver of the car resumed his grip on the back of my neck and frog-marched me into the house, I certainly wasn't laughing either. Under his direction, I quickly climbed the stairs, but on my way caught a glimpse of our kitchen, where agents were systematically pulling items out of the fridge and throwing them to the floor. It started to make sense. They were looking for performance enhancing drugs, some of which need to be refrigerated. In France, doping in sport is a criminal offence. Someone amongst us had been taking some shortcuts, and the Stups had found out.

At the top of the stairs, the agent released his grip and demanded to know where my bedroom was. I indicated the room to the left. Two more agents, who'd followed us up the stairs, went in before me. The driver, turned interrogator, motioned with his hand for me to follow them.

Our team house was basic, but clean and well kept. I had few personal items in my bedroom, a small bedside cabinet and a single wardrobe. Naturally we decorated the bare walls with cycling posters.

My interrogating agent had a distinctly military air about him as he stepped around my bedroom, nose upturned like a sergeant inspecting the barracks.

"Where are your drugs?" he demanded imperiously.

"I don't have any!" I replied.

"We know that is a lie! We have been recording your phone calls and watching your house!"

This was news to me. It must have been a bluff. Perhaps they had some information on someone else, but there was nothing to find out about me; I was riding 'clean' as they say. Not that this seemed to matter to my agent friend; guilty by association.

He suddenly calmed.

"We can do this the easy way or the hard way." With a sigh and a Gallic shrug, he turned away.

He's been watching too many movies, I thought. Suddenly he tensed and swivelled to face me again, with theatrical flourish.

"TELL ME WHERE THE DRUGS ARE!!!" He spat the words at me.

I shrugged back at him. I didn't know what to say. My interrogator looked across at his two colleagues and made a sweeping gesture with his right hand. I watched as the agent's launched into a systematic destruction of my room. They dragged the mattress off my bed and threw it up against the wall, tore my clothes out of the wardrobe and pulled every draw out of the cabinet.

I eyed the bottom draw nervously. Earlier in the season, I had bought a few caffeine pills. I used them at the end of races for a 'boost'. I also had some vitamin tablets and amino-acid powder, to help with recovery. All of these products are perfectly legal, but they were sitting there looking guilty in their pharmaceutical-style packs.

The agent ripped out the drawer, tipped the contents to the floor and rifled through them. He quickly found the white boxes and held one up with a latex-gloved hand.

His eyes burned into me. He raised his hand and, without taking his eyes off me, jabbed his finger into a poster on the wall so forcefully, the paper nearly tore.

"YOU SEE HIM???!!!" he shouted. Ironically, the poster featured a large colour photo of Robert Sassone, a French professional rider whose team had recently been implicated in a doping scandal.

To say I was intimidated would be an understatement. This wasn't what I'd signed up for. I couldn't measure this experience with my power meter.

"It started like this for him." He seethed through clenched teeth. "A little bit of 'vitamin'..." he continued, "a little bit of CAFFEINE..." the intensity in his voice was rising, "a little BIT of RECOVERY," he spluttered, with darkly comic emphasis as he built up to his finale. "And NOW...." he roared, in preparation for his punch-line, "HE IS IN PRISON!!!!!!!"

When they were finally satisfied I was an innocent bystander, dabbling in sports supplements and nothing more, they left me to reflect on what had just happened. I needed to get out of the house. They hadn't officially arrested me, but I didn't want to give them the opportunity, so I grabbed a jacket from the floor, shut my door as quietly as I could and crept out onto the first-floor landing.

Aleksy's door was open. I saw that he was back, and his room, which was full of agents, and looked in an even worse state than mine. His mattress had been sliced open. Aleksy was sitting on the floor, in the middle of his room, surrounded by piles of clothes, boxes, his cycling kit and assorted junk. An agent stood above him, holding a small box in one hand, about the size of a pencil case, and a pre-filled syringe in the other, which he held between thumb and forefinger. Aleksy, cross-legged, elbows on his knees, was holding his head in his hands and weeping. Tears streamed down his chiselled cheeks. The Terminator was broken.

DO YOU KNOW WHAT YOU WANT?

I thought that Aleksy and I were riding parallel, but somewhere along the road, our paths separated. Small decisions, a tiny alteration in trajectory, ended up taking us to very different places.

Aleksy had put everything on the line, but for what? We thought we were immortal machines, pushing ourselves to the limit, flying down descents without helmets at 80 km/hr, but somehow he lost his way. Now his cycling dream is dead.

The 'drug raid' was the beginning of the end for my career as a rider, too, though I didn't realise it then. I continued to race for another 18 months, but at the start of my final season, my health deteriorated. I contracted a nasty case of bronchitis, following a freezing stage-race where it had rained every day and the temperature never made it above 10° C. Subsequently, I returned to training too quickly and struggled with my breathing for the rest of the year. Just as I started to recover from this setback, I crashed badly in a race and injured my knee. I couldn't ride for a month and when I returned, my biomechanics were out of balance and I continued to experience pain.

I could measure these problems objectively in my power numbers: both the deterioration in my performance, then my subsequent recovery, but something else was going on that was much more difficult to quantify.

DO YOU KNOW WHO YOU ARE?

The sporting world moves quickly. There's always something around the corner to look forward to. It's full of distractions and you need to think fast. It's a fun and energizing environment, but it doesn't encourage much reflection. However, during my month off the bike while my knee recovered, I had a lot of time to think. Much of it was spent in my favourite café in the large square that dominated the town-centre.

I realised that I'd spent a lot of time reacting. My decisions were made without much consideration. Until recently, that hadn't been a problem; I was happy with where they had taken me, but as I looked ahead, I wasn't convinced I was on the right path. I began to question myself. Do I have what it takes to reach the top of the sport? Why am I doing this? Do I still want to get there?

I reflected on how quickly the adventure could come to an end. If my entire identity was based on my job-title – elite cyclist – my life was being built on shaky ground. All it takes is an accident behind a team-car, a mistake, being positioned in the wrong place at the wrong time. As I sat in the café, sipping espresso and watching the world go by, I wasn't ready to explore the deepest layers of my Core, as Aki would call it, but I did reflect on who I was and what I really wanted.

It came to me that it was the process of training that I enjoyed much more than the racing. My curiosity and love of learning defined my character much more than my identity as a cyclist and I wondered whether there were better ways to explore my potential than by riding my bike full time.

I needed to make a choice. I could continue to spread my efforts, trying to develop my career in cycling while learning in my spare time, or I could focus on a new path altogether.

I decided that directing my time, energy and attention to improve my knowledge about human performance was both what I wanted, and what was likely to yield the most impact, with the best results. I returned to England, to continue my studies in Sports Science.

THE STUDY OF HUMAN POTENTIAL

After graduating, I continued to broaden my experience, establishing a network of relationships with experts in many specialisms in both sport and business.

You could describe Sports Science as the study of human potential. It provides a systematic approach to investigate human performance and build frameworks to enhance it, integrating a wide range of disciplines, from physiology and psychology to biomechanics and data science.

In time, I established my own coaching consultancy, developing performance programmes for sports and business people that combined a range of specialist input, applying science and technology in a logical plan, to help them achieve their goals.

I continued to run this company, but there was still so much more I wanted to learn and explore. I saw a growing need to apply digital tools to translate all the data my clients were collecting into useful information, real insight and understanding. I also had a vision for using these findings to automate and augment some parts of the performance coaching process.

However, I found myself spending increasing amounts of time administrating, rather than learning and sharing a vision for how we can enhance human performance, which is what I'm really passionate about. Again, I wanted to focus my attention where I could make the biggest impact. The job offer from Hintsa was a golden opportunity for me, and an easy decision.

LOOK BENEATH THE SURFACE

Many of my amateur sporting clients were knowledge workers in professional occupations; they handled information for a living. One of the reasons they enjoyed cycling so much was that they had a clear plan for each day, week and month, and an objective way to measure their improvement. Their sporting objectives were often in stark contrast to the reactive approach they took to their working lives.

As with my former French cycling teammates, little attention is paid to intensity or the distribution of effort in knowledge work. Similarly, both endurance athletes and business people use a lot of technology, but don't necessarily get the most out of it. Many sports and businesspeople have fallen into the trap of spreading their effort too thinly, and losing focus.

I started to wonder whether it would be possible to quantify knowledge work using principles from sport and exercise. In both sport and business, the quantitative aspects of our wellbeing and performance are important; how we use our time and energy, our physical activity, nutrition, recovery, biomechanics, mental energy and general health; but like a racer finding their optimal position in the peloton, we need to integrate the qualitative factors, too.

If we really want to enhance the quality of our lives, improve our performance and become the 'best version' of ourselves, we need to consider the whole person: body, brain and mind. I once considered this approach too 'fluffy'. However, as I expanded the breadth of my reading, interacted with experts from multiple academic fields and worked with more clients, I became convinced that we cannot ignore the more nuanced and complex aspects of the human experience.

I think there is a 'sweet-spot' in life, as well as the cycling peloton. It's a position where our sense of identity, purpose and control converge, helping us to identify what is important and what we should ignore.

It's an approach that requires us to combine objective measures with the recognition that we can't quantify everything in exact terms, and that some things must be learnt through reflection and by experience.

If we take time to look beneath the surface of what it means to be human, and focus our attention and energy where we can have the biggest impact, the results on our life and performance can be exponential.

3.
BEYOND THE POSSIBLE

"The only way to discover the limits of the possible is to go beyond them into the impossible."
Arthur C. Clarke, Science Fiction Author [1]

At our core, human beings are explorers and innovators, driven by powerful, instinctive forces. Physiologically, we are rewarded for searching out novel information. When we anticipate the experience of something new, networks and regions in our brain associated with 'reward' and memory are activated, which motivates us, and encourages recollection of these novel experiences [2].

In addition to our exploration instincts, human beings apply their cognitive skills in a way that differentiates us from all other life on the planet. We have a sophisticated and powerful capacity to choose what we pay attention to, and what we ignore, to focus our cognitive resources. This has enabled us to create and use natural languages, develop complex tools and technologies, generate mathematical and graphic symbols and form intricate social institutions.

As we have continued to explore and pool our cognitive resources, we've generated increasing amounts of data and information [3]. Around 20,000 years ago, it appears that we began to record information in physical form [4]. The Ishango Bone, discovered on the border between modern-day Uganda and Congo, features three distinctive columns of asymmetrically grouped notches. These marks represent one of humanity's first numeric systems [5, 6]. From this time on, humans developed increasingly sophisticated mathematical, graphic and symbolic techniques to record and process our increasing amounts of data and information.

This data and information is an incredible resource, as we will explore later in this chapter, but it also introduces the risk that we can become chronically distracted. One of the most important concepts in this book is 'attention'. What should we pay attention to and what should we ignore, and what are the implications of this? As you read and reflect on the content in the book, please keep these concepts in mind.

BIG DATA

A tablet computer sits next to the laptop on my desk. I'm using it to display various references and source texts to inform this book. The device is 7.5mm thick and can store 128 gigabytes of data.

Ninety percent of the data in the world has been created in the last two years [7]. In 2014, if all of our data was stored on a stack of tablet computers, it would reach two thirds of the distance to the moon. By 2020, the stack will reach from the moon and back 6.6 times. [8] Every two years from now, our digital universe will double in size [8].

2014: x 2/3

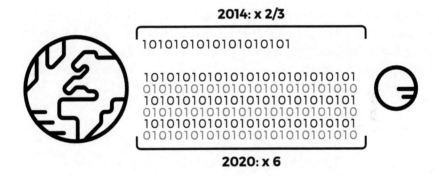

2020: x 6

PUSHING THE LIMITS OF TECHNOLOGY

The National Archaeological Museum in Athens, Greece is home to one of the wonders of the ancient world, but in 1900, when it was retrieved from an ancient shipwreck, close to the island of Antikythera, it looked like a block of corroded bronze and wood.

The artefact languished in the museum for two years until archaeologists inspected it in more detail. As they began to tease apart its components, they discovered a highly sophisticated clockwork device combining at least 30 bronze gears, elaborate mechanical timing systems and a moving model of the solar system. The device, which is known as the Antikythera mechanism, is so sophisticated, some researchers believed that it was 'planted' in the shipwreck, at a later date.

However, as the Antikythera's workings and materials were analysed, the device was dated to around 205 BC. The mechanism appears to have functioned as an analogue computer. Ancient astronomers designed its complex arrangement of cogs, gears and timing systems to replicate the patterns they observed in the solar system. It represents an unparalleled vision and technical ambition for this time period. The workings go far beyond previous understandings about what humans were capable of during that time [9].

One of the mysteries of the Antikythera mechanism concerns the reasoning behind building it in the first place. The gearing ratios in the mechanism were theoretically accurate, based on the astronomical knowledge of the day, but the concept was doomed from the start, by the manufacturing precision of the day [10]. Its design included refined solar and lunar correction mechanisms, but they were hampered by the friction and inconsistency associated with the primitive metal working of the bronze gears. It would take another 1500 years for manufacturing techniques to catch up with the vision.

BREAKTHROUGH

One of the greatest breakthroughs in information processing came in the 19th century. In 1880, after receiving his degree, a young engineer called Herman Hollerith found a job processing information from the United States census. This laborious process required Hollerith and his colleagues to arrange and sort the information from census cards.

It took around 10 years to process the census data. When the results were compiled, it was time to begin the next population count. Ahead of the 1890 census, the government launched a competition to find a way to improve the efficiency of the process.

Inspired and likely frustrated by his experience, Hollerith devised an automated electro-mechanical system to store and process the census data. The card-based machine was able to complete the task in a fraction of the time it took the humans, reducing a

10-year job to three months of work, rendering many people redundant in the process. Subsequently, Hollerith's company merged with several others to form the corporation that eventually became known as International Business Machines (IBM) [11].

Over the years, we developed increasingly sophisticated machines and created new languages, instructing them to complete increasingly complex operations.

THE RISE OF THE KNOWLEDGE WORKER

Continuing progress in computing and technology enabled humans to generate data and information in greater volumes and complexity than ever before. A new class of worker emerged as we discovered ways to create value from these new developments.

When Herman Hollerith's company changed its name to IBM in 1924, Peter Drucker was just 15 years old. He would go on to become one of the world's most highly regarded business thinkers. In 1957, Drucker wrote one of his most influential books, *Landmarks of Tomorrow* [12].

In this book, for the first time Drucker introduced his concept of the rise of "knowledge work" and imagined an era where humans would generate and demonstrate their value with brains, over brawn.

Drucker offered many prescient insights that resonate to this day. He believed that "It is information that enables knowledge workers to do their job" and suggested that the most important contribution management could make in the 21st century would be to increase the productivity of the knowledge worker [13].

Drucker foresaw that processing, access to and appropriate application of information, would be a driver of change and a key challenge in this new era.

"THE PURPOSE OF COMPUTING IS INSIGHT, NOT NUMBERS" [14]

I wonder whether Drucker imagined the breadth and depth of information we would create, and the unusual ways we would discover to take advantage of it?

Twitter, the online social networking service, or media company, depending on your perspective, boasts 313 million monthly active users [15].

The ubiquity of mobile computing and the vast amounts of personal information shared via services such as Twitter has opened some interesting and unexpected opportunities. The brief messages that characterise Twitter communication often contain personal information about emotions, thoughts and behaviours. A group of researchers decided to explore the potential embedded in this data by focussing their attention on a specific area: how language use on Twitter related to psychological states and the incidence of heart disease [15].

Between June 2009 and March 2010, Twitter made a 10% random sample of tweets available to the researchers, enabling them to capture 826 million messages.

Heart disease is the world's leading cause of death [16]. The 10 most common risk factors for heart disease include smoking, diabetes, high blood pressure, and obesity. However, it's also possible to estimate the risk of death from atherosclerotic heart disease (AHD) from a person's psychological state. Research has also demonstrated that we can infer someone's psychological state by analysing their use of language.

Based on this knowledge, do you think that it would be possible to infer psychological state from people's language use on Twitter, and use this to predict the prevalence of atherosclerotic heart disease? The researchers created a statistical model and discovered that language use on Twitter could predict deaths from AHD significantly better than a model combining the 10 most common risk factors [15].

Language patterns reflecting negative social relationships, disengagement, and negative emotions — especially anger, using words such as 'hate' and 'mad,' emerged as significant risk factors for AHD. In contrast, positive emotions and psychological engagement, expressed with words including 'our,' 'interesting' and 'thanks,' emerged as protective.

This is just one example of the insights that reside untapped, for the most part, within the huge datasets we are creating. If we focus our attention in the right place, who knows what we will find next.

IBM WATSON

IBM, the company whose ancestors revolutionised the United States' census process, have continued to develop their expertise in helping human knowledge workers make sense of overwhelming amounts of information.

The World Health Organization estimates that 13% of all deaths worldwide can be attributed to cancer [17] but the volume of research, medical records, and clinical trials associated with cancer diagnosis and treatment is vast; too much for any one clinician to keep up to date with.

IBM has developed a technology platform called 'Watson' which can reveal insights from large amounts of unstructured data. 'Watson for Oncology' analyses the meaning and context from a wide range of sources such as clinical notes, reports and publications, curated literature and rationales, 290 medical journals, over 200 textbooks and 12 million pages of text. Watson then reports back to clinicians with advice written in plain English, to help them select the most appropriate treatment pathway[18].

In January 2015, a female patient was admitted to a hospital in Japan. Initially, she was diagnosed with acute myeloid leukaemia, a blood cancer distinguished by rapid growth of abnormal white blood cells. Following a conventional chemotherapy treatment, her recovery was unusually slow. Doctors surmised that their initial diagnosis was incorrect, suspecting another form of leukaemia, but further tests proved inconclusive.

The hospital was affiliated to the University of Tokyo's Institute of Medical Science, which provided the doctors with the opportunity to access IBM's Watson for Oncology platform. Watson compared the patient's genetic data with a database of gene mutations, identifying a rare form of blood cancer. This cross-checking process would have taken a team of human scientists 2 weeks. Watson completed the process in 10 minutes.

In response to this finding, doctors altered the patient's treatment plan. Her condition quickly improved and nine months after being admitted to hospital, she was discharged. The system is not yet perfect, but it represents a significant advance, and it is a great example of how technology can augment human expertise [19].

EXPLORING OUR DIGITAL UNIVERSE

From Hollerith's automated tabulating machine onwards, computing relied on algorithms. These algorithms provided clear instructions to information processors: a specific set of rules to be followed. As data sets have grown, become more complex and interconnected, coders have built algorithms on top of algorithms. However, our data universe has become so vast, and the capacity of our computers so great, that they drastically exceed the capability of humans to program them one instruction at a time.

MACHINE LEARNING

Exploring our digital universe requires new, more independent machines. Both IBM Watson and the Twitter study I mentioned applied machine learning techniques to achieve their observational and diagnostic feats. But this technology is not isolated to a stateside technological elite.

I was working in our Helsinki office a few months ago when one of our summer interns, Joonas Myhrberg, came to speak to me about a project he'd been occupied with. Joonas is an iOS developer and he's been working on a prototype food recognition feature.

Traditionally, developers may have approached the creation of a feature such as this by coding all the necessary knowledge required to recognise foods in the form of specific, discrete algorithm-based instructions. The code required to achieve this would be incredibly complex and inherently error prone to address every possibility; there are countless types and combinations of food products, and the way the appearance of food looks can be unpredictable.

Instead of spending the rest of his life writing an algorithm for every type and variation of food item in the world, Joonas used an artificial neural network. Neural networks have been inspired by what we know of how the brain works. Large clusters of artificial 'neurons' are connected by 'axons.' A typical network may consist of 10-30 stacked layers of artificial neurons. Each image is fed into the input layer, which then talks to the next layer, which talks to the next, and so on until the output layer is reached. This final layer provides the network's 'answer' [20].

ARTIFICIAL NEURAL NETWORK

INPUT LAYER   HIDDEN LAYER   OUTPUT LAYER

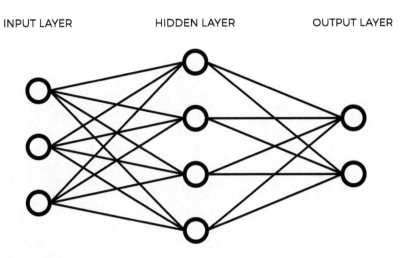

Rather than explicitly coding all the knowledge required for recognising different foods, Joonas trained the artificial neural network by 'showing it' images of food in thousands of cycles, adjusting the network parameters until it provided acceptable categorisations. As Joonas exposed the network to more images, its food recognition capability improved and the food categories became more narrow and specific.

This model is similar to the way in which some psychologists believe that the human brain learns. I have a two-year-old son, who for the moment sees every animal as a cow. However, my five-year-old son can already list at least seven different types of dinosaurs.

Our brains change in an orderly way that is consistent with our experience. However, two people's brains may not change in the same way, even if they are exposed to the same stimuli. You and I may both listen to the same piece of music, but the respective changes that occur in our brains will be built on our unique neural structures and experiences, which have developed over our individual lifetimes [20].

This variable trait is mirrored in the performance of machine-learning systems; after training, some machine learners become great problem solvers, others do not. While self-learning systems are much more capable of dealing with uncertainty, the results there may be more uncertain, too.

ARTIFICIAL INTELLIGENCE, MACHINE LEARNING & DEEP LEARNING

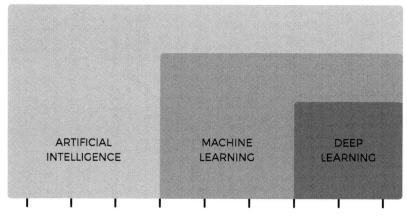

AI research has been taking place since the 1950s, but the development of significantly cheaper and faster parallel processing chips, as well as the amount of available data due to digitalization, have facilitated significant progress in recent years. Coupled with growing media coverage, this has pushed AI back into the public consciousness.

'Artificial Intelligence' is an umbrella term that is used for many concepts, but it's often spoken about interchangeably with 'machine learning', and 'deep learning' [21].

As automated and artificially intelligent systems encroach on the thinking space that has been dominated for millennia by humans, there seems to be a lot of confusion and even fear associated with them.

FEAR AND DISTRACTION

In many situations, fear is very useful. It helps to narrow our attention, focussing our physical and cognitive efforts on the information and tasks that are required to keep us alive. However, our fear of technology may be having unintended consequences.

As we will explore in more detail later in this book, fear is antithetical to the deep thinking that we need to make good decisions in the face of complex problems. To consider the best ways to apply and develop these new, powerful technologies, we need broad attention, considering multiple factors, and this will only happen if we can overcome our fear. One of the most effective ways to overcome fear is to imagine a more positive vision of the future.

Some people may criticise a Utopian vision of humans working in blissful harmony with artificially intelligent technology.

Human brains work best in a hopeful state. We will be better prepared to consider all possibilities if we reflect on what may come with hope as the starting point. Some of the systems we have created may seem scary, but perhaps that's because we just don't understand them very well, yet. We don't have all the skills we need.

While we shouldn't ignore the potential pitfalls, I contend that, if our starting point for thinking and decision-making is fearful, we will increase the likelihood that we will engineer the outcomes of which we are so afraid.

Perhaps the greatest risk is that we will pay attention to the wrong things as a consequence of our fearful and distracted mindsets. Our best opportunity to narrow our focus on what is most important is to start with a positive vision, casting the net across a wide range of possibilities.

NARROW AI VERSUS GENERAL AI

Most of the artificial intelligence we are using today relates to so-called 'narrow' or 'weak' AI technologies that can complete specific tasks. Apple's 'intelligent' digital personal assistant Siri uses a neural net system for voice recognition, for example.

Apple actually replaced Siri's 'brain' with a neural net, back in 2014, to improve its performance [22]. Other AI systems, such as IBM's Watson for Oncology platform, can already do specific jobs as well as, or even better than, humans.

Both Siri and Watson depend heavily on machine learning, which means that rather than relying on specific instructions, the machines are 'trained' and essentially learn how to complete specific tasks for themselves.

Deep learning is one of many techniques to apply machine learning in practise. 'Deep' refers to the huge number of layers, artificial neurons and the enormous amounts of data that must be fed through the system in order to train it. The food recognition feature developed by our intern was an example of this. Deep learning, combined with the huge amounts of data we are generating, promises an exciting and meaningful future of improved medical diagnoses, self-driving cars and possibilities we have yet to imagine.

Many people's fears in relation to artificial intelligence link to the idea of the 'General AI' that we've imagined in books, TV and films for generations. General AI represents a system that can replicate and even surpass the intelligence of humans in all contexts. The point of AI surpassing human intelligence is spoken about as 'The Singularity' and predicts never before seen rates of technological growth and incomprehensible changes to human civilization ranging from dystopia to Utopia, both, or somewhere in-between.

Many commentators believe that The Singularity is close. Others suggest it's an impossibility. Some think that it's likely to happen, but too far away to worry about. However, there is no doubt that technology and, specifically, artificial intelligence is having a real and growing influence. We need to think and talk about the immediate, medium and long-term implications.

It's unlikely that an all-powerful Skynet [23] will send robotic Terminators to destroy all of humanity any time soon, but research suggests that automated systems may be coming after at least 50% of our jobs in the near future [24], replacing human in entirety, or in part.

Many human jobs could be automated and replaced, but just because we can, does that mean we should? AI clearly holds the potential to significantly improve services such as healthcare; how can we distribute access to this equitably? When artificial intelligence begins to play the role of humans more frequently in everyday life, how do we embed human values in those systems, and whose values should they be?

EXTENDED INTELLIGENCE

Joi Ito, Director of the Massachusetts Institute of Technology (MIT) Media Lab, is a Hintsa client and friend. When speaking about these questions, Joi uses the term 'extended intelligence.'

> "Everybody needs to understand that how AI behaves is important. In the Media Lab we use the term extended intelligence. Because the question is, how do we build societal values into AI? [25]"

As increasingly intelligent machines work more closely with humans and even replace them in certain contexts, we encounter the tricky question of how to integrate values into our thinking and into the information processing of our machines.

A STATE OF TRANSFORMATION

Every revolution in technology has brought challenges and opportunities, requiring humans to make difficult decisions and complex judgements. We live and work as part of a wider system, but where previous transformations have impacted technology, our economy and society in a linear manner, the pervasiveness, independence and interconnectedness of the digital technologies we have created are accelerating development at an exponential rate [26].

It took over 100 years for the use of spindles – straight wooden spikes used for spinning fibres such as wool and cotton – to spread beyond Europe. The Internet extended across the globe in only seven years [27].

Peter Drucker believed that a state of rapid transformation began in the early 1990s. He suggested that the process would take somewhere between 2010 and 2020 to complete.

"Every few hundred years throughout Western history, a sharp transformation has occurred. In a matter of decades, society altogether rearranges itself — its world view, its basic values, its social and political structures, its arts, its key institutions. Fifty years later a new world exists. And the people born into that world cannot even imagine the world in which their grandparents lived and into which their own parents were born." Peter Drucker, 1992 [13]

If the process he prophesied is nearing completion, perhaps we are at the beginning of a new, exponential inflection point.

DON'T BE SCARED OR DISTRACTED

The rate of change we are experiencing may seem overwhelming, but perhaps our best course of action is to take advantage of our ability to slow down and take momentary pauses between perceptions and actions. We need to decide what we pay attention to; what information we focus on and what we ignore. It would be easy to become distracted. We could end up in paradise, or in a nightmare of our own making, but neither is a foregone conclusion and the dualism is likely a false dichotomy.

I've been reflecting on the Antikythera mechanism. The technical vision was limited by the skills they had available. Perhaps the creators and users became frustrated that they did not have all the answers. But what would have happened if they'd persevered, and refined their manufacturing skills. Where would we be today?

I can see parallels in our relationship with technology today. We certainly don't have all the skills we need to take full advantage of them, yet. But we shouldn't give up. We need to keep wrestling, move forward with care, but also with passion and vision.

WHAT QUESTIONS ARE WE ASKING?

Our cultures have equipped us for contemplation with a variety of tools for critical thinking. Questions about what it means to be human, how we perceive the world, what values we share and how we establish our goals are central to this new phase, and more pressing given its exponential progress.

What anatomical and functional systems are influencing our perceptions, decision-making and actions? Do you know who you are and what influences are moulding your perception? Do you know what you want; are you being driven by reflexes, or motivated and kept on track by a deeper sense of purpose? Are you in control of your life? Do you have systems and processes in place to help you shape your world and positively influence those around you? Are you being driven by fear or passion? By survival or purpose?

We will explore these questions, concepts and more, throughout this book.

> "Before you become too entranced with gorgeous gadgets and mesmerizing video displays, let me remind you that information is not knowledge, knowledge is not wisdom and wisdom is not foresight. Each grows out of the other, and we need them all."
> Arthur C. Clarke [28]

I believe that we are in a time of immense hope and opportunity. Throughout human history, our greatest progress has come from the pooling of our cognitive resources. We now have communication and processing tools available to address exponential potential with exponential capabilities. It's time to reconsider our existing models and metaphors, form new ones, and explore how we can apply them to improve life and performance for ourselves, and the people we lead.

LINDA LIUKAS: PROGRAMMER, TEACHER AND CHILDREN'S WRITER

When Linda Liukas talks about technology, she uses words like warm, whimsical, compassionate and full of culture: "The internet," she says "is profoundly human."

Linda sees her work as deciphering or untangling the things that people label as complicated, that distance them from technology. "Take the word algorithm, for example, it's just a step-by-step process to solving a problem."

HUMANS AND COMPUTERS WORKING TOGETHER

In teaching computers to kids, she begins by helping them understand what computers are good at compared with what humans do well. Computers love boring and repetitive tasks like factory work, they're also getting good at some professions like law and diagnostic medicine, and they never get tired and they don't need coffee breaks. But computers can't give an emotional interpretation of an artwork, even if they can make an exact copy of it.

A close relative recently passed away and Linda recalls how the nurse at the hospital comforted the family in ways that machines could never do. She advocates a future where greater recognition and higher salaries are offered to professions and jobs that require emotional commitment from people.

The future should be about combining the strengths of people and their devices. Solving what Linda calls the big hairy problems of the world, like overconsumption and climate change, will be about how humans and computers can work optimally together.

DOES SHE GET DISTRACTED?

At the time of our conversation, she's running with her smartphone through an airport in Sweden on her way to make a keynote speech. For someone who teaches children about algorithms, her own path to success has been anything but linear. Her globally successful children's book series, Hello Ruby, that teaches coding to kids, began as a side project to help Linda make sense of her own coding problems.

Now she combines a two-fold lifestyle moving back and forth from the solitary introverted world of her books to the extrovert world of teaching and public speaking.

Does she ever get distracted? She's writing and illustrating her books on a computer so she can't separate herself easily from her devices.

"I'm like a whale swimming through all this plankton in a sea of interesting information."

"My generation can at least still grasp the concept of disconnecting," she says, "if you look at the words we use – information highway, internet surfing, cyberspace, and virtual village." It's all language that implies separateness.

CHILDREN CAN'T SEE THE INTERNET OUTSIDE OF THEMSELVES

In contrast, today's children don't have this separate view. When Linda asks her students to draw a picture of the internet, they can't see it as something outside of themselves. "For them it's the hardware, but also the software, the social, the means and the culture."

But talking about today's children as digital natives is a harmful notion, reinforcing the misconception that they will naturally learn computers. "To some extent they do," says Linda, "but if your three-year-old son has mastered the iPad, you might think that's great, but it's not an education, it's not an upbringing."

She makes the analogy with language acquisition: "It's almost like saying our kids naturally learn English or Finnish because they're surrounded by the language all day." Yes they can absorb language, but that doesn't mean they really know how to use it. With language learning, parents and teachers are cognisant of the need to enrich children's understanding with grammar lessons or reading them classical literature, modern literature, poetry, and teaching them different ways to use language like irony or rhetoric. So why not with technology use?

Linda is searching for her departure gate while giving thoughtful answers to thorny questions. How do we make the most of our technologies when the very same tools that potentially enable them to create in such interesting ways are potentially the same tools that can actually corrupt the cognitive functions that underpin their creativity?

"Definitely we need to limit children's smartphone use," Linda asserts. When she's teaching, the children are stuck to their phones during every moment of downtime. "It's like an addiction." Unfortunately the grownups in the room are doing the same. "More leadership is needed in setting digital boundaries for our children, and also for ourselves."

CAN TECHNOLOGY USE BE TAUGHT IN SCHOOL?

"Children should be taught how to make the most of their devices." In fact, Linda would like to see this as part of everyday curriculum. This year, she launched her own summer camp, teaching coding to children, but they don't sit in front of screens. She designed the course to help children and their parents become more aware of how technologies should be used. "Most of my activities were unplugged."

Each day, Linda introduced fun, phenomenon-based topics, like recycling, energy use, city planning and friendship, and the children practiced computational thinking – breaking algorithms into parts but with real life context.

For example, manually sorting different kinds of trash teaches classification, and can even simulate merge sorting, bubble sorting, and inversion sorting; famous algorithms used by computers in automated recycling plants. "Children might then repeat these actions with bigger data sets in the future."

But after three days of sorting garbage, the parents started dropping hints. "All of this playtime is fun and nice but when are we going to start the coding?" The expectation is that if children are learning coding then they should be at a computer. "But this generation of kids no longer understands computers only as boxes or screens, and we need to take this into account when we educate them."

IN CODING, WE NEED TO TAP INTO
MORE TALENTS AND TYPES

Nowadays a computer can be a teddy bear or a toothbrush; a computer can seemingly react to our emotions, answer our questions and give an appearance of ordering our world for us. Linda is coming up with new ways of teaching children that's accessible and fun for all kinds of learners.

"In programming, we need to tap into more talents and types." Unfortunately, girls are underrepresented. In 2010, Linda founded Rails Girls, which has organized programming workshops for more than 10,000 women in 230 cities.

"When girls in my classes say they suck at programming, it usually turns out they're missing one semicolon in a long line of code, otherwise they're not bad at all. Finding that missing semicolon is called 'debugging' and it's an important part of programming."

Linda's advice to today's kids is "Never limit yourself in a binary way. Don't tell yourself you're one thing so you can't be another. Don't tell yourself you're good at art so you can't be good at computers." She quotes Walt Whitman, who said it well: "I am large, I contain multitudes."

4.
HIGH PERFORMANCE
BODY & BRAIN

I reached the top of the slope with burning lungs, sore knees and a dented ego, but no sooner had I celebrated my success than I lost my balance and fell to the side of the track. I was humiliated, but I welcomed the respite that came with lying spread-eagled in the snow. I tried to slow my racing heart. Cross-country skiing wasn't supposed to be like this. I stared up at the cloudless night sky, watching my rapid breaths condense into freezing clouds. An elderly lady glided gracefully beside my resting place, turned her head to offer a "Gueten Oobe" and a wry smile, before sliding from view. She'd already lapped me twice. How did they make it look so easy?

The extremes of humanity fascinate me, and world-class cross-country skiers are among the most genetically gifted and highly-trained endurance athletes on the planet. I've enjoyed studying their physiology and preparation but, having grown up in the winter sports wasteland that is England, my exposure had been limited.

We were in Davos, for the World Economic Forum, and, in my naivety, the suggestion from Juha Äkräs, my colleague at Hintsa, to go cross-country skiing had sounded like an opportunity to squeeze some exercise into our busy schedule.

In 2001, Aki became the Chief Medical Officer of the Finnish Olympic Committee, and Head of Sports Medicine at the Mehiläinen Hospital in Helsinki. Aki had vast experience across a wide range of sporting disciplines. I've enjoyed many conversations with him, where we talked about the outstanding characteristics of the multiple Olympic medallists he worked with, and about how what we could learn from world-class performers, to apply in other contexts.

WORKING FAST AND SLOW

SPRINT SYSTEM
—
FAST FOR
A SHORT TIME

ENDURANCE SYSTEM
—
RELATIVELY SLOW
FOR A LONG TIME

Our human capacity to adapt and carry out a broad range of tasks means that we're able to thrive in many climates and across varied terrain. Perhaps our greatest strength as humans, relative to some other species on the planet, is that we are 'average' at lots of things, rather than being pure specialists in one type of activity.

Our bodies can perform over a wide range of intensities and durations. We can produce a reasonable sprint performance, sufficient to escape a predator (be that an animal, or the car that is about to run us over) and our relatively long legs, foot structure and fuel stores make us well-suited for extended journeys.

The systems that supply the energy for these efforts work on a continuum relative to exercise intensity. Short, high-intensity efforts rely little on oxygen and are often called 'anaerobic'. Efforts gradually become more dependent on oxygen as duration increases and become predominantly aerobic. While these systems do not work in a binary way, it can be helpful to characterise them as a 'sprint system' and an 'endurance system' respectively, when we consider different types of physical work.

Human beings are quite good at working both fast and slow, and winter Olympic sports provide an excellent opportunity to witness extremes of performance across these domains.

BOBSLEIGH SPRINTERS

In addition to hosting the WEF's annual gathering, Switzerland is also home to the oldest bobsleigh track in the world; the St. Moritz-Celerina Olympic Bobrun, which opened on New Year's Day in 1904. The sport has come a long way since then, with today's Olympic teams populated by world-class sprinters.

The most critical part of a bobsleigh run is the first 65 metres. The crew pushes the sled from a standing start, driving their spiked shoes into the ice track to accelerate as fast as possible. Exactly 15 metres into the effort, the sled triggers a timer. The crew continues to sprint, leaping into the sled before hitting the first turn of the track. The sprint time is recorded 50 metres from the timing gate.

This short, explosive push lasts less than four seconds and is a good example of our fast anaerobic energy systems at work.

CROSS-COUNTRY SKIERS

Female Olympic cross-country skiers race up to 30km, males up to 50km, in events that require them to work close to their maximum sustainable effort for one and a half to two hours. These performances are a powerful demonstration of the human capacity to sustain high physical workloads over long durations, using our slower aerobic energy system.

MEASURING VO_2 MAX.

Sprint times over 60 metres can help us to identify the best bobsleigh crew, but a measure called VO_2 max. is used to identify the most capable endurance athletes.

VO_2 max. describes the maximum rate at which a body can take up and use oxygen during strenuous exercise, taking oxygen and fuel and turning it into physical work.

We can measure VO_2 max. by asking athletes to run at progressively faster speeds, while we monitor their breathing rates and the changing properties of the air they breathe in and out. The changing composition of the gases in the air helps us understand how the body is responding to the increasing physical workload. In the final minute of maximal exertion we can take measurements to calculate VO_2 max., which is usually expressed as a number, relative to their body mass.

In 2015, a group of researchers from Norway published a paper detailing VO_2 max. benchmarks across endurance sports in the winter Olympics [1]. In addition to technical skill (which I was clearly lacking) the study suggests that to win a medal in cross-country skiing, a male competitor requires a VO_2 max. of around 84mL/kg/min, and a female athlete 72mL/kg/min.

72
mL/kg/min

84
mL/kg/min

Most people are considered to be in good physical condition if they can achieve 50% of these VO_2 max. values; around 43mL/kg/min in men, or 34mL/kg/min in women [2].

34
mL/kg/min

43
mL/kg/min

THE ENDURANCE ATHLETE'S SUPERPOWER

Endurance athletes require a large capacity to take up and use oxygen to be competitive. A high VO_2 max. helps an elite cross-country skier to stay with the lead group or hold off chasing competitors. It means that top endurance athletes can make decisions and shape the outcome of a race, responding to rivals' attacks, solving tactical problems such as the need to quickly close the gap to a faster group.

The best way to achieve a world-class VO_2 max. is to choose your parents wisely – 25-50% of the difference in VO_2 max. among individuals is inherited [1].

CHOOSE YOUR PARENTS WISELY

Our genetic makeup represents the raw material, but we still need to train our bodies, switching on our genes to shape and mould our cardio-vascular system to its full potential. But even if we don't begin with world-class potential, we can all improve our VO_2 max. Some people may even be able to achieve improvements of up to 93% [2].

FLEXIBILITY

Another important component in a successful endurance athlete's 'arsenal' is the ability to work efficiently for long periods, but also be able to fully utilise their 'sprint system', when they need to. This could take place in the final metres of an event, when they need to produce a burst of effort for a few seconds to overtake a competitor, for example.

HOW DO ENDURANCE ATHLETES WORK?

Endurance athletes need to train their sprint system, but the majority of their training time is committed to improving their 'slow' aerobic system. Professor Stephen Seiler is a renowned researcher from the University of Agder, in Norway. He is one of the authors on the study of VO_2 max. values in winter sports, which I cited earlier, and has also spent a lot of time researching how the world's best

World-class cross-country skiers spend around 500 hours a year on sport-specific training. Professor Seiler has published extensively to help us understand how they spend this time in terms of how hard they work, for how long [4].

endurance athletes train. In particular, he has studied 'training intensity distribution,' which seeks to understand how athletes should distribute the volume and intensity of their work in the most effective and efficient way possible [3].

MEASURING PHYSICAL WORKLOAD

Determining the composition of the gas we breathe in and out provides a good indirect measure of how the body is responding to physical workload, but the test requires the athlete to wear an uncomfortable facemask, and the equipment is bulky and expensive.

However, as physical workload increases, the activity of thousands of chemical processes in the body intensifies. In addition to changes in the gas we expire, a compound called lactic acid increases in concentration in the blood. The concentration increases in a fairly predictable way, relative to workload, which means that we can measure it, to understand how hard the body is working.

During an exercise test we make a tiny pinprick, usually on the athlete's ear lobe or fingertip, take a drop of blood using a testing strip, and then analyse it using a compact machine. Some models are small enough to drop into your pocket.

LACTATE THRESHOLD TEST

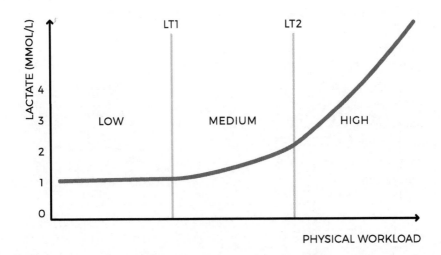

As the speed continues to increase, the subject transitions from jogging to running and eventually we'll record a sudden and sustained increase in blood lactate concentration (LT2).

The exercise test begins at the pace of an easy walk. Even at rest, some lactate is formed, so blood lactate concentration starts at around 1mMol. As the speed increases from an easy walk to jogging, we usually measure the first rise in blood lactate concentration above the baseline, known as Lactate Threshold 1 (LT1).

The physical workloads that correspond to LT1 and LT2 can be used to define three intensity zones. We can describe the three zones as three gears: low, middle and high. Even though these gears are imagined, they are a useful tool to help with planning, performance and analysis of training and racing.

HOW DO ELITE ATHLETES SPEND THEIR TRAINING TIME?

Professor Seiler's research describes how the world's best endurance athletes 'polarise' their training, spending most of their time in low gear, 10%-20% focussed on very intense work in their high gear, and very little time spent working at moderate intensities.

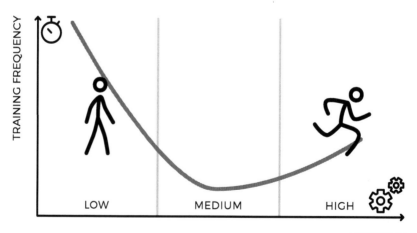

MORE WORK – SAME EFFORT

If your objective is to sustain high physical workloads for extended periods, this po-larised approach to distributing the physical work of training can be very effective. In particular, the long durations spent in low gear stimulate the body to increase the number of mitochondrial 'energy factories' in the muscle cells.

When retesting athletes, following six months of training that included large volumes of low-gear work, we often see a rightward shift in their lactate curve. This indicates that they are able to do more work for the same effort, relative to earlier periods in their training [5, 6, 7, 8].

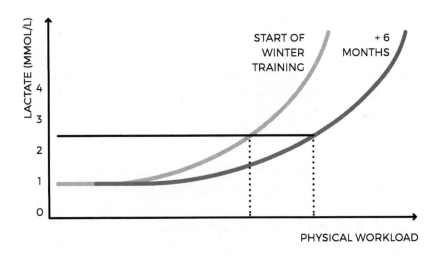

Training at high-gear intensities provides a potent stimulus to develop the athlete's cardiovascular system. In addition, the function of the mitochondria improves and their capacity to supply energy to the working muscles is enhanced [8]. As endurance athletes progress in their training, their VO_2 max. is developed to its full potential and they're able to sustain higher workloads for longer durations.

TIME IN MIDDLE GEAR IS NECESSARY, BUT LIMITED

The best endurance athletes spend some time in middle gear, but the work is limited to specific sessions, as opposed to being spread over every workout.

There are some benefits to occasional middle gear training. It can help an athlete prepare for the specific intensity of an event and individuals who have trained little in the past will benefit from almost any kind of work. However, if an endurance athlete's objective is to maximise the impact of training and reach full potential, middle-gear training does not represent an optimal stimulus for the majority of their training time.

NERVOUS SYSTEM IMPACT

Our 'autonomic' nervous system works continuously in the background, outside of our conscious control, making constant adjustments to regulate key parameters in our body within limited ranges. It features two complimentary branches: the parasympathetic system, which is dominant when we 'rest and digest,' and the sympathetic system, which leads the way when we need 'fight or flight.' In that sense, the nervous system mirrors other aspects in our body and mind; there are well-developed means to adapt to both fast and slowly occurring situations.

The response of our nervous system provides an insight into how our physical workload is impacting our nervous system, and how rapidly we recover from stress. Professor Seiler found that training in middle gear delayed the recovery of the autonomic nervous system relative to training in low gear [9].

Interestingly, the nervous system doesn't appear to take any longer to recover from training in high gear than in middle gear, even though high-gear intensities seem to be a more effective way to stimulate the body to improve. We could describe too much time spent in middle gear as 'maladaptive' and stress-inducing and the accumulated fatigue behaves like a residue, making it more difficult to make the potent high-gear efforts when the athlete needs to.

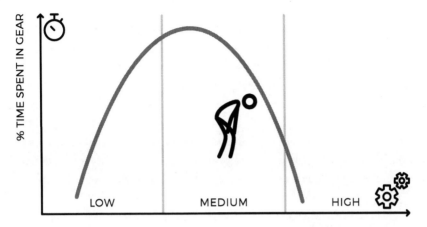

THE CONTRAST BETWEEN THE BEST AND THE REST

I've witnessed these two contrasting approaches in practise, both in my own performance as a racing cyclist and in athletes I've coached. I've also analysed thousands of files, detailing the volume and intensity of athletes' training.

Many amateur endurance athletes fall into the middle-gear trap. Their sessions are not structured, and they switch constantly between intensities: sometimes working easy, mostly moderate and very rarely at high intensity.

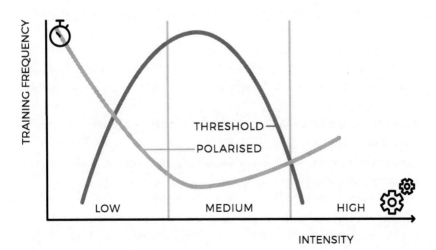

Spending the majority of your time training in middle gear has been described as a 'threshold' training model. Athletes may spend a lot of time training at this intensity, but often the work does not result in the impact they're aiming for. They get stuck. Their adaptations are compromised: they don't develop their VO_2 max. to its full potential, limiting their capacity to sustain high physical workloads for long periods.

When coaching athletes, we must take into account the individual nature of response to training. The exact distribution of volume and intensity should be tuned to the individual. However, the following observations hold true for the majority of endurance athletes:

1) The evidence is compelling that high-gear and low-gear sessions offer an excellent fatigue: adaptation ratio.

2) Planning and executing structured sessions, designed to elicit specific adaptions, is a good way to maximise the efficiency and effectiveness of your training time.

3) If you don't measure the volume and intensity of work, or your response to it, you could waste a lot of time and potentially never get close to an optimal distribution.

THE COMEBACK

Last year I had an early midlife crisis and decided to make an ill-conceived comeback to road racing. Pete and Miri McKnight, two of my colleagues at Hintsa, persuaded me to enter a semi-competitive 'Cyclo-sportive' event, held on a mountainous course not far from my home in the French Alps. I thought it could be fun, and a good way to spend some time with Pete, as he's also a keen cyclist, so we began to train together.

The problem is that I'm an 'all or nothing' character, so I created a detailed, polarised training programme for myself. Meanwhile, Pete adopted a less structured approach. On our training rides, particularly as the road began to pitch upwards, I tried to maintain discipline and ride at my self-prescribed low gear intensity. Pete is an outstanding coach, and knows all the benefits of polarised training but, unlike me, he has somehow managed to find a way to ride his own bike for fun most of the time, and he doesn't worry too much about power outputs and training load. It's obviously good to ride your bike for fun, but if you are trying to achieve a specific, demanding goal, you need to commit significant energy and time to periods of focussed effort, as well as recovery and enjoyment.

While I rode faithfully to the power numbers displayed on my handlebar mounted computer, Pete enjoyed the sensation of sprinting up steep gradients and cruising over shallow rises, switching between low, medium and high gear. Soon, the sight of Pete disappearing up the road proved too much for my ego to take. My polarised resolve cracked and I chased him down to prove my strength as a has-been endurance athlete. But these repeated efforts accumulated and I was often too fatigued to complete my high-intensity sessions later in the week. I was also over-ambitious in designing the duration of intervals in my high-gear sessions. After 10 years without racing, I wasn't accustomed to the intensity. I got stuck in middle gear, making the easy rides too hard and taking the hard rides too easily.

WHY DON'T ALL ENDURANCE ATHLETES POLARISE THEIR TRAINING?

You may be wondering why all endurance athletes do not polarise their training. I have identified three consistent themes:

1) Many athletes would like to take a polarised approach, but train with other athletes who distract them from their efforts. Like I did, they make the easy rides too hard and the hard rides too easy.

2) Some athletes struggle to build their capacity to tolerate the intense, repeated, uncomfortable efforts that characterise the high-gear intensity sessions. (The truth is that you never really get used to it, but you learn to push through).

3) Training in low gear feels too easy. Many endurance athletes have spent the majority of their time riding in highly fatiguing middle gear. As the literature describes, they notice that low-gear training is less demanding on their nervous system and they recover more quickly from it, but instead of enjoying it, they feel guilty that they are taking it 'too easy', so they speed up into middle gear again!

Endurance athletes aiming to adopt a polarised approach to their work need to choose their training partners carefully, recognise when they need to work in isolation and provide time to cultivate their capacity to maintain the high intensities required to reach their full potential.

THE COGNITIVE ATHLETE

I often reflect on the parallels between endurance athletes and the 'cognitive athlete,' otherwise known as the knowledge worker.

COGNITIVE ATHLETE	ENDURANCE ATHLETE
• Does knowledge work. • Deals with cognitive workload. • Handles & uses information with their brain. • Measure cognitive exertion.	• Does physical work. • Deals with physical workload. • Handles physical challenges with their body. • Measure physical exertion.

Knowledge workers, like endurance athletes, must sustain high cognitive workloads as they handle and process information over extended periods. My position as a former athlete and current knowledge worker has fuelled my interest in the comparison. Just as endurance athletes aim to improve their physical capacities, many of us would like to optimise and improve our cognitive capabilities.

INSIDE THE BRAIN AND MIND OF A KNOWLEDGE WORKER

To understand any kind of human performance in detail, we need to look beneath our skin. When we consider physical performance we often explore the complex interactions taking place in the organs and tissues associated with how we use energy and turn it into physical work.

Two athletes running on a treadmill at the same speed may have very different physiological responses, depending on what his happening inside their bodies. You and I could engage in the same task in our workplace, but we could experience very different cognitive loads, depending on how we approached it.

To consider the cognitive performance of knowledge workers, we can't begin with the tasks. We first need to understand more about the structures and processes of the brain and mind. Specifically, we need to explore what's happening when we handle information and engage in cognitive work.

Whenever I walked into Aki's office, I would generally find one of two sketches scrawled on his flip-chart: a circle of better life, or a brain. He often talked with clients about the brain, and Aki and I had many interesting conversations about brain anatomy and function and what they could mean for wellbeing and performance.

ANATOMICAL PERSPECTIVES ON THE BRAIN

We can describe observations about the brain in two broad categories:

1) Anatomical perspectives: these consider the complex interactions of the brain from a structural point of view.

2) Functional perspectives: these explore the human experience of the mind.

Both are useful means to understand more about knowledge work.

The anatomical perspective has provided valuable insights into what is going on in our brains. Neuroimaging technology such as near-infrared spectroscopy (NIRS) and functional and Magnetic Resonance Imaging (fMRI), allows researchers to detect changes associated with blood flow in the brain, and measure brain activity in real time. While a subject is engaged in a task it's possible to measure which brain regions are activated to understand more about how the task is processed.

This has helped researchers to understand more about the regions of the brain that are associated with different types of thinking. For example, we can see that a portion of the brain called the right inferior frontal cortex (IFC) is very important in our capacity to think more slowly and carefully, resolving reasoning problems and how, if we stop paying attention, this portion of the brain is not so effective, and we revert to fast, reflexive actions. Keep this portion of the brain in mind, as we will be exploring the subject of attention throughout this book.

SYLLOGISMS AS A COGNITIVE WORKOUT

A good way to give the brain a workout is to use a 'syllogism'. A syllogism is a kind of logical argument. For example, researchers sometimes use syllogisms to present arguments in two forms, designed to provoke two different responses. The contrasting responses can then be measured and compared using an imaging technique such as fMRI. Previous studies have presented syllogisms that contain two contrasting statements; one that the subject is likely to have a belief about, and another that they are likely to consider as neutral.

Read the following two statements.

"No reptiles are hairy; some elephants are hairy; no elephants are reptiles."

This is a belief-laden syllogism, because you are likely to have some form of pre-existing beliefs about the characteristics of reptiles and elephants.

"No codes are highly complex; some quipu are highly complex; no quipu are codes."

This second syllogism is considered to be neutral, because most readers will not recognise, and therefore not have pre-existing beliefs about quipu. If you're interested, a 'quipu' is a kind of knot that was used by ancient Andean cultures to keep records and communicate information. You never know, that may be a piece of information you can put to use, one day. Perhaps you can become an outlier in someone's brain study.

Neuroimaging technologies and research techniques are providing us with a rapidly growing body of knowledge about the structure and function of the brain, which can even extend to abstract concepts such as 'belief' [10, 11]. Measurement is an important step in learning how to optimise and improve our cognitive performance.

FUNCTIONAL PERSPECTIVES ON THE MIND

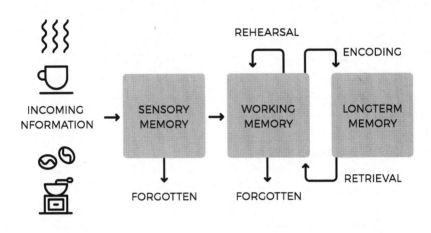

(10)

It's Friday morning and I'm writing this chapter on my laptop, in a café. The diagram helps to explain what's happening in my mind. It's based on the 'human information processing model' that can be used to describe some of the functional processes inside my head and my experiences as a knowledge worker. I'm being bombarded with sensory input: the whirring sound of the grinder, the smell of the coffee, and the murmur of conversation in the background, but I'm not really aware of it.

Think about your own context, in this moment. Can you feel the chair you are sitting on, or the object you are leaning against? Before I mentioned it, it's likely that you were not aware of the sensations of the objects pressing against your skin. Your sensory memory is selectively forgetful; it filters out most of the input, keeping only what is necessary to form an impression of the most important items. These items are then passed to your working memory. When we speak about working memory, we're most often referring to the actual holding and manipulation associated with information processing. This is one of the most important capacities for knowledge workers, where most of our conscious information processing takes place.

The information processing model describes how information is processed in our working memory by grouping it as 'chunks.' These 'chunks' are either stored somehow in the long-term memory for later retrieval or reflection, or they are forgotten. Memory is not a static store of information. It has a continuing interaction with our experiences [13].

Most people can only hold around four 'chunks' of information in their working memory at one time [12], but it's the place where the majority of our knowledge work takes place. We need to manage it carefully and be conscious about where we direct our attention in filling this limited capacity.

EXECUTIVE FUNCTION

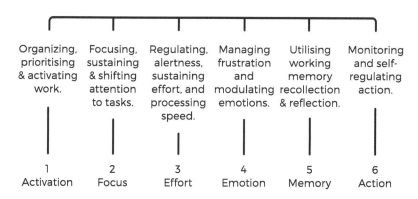

EXECUTIVE FUNCTIONS
(Work together in various combinations)

Organizing, prioritising & activating work.	Focusing, sustaining & shifting attention to tasks.	Regulating, alertness, sustaining effort, and processing speed.	Managing frustration and modulating emotions.	Utilising working memory recollection & reflection.	Monitoring and self-regulating action.
1 Activation	2 Focus	3 Effort	4 Emotion	5 Memory	6 Action

(14)

Executive function is often spoken about as an umbrella term for the supervision, coordination and control of cognitive processes. While we consider the information processing model and working memory, it's helpful to keep the concept of executive function in mind. Without executive functions, we would not be able to start, maintain or complete a task, for example.

Executive functions include evaluation, decision-making, organisation and planning, and this relates closely to our attention and goal management. These activities make up the cognitive work that knowledge workers are engaged in throughout the day as we evaluate and organise information, make decisions and plan multiple behavioural goals, but the implications reach into every aspect of our lives.

If you consider the diagram, which describes how **executive functions** work together in various combinations, you can probably imagine multiple examples of these functions being used throughout your day as you start tasks, direct your attention, resist the urge to do something else, manage your emotional responses, reflect on past experience and make countless decisions about how to act.

Executive functions and working memory share a common underlying attention component. Attention helps us to manage all of the conscious systems in our body; how and where we invest our physical and our cognitive efforts.

COGNITIVE ABILITIES

COGNITIVE ABILITIES

Our cognitive abilities can help to describe how we use our brain. Like most abilities, they have limits. One of the main roles of attention is to make sure that our cognitive resources are allocated efficiently and effectively within these boundaries [15]. To process information in our working memory in a helpful way, we need to choose what we pay attention to and what we ignore. Attention is the cognitive control process that keeps us on track and helps us to achieve our goals.

Executive function and working memory work together from when we get started on a task, to the process of focussing on what's important, keeping going when we feel like stopping, thinking about how we're feeling and the impact that we're having on those around us, reflecting on our previous experience, simulating possibilities for the future, making decisions and, finally, acting in a particular way.

Many attention and concentration processes are associated with the frontal lobes of the brain, such as the inferior frontal cortex (IFC) I mentioned before. The importance of attention to everything we do is highlighted if these regions are damaged. The injured person may struggle to ignore distractions and find it very difficult to maintain their focus and sustain attention to achieve even small behavioural and cognitive goals [16].

GOALS HAVE A TOP-DOWN INFLUENCE ON ACTIONS

'Goals' are a way to describe our internally generated plans [17]. Unlike many other organisms, our well-developed executive functions mean that we do not have to be slaves to our reflexes. We can think in the long-term, as well as short-term. My colleague, Juha, trains his hunting dog, Jade, and he's spoken about the lengthy process of teaching her to wait for instruction, rather than chase every interesting object she sees.

There is a delay between human perceptions of a situation and our actions that equips us with the potential to consider a situation in more depth than any other species on the planet. We can use the opportunity provided by this pause to make evaluations and engage our cognitive capabilities, simulating multiple future possibilities, and choosing where we focus and sustain our attention, rather than chasing the next squirrel.

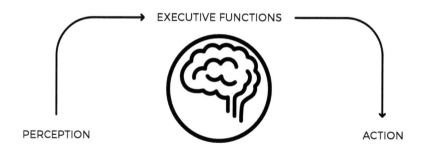

EXECUTIVE FUNCTIONS

PERCEPTION

ACTION

During the delay between perception and action we organise information, simulate what the future will be like, to imagine future possibilities [18] and create a plan for how to respond. Goal management is a form of higher-level cognition that is actually associated with physically higher regions of our brain. We can describe goal management as having a 'top-down' influence on our actions. Goal management means that we can think in the long-term, as well as the short. We can think slow and fast, depending on the requirements of the situation.

For example, reading this paragraph could be perceived as a goal. Your management process involves you first making an evaluation to set the goal, perhaps about the importance or entertainment value of these words, so you respond by continuing to focus and sustain your attention. You might decide that it's worthwhile to think slowly, and with effort, rather than darting around between the multiple screens that are likely within your field of view.

This creation of goals and allocation of your attention is a fundamental aspect of leading a life of meaning and purpose. This may sound lofty, but it's true.

BOTTOM-UP INFLUENCE

We don't always act in this way. Sometimes, there is no delay between perception and action, and we act reflexively. This is a 'bottom-up' influence, when our attention is externally driven, without a pause. These reflex actions are associated with physically lower regions, towards the bottom part of our brain.

While writing this book in a café, someone accidentally tipped a hot coffee into my lap. My attention immediately switched from my contemplative internal reflection, about what to write next, to the external work. My reflex was to withdraw from the painful stimulus.

I'm thankful that I didn't pause. I acted on instinct, driven by a powerful bottom-up influence. I did not have time to generate a plan that considered multiple factors or consequences.

However, immediately after this unfortunate event, my capacity to pause and set goals helped me to avoid being thrown out of the café. I was angry, but decided that the urge to shout and scream at the person who spilt the coffee was inappropriate, so I acted accordingly, as a good Englishman should, by apologising to him, before he apologised to me.

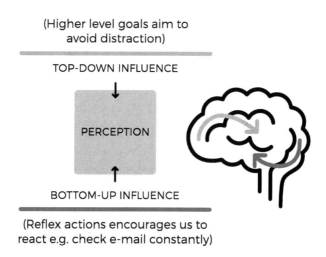

(Higher level goals aim to avoid distraction)

TOP-DOWN INFLUENCE

PERCEPTION

BOTTOM-UP INFLUENCE

(Reflex actions encourages us to react e.g. check e-mail constantly)

We have the chance to suppress some of our reflexive urges and this capacity differentiates us from animals and young humans. You may have noted that this pause takes time to develop. I've written the majority of this book wearing headphones, to block out the sound of my two sons fighting over Lego bricks. Their capacity to suppress inappropriate, violent responses is yet to mature.

GOALS SHAPE OUR PERCEPTION OF THE WORLD

Our goals influence our actions, but they also shape our perception of the world. We filter and tune the information we retain to fit the goal we have made. We use associations, reflections, expectations and emotional weightings to decide what's important – what we should focus on and what we should ignore.

Our perceptions are an interpretation that is strongly influenced by what we are aiming to achieve, rather than an entirely truthful representation of reality. For example, I sat in the café concentrating on my writing. My attention was focussed on reflecting on and translating my abstract thoughts into coherent prose. There was a powerful top-down influence on my actions. I was unaware of the conversation occurring at the table next to me. I also did not notice the customer who was walking towards me with an overloaded tray of hot coffee. This customer existed, he was even in my field of vision, but I did not perceive him until it was too late. My attention was internally driven, focussed on my memories, ignoring many of the stimuli in the environment around me until they were forced into my consciousness, bottom-up. These kinds of top-down and bottom-up processes and pressures are a continuous feature in our daily lives. Some of them are imposed; interruptions from devices, colleagues or other unexpected events, but many are a result of us failing to exert sufficient control over our choices and environment.

We are able to shift our attention from ourselves, to others and to the wider world. This capability and flexibility is also very important to help us achieve our goals, but it needs to be managed carefully.

MULTI-TASKING

Our brains are constantly processing information. Multi-tasking is actually possible, but only one of the tasks we're engaged in can be carried out automatically, with little conscious control. For example, I can eat a piece of fruit while reading back over this chapter without much difficulty.

However, if two tasks require cognitive control and demand more of my executive functions, they compete with each other for limited resources.

> *Exercise:* Try to calculate the answer to 15 x 19 in your head, while continuing to read this paragraph. Is it difficult? Is it stressful? Is it taking a long time? It's almost impossible! Your working memory and selective attention are competing for 'brain power.' You can switch between neural networks and tasks, but you cannot undertake effortful, conscious information processing in parallel. As we'll discuss in more detail later, this switching process significantly diminishes performance and can increase stress. It would be significantly quicker, and less stressful, to complete the tasks in sequence; finish reading the paragraph, then tackle the mathematical problem.

Do you consciously manage your attention to account for the limitations of cognition and focus on tasks in sequence, or interweave everything that you do?

IN TWO MINDS

It's now Friday afternoon. I went home to change my jeans after the incident with the spilt coffee and I'm now sitting at my desk at home. The shelves in my office are populated with a diverse selection of books. I've assembled a wide range of physiological texts, but my collection of books about the brain and mind has grown more rapidly in recent years. I've been interested to note the similarities and parallels between our physiological, psychological, and neurological systems.

The fast and slow systems in our bodies enable us to perform over a wide range of intensities and durations, from bobsleigh sprints to 50km cross-country ski races. Our brains are equally well equipped to respond rapidly or in a more considered, prolonged manner, depending on the demands that are made.

Humans can identify and assimilate complex stimuli in fractions of a second as they pilot a car through a street circuit at hundreds of kilometres an hour. This same brain can recall events that occurred decades before; evaluate them and form an opinion about them.

THINKING, FAST AND SLOW

In his prize winning book *Thinking, Fast and Slow*, Daniel Kahneman introduced many to the idea of 'dual-processes' in our thinking. He presented two characters to help us understand it: System 1 and System 2. System 1 is a proxy for our fast, instinctive and emotional thinking. System 2 is its slower, effortful and more deliberative counterpart [19]. System 1 may be associated with bottom-up influences on our actions; System 2 with our top-down higher-level goals and our executive functions. However, it's important to note that System 1 and System 2 characterise functions of the brain, rather than separate brain systems.

Question: What is 2+2?

It's likely that the number '4' popped into you head, without requiring much effort. Could you explain clearly how you arrived at the answer? Probably not.

We don't have much of a sense of voluntary control of System 1; it runs quickly and efficiently. System 1 maintains our model of the world, relying on what it already knows based on impressions, intuitions, intentions and feelings. System 1 assesses our present situation, delivers updates and is the main source of information for many of System 2's decisions.

System 2 spends most of its time idling in the background, continuously monitoring System 1's stream of suggestions, looking for new or missing information and helping us to form higher-level goals that guide our attention. Most of the time, System 2 uses a fraction of its capacity. Occasionally, in the pause between perception and action, System 2 modifies System 1's suggestions, if it thinks that it's necessary and providing it has the cognitive capacity to spare.

SYSTEM 1
—
INTUITIVE
FAST & AUTOMATIC

SYSTEM 2
—
EXPLICIT
SLOWER & EFFORTFUL

In the gap between perception and action, System 2 is also responsible for self-control and applying executive functions, but it tries to minimise its workload. Most of the time, System 2 approves System 1's suggestions, without making too many changes. When System 2 functions, we're more aware of the processing. Consequently, we may be able to describe and reflect on our thinking in more detail. For example:

What is 15 x 19?

You are more likely to be able to explain how you arrived at the answer, relative to the '2+2' question.

System 1's processing is more automated and implicit; System 2 is more conscious and explicit, but while System 1 has been characterised as being 'dumb', unreliable or even unsophisticated in the past, this appears to be far from the truth [20]. System 1 is vulnerable to biases and faulty assumptions, but it appears that a significant amount of complex and sophisticated forecasting and intuition is taking place. Evidence also suggests that, if we are provided with good information and sufficient relevant and meaningful experience, we can reduce System 1's errors [21, 22, 23].

Both System 1 and System 2 are critical to our optimal functioning as human beings, how we evaluate possibilities and plan of our actions, but both require some degree of deliberate effort. We need to prime System 1 with good information and a pool of experience that it can draw from to make effective, intuitive suggestions. We also need to take advantage of the gap between perception and action, to consciously consider the best course of action towards our goals, applying our executive functions.

A MISMANAGED MIND

One of the challenges in knowledge work is that our faulty beliefs about what the brain is capable of (multi-tasking for example) may be priming System 1 with poor information. Consequently, we set up System 1 for failure in decision making and evaluation. In addition, if we don't consider the possibilities, as well as the limitations of our brain, we may not use our conscious cognitive abilities (System 2) to their full potential.

In addition, our sympathetic nervous system begins to dominate in many of the stressful situations we encounter at work and home. This narrows our attentional field, as we enter a 'fight or flight' survival state, and we are more likely to allow implicit System 1 thinking to dominate. This may degrade our decision making and also compromise the complex and conscious cognition that is so fundamental to modern knowledge work.

At the same time, we may be failing to train and apply our executive functions as a consequence of our distracted habits at work and home. This means that we are more likely to pay attention to the wrong things, quickly fill our limited working memory, further increasing the stress associated with our work.

WE ARE EASILY LED ASTRAY

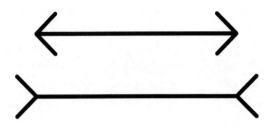

Look at the two lines. Which line is longer? It's obviously the bottom line, right? Even if you've seen this optimal illusion before, your attention is drawn to the fins at the end of each line, which distorts your perception.

The only way you can determine that they are the same length is to base your decision about what is true on more reliable information – either someone you trust telling you that the lines are the same length, or by taking a tape measure and finding out for yourself.

We face this challenge in knowledge work frequently. How do we measure the work that is taking place inside our head? Who is to say what the best way to approach it is? If we don't manage attention and working memory carefully, feeding our intuition with good information and consciously considering possible outcomes of our decisions, we may act in ways that limit our wellbeing and performance potential.

If you work in a business where long hours and little sleep are lauded as examples of what it takes to succeed, and where everyone expects e-mails to be answered within minutes, for example, you will be more likely to fall prey to the 'bandwagon effect'; the probability that we believe something increases, based on the number of people we know who hold that belief. This may make you less likely to challenge these assumptions, and more likely to miss out on the opportunity to release your 'locked potential'.

But what if higher performance is possible? What if you could maintain the same level of performance, but increase the margin in your life and experience greater wellbeing?

We have a sophisticated control system, in the form of our attention and executive function, with enough space in our working memory to consider complex problems and arrive at sophisticated solutions. Human beings have proven they are able to adapt to a wide variety of demands.

THE BODY AND MIND HAVE WELL DEVELOPED SYSTEMS FOR ALL CONDITIONS

As we consider some of the challenges and opportunities presented by our changing world, I encourage you to remind yourself that our human body and mind is equipped with well-developed systems to manage our resources in a wide variety of situations. We have fast and slow systems for managing physical energy, cognitive energy and our nervous system can respond quickly to changing demands.

MANAGING ENERGY, EFFORT AND TIME

However, these systems need preparing and training. Cognitive work is effortful and it needs directing. Where we pay attention and allocate our cognitive resources has an implication for everything we do.

When I began to transition from working with athletes to working with business people, I started pondering a series of questions: Was there a way to measure cognitive workload in a similar way that we measure physical workload? Could we assess the cost of not paying attention or switching tasks? Could we measure cognitive load in terms of volume and intensity? Would we discover parallels between patterns of knowledge work and the training patterns of athletes? Could we use our findings to help people to distribute their cognitive efforts and attention in line with what they value most and where they can have the biggest impact? How can we prime System 1 with good information and develop System 2, our executive functions and cognitive control? What happens when we work hard on a task? What is going on when we let our mind drift? How can we release more of our potential to improve wellbeing and performance, or do what we are already doing, with a little more margin?

ENERGY AND AGILITY

Previously, people have spoken about trying to achieve 'work-life balance.' Unfortunately, I think the idea that we can find a perfect balance is a myth. In the same way that the body is always working to maintain homeostasis within ranges, our lives will never be static. There is no 'neutral.' While we are alive, humans are always changing. We are always growing or decaying.

Many people express a desire to step back and disconnect from it all, but I wonder whether this craving is more an expression that we feel poorly equipped to cope with the changes around us and that we are struggling to prioritise and eliminate the unnecessary, rather than there being a real need for the world to stop. Perhaps our goal should be to become better navigators on our journey.

Rather than balance, I think we should find ways to better manage our time, our priorities, our cognitive and physical resources, so that we can invest them in what we think is important. This requires us to develop our skills of attention and flexibility, so we can consider what matters most to us, live with agility, efficiency and be effective at work and home.

THE MASTER REGULATOR

How we manage attention determines how we connect our perception of the world with what we actually do. Attention and motivation are so closely linked that you could almost see attention as a 'master regulator.' At a neurological level, evidence points to a common motivational 'node' for both mental and physical effort [24].

What we pay attention to also influences how effectively our brain prepares itself for action, our motivation and how much effort we apply to a task [25]. If we think something is important, if it offers a reward for example, humans increase attentional effort and performance [26].

Our attention helps us make 'cost-benefit' decisions, weighing the investment of effort against the potential gains. [26] We will only direct physical or mental energy towards what we think is important enough to pay attention to.

We will only be able to make good decisions about what is important, automatically and consciously, if we provide better information to prime System 1 and create improved tactics and strategies to enhance the conscious control of System 2.

We also need to manage our attention between task focus and 'task-negative' states. We need to learn to do and be. Rather than dreaming of stepping out of the 'rat-race', let's envision a future characterised by purposeful work and replenishment, meaning and adventure. We need to start a new conversation about the journey that we are on, what we think is important and worth paying attention to, what's happening behind the scenes in our body and mind, and how we can improve life and performance.

There is a lot of latent potential in our physical and cognitive systems. To release it, we need to upgrade and manage our 'control system,' but we should begin by taking a deeper look at how we are living now.

LEARNING FROM SPORT FOR BUSINESS

1) Can you see any parallels between how endurance athletes distribute their workload and how you approach knowledge work?

2) What proportion of your decisions about how to invest your time and energy are made consciously.

3) When you consider the different components of executive functioning: activation – getting started on tasks; focus – directing attention; effort – resisting the urge to stop and do something else; managing emotion; retrieving and reflecting on memories and putting a plan into action; how well do you think you are applying these at work and at home?

4) The best athletes structure their time with carefully considered distributions of work and rest. Could you apply this principle to your life and work?

5) Are you looking for work-life balance, or better tools to manage your time and energy?

MIKA HÄKKINEN: TWO-TIME FORMULA ONE WORLD CHAMPION

Mika Häkkinen looks out the window on the morning of a big race and says: "I'm so happy it's raining, this is fantastic!" Even non-enthusiasts know that rain is rarely welcome in motor sport. But this is all part of Mika's lifetime commitment to staying positive.

The two-time Formula One world champion, ranked among the greatest Formula One drivers of all time, says: "You can choose your reactions to things and you can also choose who you spend time with. I always try to surround myself with positive people."

STAYING THE COURSE

It's this proactive life view that helped Mika stay the course for seven years, competing in 100 races, before finally clinching his first Grand Prix victory in 1997. "I was close to winning many times," says Mika, "but close doesn't count."

He went on to win eight races during the 1998 season, to become world champion, then repeated his world championship success in 1999 with five more victories.

During the journey, Mika recalls constantly working with his team and trusting together that the wins would come, if not today then tomorrow. A sense of humour was also important as well as constantly keeping people motivated towards their shared goal. But at times, Mika admits it wasn't easy. "I knew I had the talent and I was putting in the hard physical training, the mental training and all kinds of exercises, but I just wasn't winning. Seven years was a bloody long time for losing!"

LEARNING HOW TO LOSE WELL

It was these times when Mika would go back to his lessons of childhood. For example, he credits his parents with not only teaching him how to win, but also how to lose. "Losing is always disappointing but throwing tantrums never works." As a child,

Mika's father would send him into the forest to kick some trees then come back calm. "It's so important to learn how to control your mind and your body," Mika asserts, "because after a failure, if you put your emotions in charge then your judgement of that failure will never be clear."

Mika's analysis of his losses during the years up to his first victory showed that 90% were linked to some kind of mechanical failure. This knowledge helped him refuel his self-belief and remind himself that "Hey, if the car breaks down Mika, it's not your fault!"

As we speak, Mika is driving through the streets of Monaco, having just dropped his daughter at school. The conversation moves to an early career success in 1993, when Mika famously out-qualified Ayrton Senna for a pole position.

FACING OFF AGAINST AYRTON SENNA

As a relatively new guy on the circuit, how did he mentally prepare himself to face off against a three-time world champion? Mika recalls having felt very focused in the lead up to the race and confident of what he and the car could do. As he walked to the car, he remembers concentrating his energy inward: "I was this young Finnish guy, who didn't want to make any noise or attract attention. Just go out there and do my job."

In this case, the job was to secure pole. But the rational side of Mika's brain was telling him that beating Ayrton Senna was an unrealistic goal and couldn't be done. He would have to find a way to trick himself out of this mental conundrum.

"It sounds weird but I got around this by only making space in my brain for one goal then shutting out everything else. I knew I couldn't beat Ayrton Senna, so instead I concentrated my attention only on winning the pole position."

Mika knew his car and its capabilities so well that he was able to take every corner to the ultimate limit and win. And the other result, "I was quicker than Ayrton Senna, the three times world champion."

HOW DID HE FIND THE CONFIDENCE TO CARRY THIS OFF?

Mika believes his self-confidence developed over time. He wasn't born with it, although, he admits to having always had a strong competitive drive.

"Since I was very young, I've always told myself I want to win; I need to win!"

As a boy, Mika competed in diverse sports, including ice-hockey, karting, cross-country skiing and downhill skiing. "I've put on a crash helmet more times in my life than some people have put on shoes," he laughs.

Mika wanted to win in every sport he took on, but wasn't always capable. Sometimes the other guys were stronger, bigger or faster. But when Mika got into motor racing, he suddenly understood he now had a tool that he could build around himself, and together they could reach an ultimate level.

FEELING THE FEAR THEN RATIONALISING IT

Mika became publicly known as a fearless driver. But he does admit to sometimes feeling scared. "But still I wanted to win so the only solution was to stop thinking and put my foot down flat."

In motor racing, Mika explains that drivers rationalise their feelings of fear by calculating risk. The process is surprisingly analytical. He remembers a grand prix early in his career when the risk became too high. During a massive rainfall, he was driving down the long and infamous Brabham straight in Adelaide. "I was approaching 300 and visibility was zero. I had to guess the distance to the turn, which meant keeping my steering straight and counting up to the turn." It was at this point, Mika began telling himself he had to slow down. If there was something on the track or he missed the turn, he really could die.

"It wasn't so much that I was giving in to the fear," Mika explains, "but more that my calculation of the risk of serious accident had just outweighed my need to win."

CONTINUING HIS CAREER OFF THE TRACK

In his life after retirement, in 2002, Mika now has a number of business and mentoring projects in play. He's preparing to leave tomorrow on a three-week business trip to Asia. But today, after this call, he's planning an 80km cycle ride.

"I do it because it's so good for me and it's wonderful!"

Mika's ability to stay faithful to his goals has continued from his career on the track into the present. Right now he is analysing and scripting himself in advance of his trip; preparing the way for positive outcomes.

"I know it will be a long journey, it will be hard," he says "I need to prepare myself mentally and physically. But when I come back with a big smiling face, I want to say, yes, I did it and everything was perfect!"

5.
HUMAN INTELLIGENCE

How do you measure cognitive work? How can you ensure that you direct your mental efforts to maximise efficiency and effectiveness? This chapter is divided into 3 parts, where we'll explore these questions in more detail.

Part 1: How do you measure cognitive work?
Part 2: What does a day in the life of an average knowledge worker look like?
Part 3: Why attention is the key to realising our potential.

PART 1: HOW DO YOU MEASURE COGNITIVE WORK?

In 1965, Daniel Kahneman, who I introduced in the previous chapter, was on sabbatical leave at the University of Michigan. During this time he observed a group of volunteers carrying out cognitive tasks under hypnosis. (It was the 60s, after all!) The original experiments were designed to explore the influence of emotional states on participants' abilities to complete the tasks, but Kahneman made an unexpected discovery.

THE EYES ARE THE WINDOW TO THE SOUL

Volunteers in the study were asked to remember a series of digits then recite them back to an observer. As they recited, an image of the volunteer's eye was filmed. Ostensibly to amuse passersby and increase the visibility of the department, the researchers projected a live image of each volunteer's eye onto a wall in the corridor.

While watching the projection one day, Kahneman noticed that the volunteer's pupils dilated progressively as they listened to the series of numbers, and tried to remember them. Conversely, their pupils contracted as they unloaded their memory and recited the numbers back to the research assistant. He also noted that there was a relationship between the difficulty of the task and the degree of dilation; the more difficult the tasks, the larger the pupil dilation, and vice versa [1]. This observation led to the discovery that pupillary responses reveal the relationship between a cognitive task and the amount of working memory that is required to complete it. Kahneman's discovery can be used as a reliable indirect measure of the mental effort associated with a task, in a similar way that expired gases can help us to understand a body's response to increased physical exertion in a VO_2 max. test.

COGNITIVE LOAD

Athletes use various measures, such as heart rate and power, to manage and monitor their physical work. It helps them to pace their efforts and maximise performance. Applying knowledge and using our skills is effortful, but we rarely consider the intensity and distribution of cognitive work through the day. Measuring cognitive work, in terms of cognitive load, and considering how we 'pace' knowledge work in terms of effort and recovery, can help us to understand and improve this distribution.

There are multiple definitions of cognitive load depending on whether you are coming from the perspective of cognitive psychology, instructional design, or neurobiology, but the most commonly used definition describes cognitive load as the amount of working memory that is required to carry out a cognitive task [2, 3].

MISSION TO MARS

Many knowledge workers would like to upgrade their cognitive performance, perhaps to differentiate themselves from their peers, or simply to make their workloads more manageable and improve the quality of their life. But, if you're a knowledge worker flying through space at 27 km/second, on a collision course with Mars, your cognitive performance may have more pressing consequences [4].

On November 4th, 2011, a team of six astronauts emerged from a five-module isolation facility, following a simulated mission to Mars. The 'Mars500' mission was a psychosocial experiment to prepare for a future manned spaceflight to the Red Planet. The volunteers lived and worked for 520 days in a mock-up spacecraft, situated at the Institute of Biomedical Problems (IBMP) in Moscow, Russia. The experiment was designed to study the effects of long-term close-quarters isolation [5].

The five modules consisted of a living area, utility module, medical centre, main spacecraft, Martian-lander and simulated Martian surface. The combined volume of the facility was 550 m^3; not much larger than an average two-story home.

MARTIAN SURFACE SIMULATOR   UTILITY MODULE   MEDICAL MODULE

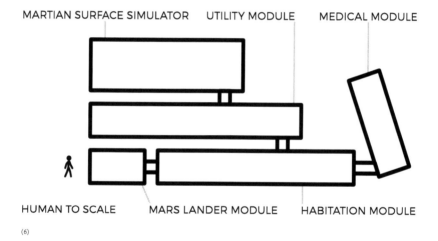

HUMAN TO SCALE   MARS LANDER MODULE   HABITATION MODULE

(6)

In space flight, impaired cognitive performance can have devastating consequences. Researchers were interested in how the subject's cognitive performance could be negatively affected by emotional responses to events and the conditions of their extreme working environment during a mission [7]. Specifically, they wanted to measure the cognitive demands of mission tasks and how performance was impacted by emotions, task complexity, speed at which they performed the work and the number of times they switched tasks.

It would not be practical to measure pupil dilation throughout the entire mission – the equipment is too bulky. They instead used a model based on the Cognitive Task Load (CTL) approach. The researchers used this model to create a subjective, yet reliable, method for assessing the interaction between cognitive load, performance and emotion.

In a great example of scientific understatement, researchers concluded that isolating yourself with five other people for 520 days on a simulated Mars mission "inflicts unique stressors such as social isolation, incidents and boredom" [7]. They also noted that long-term missions should consider cognitive task load and emotional state in task scheduling.

MEASURING COGNITIVE WORK IN KNOWLEDGE WORKERS

My working days often feel like a long-term mission. I've often wondered if I'm applying my cognitive efforts in the most efficient and effective way. Many of us would benefit from considering cognitive task load and emotional states in our work; where are we applying our best effort, where is it wasted and how can we restore it?

Aki and I often talked about how we could measure 'Mental Energy' – the energy we have to manage our life and environment. As I was looking around for a solution, I came across the CTL method used in the Mars500 mission.

CTL provides a simple and portable way to indirectly measure how hard our brain is working. We can use it as a simple heuristic device, to help us assess the cognitive load associated with our tasks and try to optimise our mental performance.

THE CTL TOOL

We use our cognitive abilities to carry out cognitive work. These abilities include our executive functions, such as decision-making, organisation and planning and our cognitive control, including our attention, working memory and goal management. The CTL tool summarises how we apply and distribute these capabilities, and how this impacts our cognitive workload, using three dimensions:

Dimension 1) Time pressure:
The amount of time we spend working on an activity, relative to the time available, influences cognitive load. If we feel that we are under time pressure, resulting in us focussing attention and working without pauses, cognitive load increases.

Dimension 2) Switching:
During an activity, switching between tasks increases cognitive load. The more we switch, the more the cognitive load increases.

Dimension 3) Complexity:
Activities that require effortful thinking, rather than relying on automated or routine knowledge, increase cognitive load. The more complex the task, the higher the cognitive load.

DEFINING THE COGNITIVE LOAD OF AN ACTIVITY

Each dimension in the CTL method features a question to help you assess the cognitive load of a task. For example, imagine that you have a 10-minute break and decide to use your smartphone. You're not under too much time pressure; however, you begin your smartphone session by browsing through your e-mail, then switch to Twitter. You see a link you are interested in, so you click on it, which opens your browser. You read the first paragraph on the page, but get bored, so you open Facebook: you're switching tasks, a lot. Finally, consider complexity. The interface feels intuitive, which may trick you into thinking that complexity is low, but you are actually making a number of fast and conscious decisions: reading text, deciding on search terms, thinking about what to look for next.

We rarely consider our cognitive load and, as a result, we can miss opportunities to produce great work in periods of focussed attention, and also compromise our recovery by engaging in relatively demanding tasks, when we could be resting.

Consider a typical hour at work and answer the questions.

CONSIDERING YOUR CTL

Question 1) Time pressure:
How much of the available time are you focused on your work? Have you allocated enough time for specific tasks?

Question 2) Switches:
How often are you switching from one process to the other?

Question 3) Complexity:
How complex, or routine, are the tasks that you're engaged in?

COGNITIVE GEARS

The three dimensions accumulate to give us a sense of the overall cognitive load for an activity, or given time-period. You can think about this cumulative load in the context of three ranges, which represent three 'cognitive gears.'

LOW	MEDIUM	HIGH
RELAXED, UNFOCUSSED CREATIVITY, INTERACTION & RESTORATION.	HIGH ENVIRONMENTAL ATTENTION & SWITCHING	UNBROKEN CONCENTRATION & FOCUSSED ATTENTION

Low-gear tasks
Relaxation and recovery (low complexity, low switching)
E.g. Unfocussed creativity, relaxed interaction & restoration.

Medium-gear tasks
Routine and quick tasks (medium complexity, higher switching)
E.g High environmental attention & switching

High-gear tasks
Focused and demanding tasks (high complexity, low switching)
E.g. Unbroken concentration & focussed attention.

These three gears provide us with a useful heuristic device. We can use them as a quick and simple way to plan and reflect on how we are allocating our cognitive resources, and distributing cognitive work through the day. One of the starkest findings, when I tried this method on myself, as well as with clients, was how widely we distribute our attention. We rarely focus and we are often interrupted.

PART 2: WHAT DOES A DAY IN THE LIFE OF AN AVERAGE KNOWLEDGE WORKER LOOK LIKE?

Scott works as a middle manager for a large firm in a major city. His weekdays follow a similar routine. Scott wakes at 6:30am. Like 79% of smartphone owners, he's looked at his device within 15 minutes of waking [8]. He then spends 30 minutes on 'household activities' and is among the 42% of people who admit to using e-mail in the bathroom [9]. Scott makes himself breakfast and spends a further 30 minutes scanning

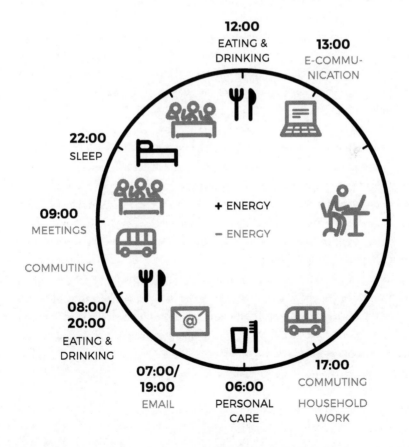

12:00
EATING &
DRINKING

13:00
E-COMMU-
NICATION

22:00
SLEEP

+ ENERGY

− ENERGY

09:00
MEETINGS

COMMUTING

08:00/
20:00
EATING &
DRINKING

07:00/
19:00
EMAIL

06:00
PERSONAL
CARE

17:00
COMMUTING
HOUSEHOLD
WORK

his phone and checking e-mail while sipping coffee. On average, we spread six hours of e-mail use over each day, so it's important that Scott starts early [9].

At 8am, Scott gets in his car and drives to work. He listens to some relaxing music and daydreams on the way; he is not among the 18% of workers who admit to checking their e-mail whilst driving [9].

Scott arrives at work. The first three hours of the day are spent in meetings – the average time for someone in middle management. During meetings, he switches between checking his smartphone and replying to e-mails, while pretending to write meeting notes on his laptop (92% of workers admit to multi-tasking during meetings [10]). Scott goes for a short walk at lunch to get some food from a local café. He is disciplined and doesn't check his smartphone during this time.

Scott's afternoon is spent interweaving tasks, mainly phone calls, e-mails, instant messages and social media (Scott is amongst the 40% of workers who admit to using the internet and social media during the workday [11]). Mixed into this digital concoction are the other distractions of the office: gossip, snack breaks and noisy co-workers.

Scott leaves the office at 5:30pm and drives home. He does a few jobs around the house, has an evening meal then enjoys three hours of leisure time. This is likely to be made up of a combination of TV, internet and on-demand entertainment. As we know, this does not represent true cognitive down time. As 70% of people do, he checks his e-mail whilst watching TV [9] and responds to a few 'urgent' work-related messages. He spends most of his time switching constantly between the TV, his smartphone and his tablet computer [12].

After checking his phone for the final time (he has already checked it 149 times today [13]), he tries to fall asleep, but the blue light from his phone has suppressed his melatonin production by 22% [14], so it takes him longer than it should. He finally falls asleep, exhausted.

LOOK BACK AT SCOTT'S DAY:

- How much of the available time did he focus on his work?

- How often did he switch from one task to another?

- How complex were his tasks?

- What was the overall distribution of his cognitive load?

HOW DID SCOTT SPEND HIS TIME?

Does this distribution look familiar? It's very similar to the inefficient 'threshold' model of endurance training I described earlier. Like most of the knowledge workers we speak to, Scott spends the majority of his day stuck in cognitive middle-gear, in a state of constant partial attention. Very little time was spent in low gear, and a fraction was invested in focused and intense high gear. What are the consequences of this way of working?

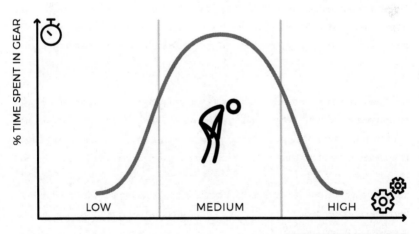

PAYING ATTENTION

Our management of attention determines which cognitive gear we are in, and how we distribute and apply our cognitive resources. It can be the difference between sitting on the start-line spinning our wheels, or surging into the lead.

Whether you are an athlete or businessperson, you need to consider how you are distributing your cognitive load. In particular, how you are using your executive functions and what you are paying attention to.

Many of us spend our days managing competing tasks and obligations, trying to stay clear of the barriers while working at the limits of our potential. Do you find it difficult to accelerate to high gear when you really need to focus on a task?

Do you have trouble relaxing and switching off when you get the opportunity for some downtime? How many times have you pushed a little too hard and spun off into oblivion, finding yourself staring blankly at your computer screen?

We interweave our tasks continuously. We spread six hours of e-mail activity over the day. Between the first glance in the morning and the final check at night, we look at our phones 150 times. Most of us switch between tasks without noticing, taking small bites from the technological buffet as we move among our inbox, social-media feed, internal messaging systems and smartphone [9, 11, 15, 16, 17].

Our workplace environments can make us feel productive and efficient. We get a lot of things done. But are we making our lives more difficult than they need to be? Is our rest and recovery being compromised? Are we on the right track to maximise our impact and the unique value we can bring, or are we driving fast but getting nowhere?

The challenge that we all face, but that's particularly evident in knowledge workers, is that our cognitive control resources are finite; attention, working memory and goal management must be applied carefully to maximise our wellbeing and performance.

PART 3: WHY ATTENTION IS THE KEY

In motorsport, attention is everything. Attention is a skill that we can all develop, but some drivers stand out more than most.

> "I suddenly realized that I was no longer driving conscious, and I was in a different dimension for me [sic]. The circuit for me was a tunnel which I was just going, going, going, and I realized I was well beyond my conscious understanding." Ayrton Senna describes a qualifying lap of the Circuit de Monaco [18]

There's perhaps no better example of attentional control, and the fast handling and manipulation of information, than a driver racing on the Circuit de Monaco. Each year, for one weekend in May, the Principality of Monaco hosts one of the most glamorous and prestigious rounds of the Formula One circus. It takes organisers six weeks of work to thread the circuit between buildings and through tunnels, and three weeks of disassembly to untangle it. The 19 turns, over 3.337km, are considered by many to be the ultimate test of driving skill.

> The onboard camera sits to the right hand side of Ayrton Senna's gold and green striped helmet. We pick up the footage somewhere into his qualifying lap. Senna's McLaren-Honda accelerates, the buildings, boats and people stream by, at the edge of our field of vision. The camera vibrates as the engine howls its way to maximum rotational speed before each change of gear.

Senna still holds the record for the most victories in Monaco, including five consecutive wins between 1989 and 1993. "His concentration on one lap was just… uncanny," says Jo Ramirez in 2013, a former McLaren team member [19].

In 1988, Ayrton Senna took pole position in Monaco, qualifying 1.4 seconds ahead of his nearest competitor – a huge margin in a sport measured in fractions of time. Senna led the race from the start and offered a virtuoso performance ahead of the chaos and drama that ensnared those behind him.

> Senna is in another world, driving at the boundaries of possibility, choosing his line with masterful control, hugging the barriers as he places the car with

millimetre precision. He accelerates to over 250 km/hr, the g-force pushes him into the leather-clad bucket seat before the tires squeal and his head is forced forward as he takes the Fairmont hairpin at less than 50 km/hr.

Senna maintains a gap of around 50 seconds to his teammate, Alain Prost – a breath-taking lead. All he has to do is bring the car home. With 11 laps remaining, Senna receives an instruction to slow down to ensure a safe 1-2 finish, but the Brazilian champion is mesmerized. Perhaps he's in 'flow state,' but his meditation is rudely interrupted.

Some say he lost concentration, but whatever the case, Senna spun into the barrier at Portier on the 65th lap; the car irreparably damaged, he retired from the race.

THE COGNITIVE DECK IS STACKED AGAINST US

Even the best of us make mistakes. We are not robots. We are human. Attention is an essential capacity for everyone. It determines where we direct our cognitive resources and ensures the efficiency and effectiveness of our work, in line with our goals; what we think is most important. But attention is a limited resource; if we don't direct our attention in the most appropriate way, we may end up on the wrong track, or in the barriers.

Humans are hardwired explorers. Regions of our mid-brain associated with dopamine and reward processing activate when we're shown images we've never seen before. In addition, activity in the area of the brain known as the hippocampus enhances the encoding of novel images in our memory [20].

This means that we anticipate feeling good when we find new information and that novelty enhances the memory of those experiences. These powerful motivations to keep humans probing and searching worked very well throughout history, as we've explored our planet and beyond.

A WORLD WHERE NOVELTY BECOMES THE NORM

Until relatively recently, the physical limitations of movement and communication limited the speed and quantity of the information we encountered and discovered.

Today, our world overwhelms us with novel stimuli. Our devices provide instant access to a multiverse of content, which creates intense competition for our attention.

This morning I sat down at my computer and opened my laptop. E-mail notifications began to pop up, begging to be noticed and encouraging a reflex bottom-up influenced action. My brain's System 1 suggested that I look at my many unread messages. They promised entry into an exciting world of novelty and reward and my brain was already anticipating the dopamine hit I'd receive. System 1 didn't worry too much about distraction, or limited attention. I'd been awake for 30 minutes, and the race to grab my attention was already underway.

DRIVEN BY SURVIVAL AND REPRODUCTION

Human beings are social. For most of our history, we've lived in tribal societies where keeping on the right side of each other has been fundamental to our survival and reproduction. Our social systems are built on the sharing of information, morality, trading and the pooling of cognitive and physical resources [21]. For most of human history, ignoring messages from our fellow humans would have, in many cases, been profoundly unhelpful in the context of survival and reproduction. However, technology has provided us with the opportunity to contact almost anyone, anywhere on the planet, at any time, and even at the same time (if your accidentally select 'reply all'). In addition, the apparent importance of these messages is often artificially inflated, using sophisticated techniques to harvest our attention.

The only way to manage our attention and energy is to consciously ignore some of these messages, even if our implicit judgements suggest that they are important or even urgent. This requires some 'retraining'.

ONLY 24 HOURS IN A DAY

There are only 24 hours in each day. Our continuous search for information has an opportunity cost associated with it. Our capacity to pay attention and process information is limited, so we need to be selective.

We often react to the bottom-up influence of digital notifications without considering that we do have a choice about how to respond. If I notice an e-mail in my inbox, I can use the gap between perceiving a notification and acting on it to engage System 2, apply selective attention and focus my cognitive resources, so that my higher-level goals can have a top-down influence on my actions and keep me on track. But this is a habit that needs to be nurtured; many of us need to relearn how to inhibit our instinctive responses to notifications.

In the same way that my two young sons are training their capability to inhibit reflexes while they play with Lego bricks, we can retrain our attention, and develop our capability to apply our executive function in the gap between perception and response.

When coffee was spilt all over me, while I was writing the last chapter, I reacted instantly to the hot stimuli. However, as I've got older, and my brain has matured, I've become better at inhibiting some of my reflex actions. I was angry that the customer had been clumsy, but I did not hit him.

The problem is, while many of us grew up being told that hitting our siblings or friends was not helpful or appropriate, not many people have learnt how to use e-mail effectively. Resisting the urge to check our e-mail is an effortful self-control process. It doesn't come naturally. We need to inhibit our reflex response. This provides System 2 with an opportunity to create a higher-level goal, and for our attention to focus on what we really want to achieve in the 24 hours we have each day.

SELECTIVE ATTENTION FOCUSES AND IGNORES

If we don't focus on something, this does not mean that we are ignoring it. Focussing and ignoring are not two sides of the same coin [22], they are both active selective processes. What we choose to pay attention to influences our perceptions – what we think the world looks like – as well as our actions – how we respond.

It's not enough to simply say that we will ignore our e-mail notifications; we need to make an active decision to shift our perception of the world, either by modifying our thinking, or adapting our environment.

If our attention is applied optimally, it helps us focus on what's most important and ignore what's not. But selection is just one part of our attention mix. When we're considering how attention influences cognition and how to approach knowledge work tasks optimally, it's helpful to consider all of these elements. We need to go back to the basics of attention, because we have fallen into the trap of believing that we are sophisticated power users of technology who can bend the systems to our will in pursuit of ultimate productivity.

Our technology can be powerful and effective, but it is a double-edged sword. We need to learn to wield it carefully, with great skill, which many of us have not been doing.

We have ancient brains and we've not yet figured out how to make best use of them with the tools we have created.

THE BATTLE FOR OUR ATTENTION

Writing this book has been a constant battle between higher-level goals and the bottom-up pressure from reflexes that reflect my brain's hunt for novelty and desire to stay in touch with my 'tribe'. I've had to ignore some messages, avoid meetings and phone calls in pursuit of my target, but the reflexive part of my brain worries about upsetting people. At some basic level, my brain wants to reply to the messages, so I don't get thrown out.

The top-down pressure of deadlines means that I know that I should focus my attention on writing, and avoid the vortex of e-mail reading, replies and social-media checks, but embedding new patterns of behaviour takes effort and 'training'. On a very practical level, it also means that we need to set expectations clearly with our clients and colleagues, to provide the opportunity for this training to take place!

I have repeatedly checked my notifications over the years and built an association between opening messages and the transient but still pleasurable emotion of discovering something new or interesting. It feels so much easier to respond to my reflex and click the mail icon within 15 minutes of waking up in the morning, as opposed to resisting the urge and applying my effortful attention to important work. However, I know that if I don't resist, I risk falling into the middle gear of cognitive work for most of the day, where I will be busy but reactive. I will limit the value and meaningful work I can produce, and increase my stress.

AVOID DISTRIBUTING ATTENTION
BY PRIMING YOURSELF

Take a moment to reflect on how you approach an average day. How often does checking your phone first thing in the morning work out well for you? When we distribute our attention by switching tasks regularly and permitting frequent interruptions, our performance declines. However, we can increase the likelihood that we will stay focussed on our priorities by priming our attention. This increases the likelihood that we will engage System 2 and use the gap between perception and action, to make a good start and stay on track.

We need to draw on our previous experience to prime our brains and plan our days proactively. Fortunately, we have an inbuilt system to help us achieve this [22].

Some of my friends are 'paleo' enthusiasts and they often remind me that, for the majority of human history, we've roamed the open plains hunting animals and gathering food. Ironically, they will often follow up this message by directing me to a helpful paleo-themed website.

The evidence is clear that our brains are very well adapted to this kind of world, providing we train them appropriately. I've never gone hunting before, but I have friends who enjoy it, and they've shared some of their experiences with me.

Hunters train their ability to pay attention to important cues in their environment. They prime their attention with the memory of past experiences, about hunts they've been on before and animals they've managed to track down. They think about the times that they moved too quickly and scared off their quarry. They prepare themselves with the memory of tracks they've identified in the past and simulate possible scenarios to help them capture their prey. Hunters pool their cognitive abilities, working together as a team to increase their chances of success. They also use tools with great skill, such as trained dogs, to improve the efficiency and effectiveness of the process. This makes it more likely that they'll be successful and achieve their goals.

The same principles and cognitive abilities can be applied to knowledge work. What are you trying to achieve in your day? What has your previous experience taught you about where you need to focus your attention? How can you distribute work more effectively across your team? Are you using the right tools, at the right time? How often has sprinting through the digital forest worked out well for you?

By preparing your attention with the memories of previous experience, good and bad, you'll increase the likelihood that you will ignore the next Twitter notification and keep devouring this book, rather than thinly distributing your attention across a digital smörgåsbord. In later chapters, we'll explore some specific tactics to apply priming in practise.

SUSTAINABILITY

How can we sustain attention over the course of a typical eight-hour workday? Many studies have explored the limits of sustained attention in the context of vigilance, but this research is often based on being alert and watchful while carrying out a repetitive task [23].

There's a limit to the amount of time we can maintain attention, particularly if our work is boring.

These studies may be relevant to some knowledge workers, but a more pressing challenge relates to how we can sustain attention associated with more complex, non-routine tasks, over the course of a typical eight-hour workday.

Research and experience suggests that breaking our days into shorter working sessions, with more precise goals, appears to be a more effective way to allocate attention. It's better to work in high cognitive gear for a short period, than in middle gear for a longer amount of time.

This is a view supported by Anders Ericsson, widely regarded as a world-leader in the study of expertise and skill acquisition [24]. In practise, we need to gradually increase our capacity to tolerate high-gear cognitive work, in the same way that an endurance athlete increases the percentage of time they can spend doing demanding workouts at high intensity.

The best performers appear to focus for between 60-90 minutes before taking a short break. Whatever our approach, our aim should be to prime our attention by reminding ourselves what we are really trying to achieve; create clear goals for our time; and try to incrementally increase the total time that we spend in periods of sustained attention from week to week.

REASONS TO KEEP GOING AND REASONS TO STOP

The challenge to sustained attention often comes from the pressure imposed by our reasons to keep going and our reasons to stop. When the novelty of information degrades as we become familiar with it, the bottom-up pressure to search for something new begins to exert itself. If the top-down higher level goals of producing meaningful work, or enhancing our capacity to tolerate high levels of cognitive exertion, are not strong enough, we are much more likely to switch tasks and focus our attention elsewhere.

When I started writing this book, I enjoyed the novelty, but as the project has progressed, it's become more routine and I've been more aware of distracting temptations. If we don't feel enough pressure from above, we are less able to ignore the irrelevant stimuli in our environment.

I've sometimes wondered, whether the instruction Senna received to slow down in the final laps of the 1988 Monaco Grand Prix might have diminished the top-down pressure that was maintaining his focus? Could that have played a role in his apparent moment of distraction on the 65th lap? We'll never know for sure, but it's clear that many knowledge workers would benefit from creating meaningful higher-level goals that would form a cognitive insulation from some of the distractions around them.

If you are working on a task, but cannot perceive the value, do you find it easy to concentrate? It's unlikely. You'll be looking for any opportunity to do something more interesting. In contrast, if you believe in what you're doing and have a clear goal in mind, you may not even be aware of the phone ringing or the people trying to speak to you.

We'll explore our deeper motivations in more detail later. If you can find a sustained source of meaning and purpose in your work, like Senna on his famous qualifying lap, it's as if you're in a tunnel that just keeps going, going, going...

SPEED

There is a limit to how fast our brains can work. Cognitive work requires a network of brain regions to work together. The transfer of these signals takes time. In the context of attention, when we focus on something new, it takes time to disengage from the previous item and focus on the next one.

For example, using a mobile phone during driving is incredibly dangerous, as the car is not under our control while we switch attention from the road ahead to our phone and back again. Driving and using a phone requires too much conscious processing to take place simultaneously, and there is a delay when we switch. During this delay, the car moves a long way. At work, our constant switching means that we unnecessarily increase the time it takes to complete tasks.

Even if we don't consciously choose to switch our attention between tasks, if something interrupts us, such as a notification, we can't help but direct some of our attention to it. Then it takes time to resist the urge to respond and reallocate our attention to the original task. This phenomenon makes a strong case for turning off notifications when we are trying to concentrate, or rest.

Many of us feel that we don't have enough time to do everything we want to do. Some of this is a reality imposed by our multiple responsibilities, but we could liberate a significant amount of time by reducing switching and distractions in our environment.

DISTRACTION IS INEVITABLE

Some distraction is simply part of life. A study in 2012 set out to explore the tempting distractions that we feel throughout the average work day [25]. The researchers gathered 7,827 samples from 205 adults and found, perhaps unsurprisingly, that we battle with sensations of desire and temptation for most of the time we are at work. The most common temptations reported by the study group included:

1) Eating

2) Sleeping

3) Sex

4) Taking a break from hard work

5) Watching TV

6) Checking e-mail

7) Using social-media

8) Surfing the internet

THE INTERNET IS DELICIOUS

The final three temptations in the list are particularly potent. The internet is a delicious source of novelty for our dopamine-hungry brains. In many cases, digital experiences are explicitly designed to exploit this.

There's a formula for building products that nurture dependent relationships and a cycle that reinforces our relationship with them. Nir Eyal described this increasingly complicated relationship with technology as a four-step cycle [26].

1) **Trigger:** A notification on the home screen of my smartphone alerts me that someone has liked one of my Instagram photos.

2) **Action:** Anticipating the reward associated with clicking on this notification, I open the app.

3) **Variable reward:** I scroll through the feed and find suggestions for content that I have not come across before. The unpredictability of what may be displayed enhances my feelings of pleasure and positive emotion [27].

4) **Investment:** I decide to upload a picture I took recently. I spend some time and effort editing and filtering the image until I'm satisfied with my 'virtual asset'. This investment makes me more likely to enter the cycle in the future.

ROLLING THE DIGITAL DICE

The cycle repeats, initially driven by external cues in the form of notifications, but eventually these aren't required. My motivation is internal, as the feedback loop between the action and the sensation of reward and pleasure is reinforced.

This cycle could equally be applied in professional contexts. Take our use of e-mail, for example. I receive a notification, I anticipate the novelty reward associated with new information and so I open my inbox. I never quite know what to expect in there but, anticipating the brief good feeling, my brain is willing to take the chance. Once I get inside, I invest time and energy writing new messages and saving old ones that I think may be important in the future.

There's a reason why 79% of people check their smartphones within 15 minutes of waking, then on average 150 times during the day [8, 13]. Our smartphones are a portal to rewarding experiences.

It's like gambling. I may not find something good in my inbox, but because I sometimes do, and because of the fact that I can't predict this pattern, the feelings of pleasure and positive emotion associated with the e-mail process are actually enhanced. I also experience a powerful urge to attend to the needs of my 'tribe,' and avoid the unpleasant experience of disappointing someone who is trying to contact me, regardless of how that may compromise the higher-level goals I am trying to reach.

We often approach our workdays like amateur endurance athletes.

1) We don't plan our sessions: we simply head out the door and hope for the best.

2) We easily get caught in low-value, moderate load middle-gear work as a result of constant distraction and switching.

3) Most of us have never measured the volume or intensity of our work, so it's difficult to know whether we are anywhere near to an optimal distribution.

ATTENTION MATRIX

We've developed a simple tool at Hintsa, called the 'Attention Matrix,' to help people consider how they are distributing their attention, and therefore their cognitive load, throughout each day. I've included one below, populated with some typical tasks.

The attention matrix often highlights how much of our time we spend in different states of mind, and how consciously we allocate our cognitive resources and pay attention to proactive planning, relative to reacting and shifting our attention to whatever is happening around us. The matrix is a continuum, but it's also helpful to demarcate some sections, to make it easier to provide examples.

COGNITIVE GEAR	REACTIVE	PROACTIVE
HIGH	TACTICAL PROBLEM SOLVING CRISIS MANAGEMENT	COMPLEX & IMPORTANT STRATEGIC & LONG-TERM
MEDIUM	ADMINISTRATION E-MAIL PHONE CALLS	
LOW	LIGHT CONVER- SATION WITH A FRIEND	READING A BOOK
ZERO	NAPS	NIGHT-TIME SLEEP

Many knowledge workers find that they are biased towards reactive activities in high and medium cognitive gear, as highlighted in the table. You may be wondering why the box for 'medium gear – proactive' tasks is left blank. This is to highlight a point. How often do you proactively plan time to spend under modest amount of time pressure, switching fairly regularly between tasks of moderate complexity? We rarely plan to work like this, but it's how we spend the majority of our day.

RUSHING THROUGH THE DIGITAL FOREST

Our attention must be selective because it's limited, but we have not trained our brains to cope with our modern environment. Competition for our cognitive resources is greater than ever before and the novelty our brains crave is overflowing from the technology that surrounds us. We have unprecedented opportunity to apply our powerful, but sometimes misplaced, tribal survival instincts. We haven't really figured out how to use our tools, yet.

Too much of our time is spent on digital devices, consuming content that creates little value. We're rushing through the digital forest, switching this way and that, and we're unlikely to catch anything important.

MIND THE GAP

1)   How much of your day are you spending in each cognitive gear? Experiment with the CTL model to quantify the distribution of cognitive load during a typical morning.

2)   Our management of attention determines how we distribute and apply our cognitive load. Are you aware of how you distribute cognitive load through the day?

3)   Are you using the gap between perception and action to direct your attention towards what is most important, or making dopamine driven unconscious decisions?

4)   Can you relate to the concepts of novelty and survival influencing your attention and decision making?

5)   Consider dividing your workday into shorter working sessions, with more precise goals. It's better to work in high cognitive gear for a short period than in middle gear for a longer amount of time.

JYRKI TÖRNWALL: FACE-TRANSPLANT SURGEON AND CELLIST

Jyrki Törnwall began his career as a cellist, studying at Helsinki's prestigious Sibelius Academy, before giving it away to move into medicine. Yet, even now as a world-leading oral and maxillofacial surgeon, music is still very present in his life.

MICRO SURGERY LIKE MUSIC

"The surgeries themselves follow their own rhythms and intensities, like music, but pumped along by a lot of adrenalin," says Jyrki. He also identifies different styles of music to go with different types of surgery. Jazz is a good fit for more routine surgeries. He recently listened to Miles Davis while removing a neck tumour. "But for microsurgery never jazz, it's always classical."

Classical music for Jyrki fits the precision of putting together arteries, only 2 to 4mm in diameter, using thread one-tenth the thickness of a human hair. He usually needs to make 8 to 10 stitches about 3mm long for every artery. "Nerve cells are easier," Jyrki explains, "but veins can be the toughest because the walls are like jelly." He began by practicing on rats and mice. "Gradually you learn and learn."

Jyrki's 15 years of cello-playing and high-level recitals not only taught his brain and hands to work well in concert together. But he believes they also helped him prepare for the intense focus that microsurgery requires, particularly in dividing attention from precise actions of manipulating each note to the performance as a whole.

According to Jyrki, operations also have their adagios and andantes. "There are some parts I know I can move through quite quickly but then for certain things like tissue manipulation I need to slow down again." But like all great performances, surgery can be intoxicating. "Without the big picture I could easily just get lost in what I'm doing."

PLANNING AND MENTAL REHEARSAL

How does he prepare for such intensity? Jyrki is again able to make the comparison with musical recitals and surgery. Both have very long lead times and require quiet and careful planning. Jyrki and his team have to plan each surgery meticulously in advance. "We don't just go in and open someone up then see what to do."

With surgery, there is no cello in a case to practice on either, so Jyrki has trained himself to perform carefully orchestrated mental rehearsals either the previous evening, or the morning before every operation. A face-plant surgery has 83 checkpoints and Jyrki goes through each, simulating and working through them with his mind. Of course things don't always go the way of rehearsal.
"It doesn't work like in movies," Jyrki says.

He recently, opened someone up to discover that a tumour had grown extensively during the waiting period. In this case, he had to make a snap change of plan. "That's why you always the need a plan B, C, and a D and then, most importantly, you need a very clear exit plan for if things go wrong."

LETTING THE GUT GUIDE YOU

As a seasoned surgeon, who's performed close to 1000 microsurgeries, Jyrki also has the benefit of his experience to fall back on, meaning that he's learned to combine precision planning with the occasional need to follow his gut. "It's a blend between conscious and unconscious control," says Jyrki, who can recount times in his blood vessel work when a gut feeling had told him something was wrong even though everything in front of him looked right. Times when he didn't act on this intuition, always brought post-operative problems.

SUSTAINING CONCENTRATION AND DEALING WITH STRESS

One face transplant surgery takes a whole 24 hours, and the working time around it is even longer. How can one human being perform optimally for such a long period? Along the way, the nurses change every six to eight hours, but the surgeons have to keep going. "You can't just put down your scalpel and say now I'll take a six hour break," laughs Jyrki.

His first experience with the stress that comes from this kind of prolonged concentration surprised him and taught him a good personal lesson. "I've always thought of myself as a very easy-going guy but on this occasion I had to fight against starting to shout and throw things."

The nurses weren't concentrating 100%, talking about boyfriends and girlfriends and holiday trips and then one of them took more than 10 seconds to find an instrument he needed. Jyrki remembers being enraged to an extent that perplexed him. "Before then, I'd never found it that difficult to control my temper. I always want to be kind to my team around me."

What Jyrki later understood is that circuits in his brain responsible for attention span had actually been competing with others related emotional control in order to help him through the long and difficult task. "Becoming aware of this helped," he says, "and I've been able to build up my abilities to deal with it over time."

RECOVERY AND RESTORATION

What about recovery? When it comes to taking care of the body, doctors traditionally don't follow their own advice, and Jyrki admits he could still do better. Towards the end of his first face-transplant surgery, when he saw with elation that it was actually working, he recalls suddenly being hit by a wave of tiredness that he likened to physical pain. "Even though, I hadn't hurt myself I was feeling pain over my whole body."

In retrospect, Jyrki says "We should've chosen a better diet." The team survived on coffee, coke and sushi for the whole 24 hours. They also didn't plan their breaks very well, "Instead of just sitting and talking, we should've slept."

Jyrki is on call now for another face-transplant operation and it's time to wrap up the conversation.

6.

ATTENTION PARADOX

Robots are an attractive option for many employers. They don't need to go to the gym. They rarely get sick. They don't need sleep and never turn up to work drunk. They make reliable, fast and predictable decisions and they don't get distracted by Instagram.

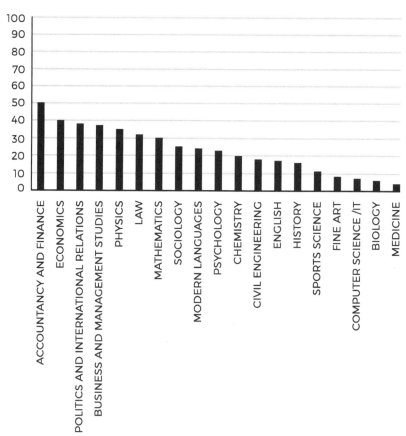

(33)

Scientists at the University of Oxford published a research paper evaluating the likelihood of various human professions being replaced by automation. They used a machine learning based statistical technique to classify 702 occupations, estimating that 47% of human jobs were at risk [33]. Jobs with higher wages, that required greater educational attainment, were generally more secure, but not across the board.

But if two companies have equally capable robots and automated systems, perhaps even purchased from the same vendor, where do they find their competitive advantage? Sustainable human high performance becomes the principle differentiator. Knowledge workers need to find ways to set themselves apart.

We'll consider three trends, and 10 challenges, as we explore these questions.

1) *Trend 1 – Automation.*
What can be automated will be. What cannot, will become increasingly valuable. As more capable machines take over many of the tasks previously assigned to humans, the knowledge workers of tomorrow will be differentiated by their capacity to engage in complex work that is difficult to emulate artificially.

2) *Trend 2 – Augmentation.*
We will either stand out for our exceptional ability to work with machines and/or produce rare insights that set us apart, but the same technology that facilitates our work may also be responsible for harvesting our attention in unhelpful ways.

3) *Trend 3 – Agility.*
We're going to be working for a long time, and the world will continue to change. We need to care for our bodies and minds in a proactive and thoughtful way so that we can adapt, continue to learn new skills and maintain our wellbeing and performance at a high level, for as long as possible.

CHALLENGE 1:
OUR WORKING MEMORY IS LIMITED

Our working memory connects our perception of the world and our actions. Much of our valuable knowledge work takes place in our working memory. For some knowledge workers this could require them to solve complex mathematical problems. For others it may involve crafting a diplomatic response to an important but frustrating client, or even something as simple as considering whether to read your e-mail now, or later. Regardless of the context, if a task requires deliberative and effortful thinking, we will draw on the resources of our working memory.

As we explored earlier, our working memory can only store around 4 'chunks' of information at one time [1]. This figure varies according to the type of information we are processing. For example, whether it's short or long words, letters or numbers, makes a difference [2]. The capacity of our working memory varies among individuals, but every human's capacity has a limit, and knowledge workers bump up against this, throughout the day.

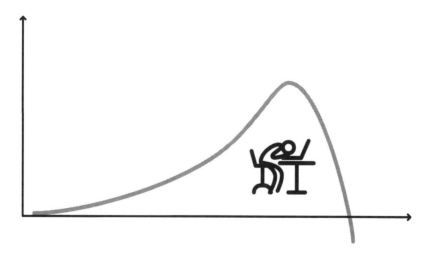

If we tracked our eyes throughout the day, we would see continuous waves of dilation and contraction in our pupillary response, as our cognitive load progressively increased then diminished. If we were looking carefully, we would also see the exact moment we gave up on a task. When our working memory is defeated, our pupils constrict rapidly.

In addition to the number of 'chunks' of information we can store in our working memory, the quality of the information we hold, known as 'fidelity' is also finite. If we're distracted or interrupted, the quality degrades. Imagine you are sitting at your desk, thinking about a difficult problem, and a colleague begins to speak to you. You will feel the sensation of the information in your mind becoming messy and blurred with the interference.

Competitive interactions are taking place continuously in your working memory, but are you consciously managing this competition? Are you unnecessarily increasing the demands on your working memory by trying to do everything at once: speaking on the phone, while you check your e-mail and order something from Amazon?

We rarely apply any filters to the items that are vying for space in our head. We need to manage our working memory proactively, using our selective attention to fill it with the right things, at the right time, to optimise wellbeing and performance.

CHALLENGE 2: SWITCHING TASKS MAKES OUR WORK HARDER

If we choose to pursue more than one higher-level behavioural goal during a given time period, there is a cost. Much of this cost is associated with network switching. We can pursue multiple behavioural goals, but if two of our goals require cognitive control, as opposed to relying on reflex actions, they compete for the limited resources in a region of the brain called the prefrontal cortex.

Most of what we call multi-tasking is actually the prefrontal cortex acting like a policeman, directing traffic at a busy intersection, switching between the various neural networks required for the flow of processes associated with each task. Switching tasks increases cognitive load. Combining two effortful tasks is harder than completing them separately.

Over the course of writing this book, I've enjoyed a number of deep conversations, many of them over a good cup of tea. When in the midst of an intense debate, I've noted how long it takes to make a cup of tea, due to the switching cost as I move between speaking, listening, considering my response and trying to find the tea bags.

SMOMBIES

Have you ever walked down the street while trying to send a text message or e-mail? I'm not sure why I bother. It would be so much more effective and efficient to simply stop by the side of the road, or wait until my destination, but I insist on switching between the process of navigating through the oncoming stream of pedestrians and typing my critical communiqué.

During our workdays, we often make our work harder than it needs to be by trying to interweave simple tasks, rather than working on them sequentially.

When I found out that people like me are called 'Smombies' (smartphone users who stagger around their urban environments like zombies) I resolved never to use my device this way again. A municipality just outside of Munich, called Augsburg, has

gone as far as to install a ground level light system at tram crossings, to alert the digitally engrossed living dead to the impending peril of fast-moving public transport [3].

We've become inseparable from our smartphones, and this may be associated with some strange phenomena.

> Have you ever felt the sensation that your phone was vibrating in your pocket, only to discover that you imagined it? You are not alone. The perception is significant enough that a systematic review of the literature on the subject was published in 2015 [6].

While the exact causes merit further investigation, the phenomenon speaks to our increasingly complex relationship with technology.

COGNITIVE CONTROL IN MEDIA MULTI-TASKERS

I used to believe that multi-tasking worked well for me. It's a view that I've encountered frequently in others. I also liked the idea that multi-tasking regularly should improve my ability to manage my competitive cognitive environment, but this does not appear to be the case.

Parents of teenagers often ask me whether young people are immune from the negative effects of switching between tasks. They certainly appear to be very comfortable moving between activities and devices, but the evidence suggests that there is still a significant cost associated with this behaviour [4].

Studies demonstrate that heavy media multi-taskers, those of us who switch frequently and quickly among multiple sources of information, actually erode our capacity to ignore irrelevant information in our environment and memory. We make it harder for ourselves to filter out interference and, as a result, perform worse on tests of task-switching ability [4].

SWITCHING TASKS
MAKES IT HARDER TO CHANGE GEARS

Switching tasks regularly increases cognitive load, often unnecessarily if we have the option to complete tasks sequentially. It may also distract us from completing more meaningful work, but there is a more subtle, longer lasting impact. When we switch tasks frequently, it also makes it harder to switch cognitive gears.

When we move to a new task, some of our attention stays 'stuck' to the previous task. It takes time to withdraw our attention from one thing and return to our primary task. This 'attentional residue' results in wasted time when we re-engage with the primary task and slows our acceleration into cognitive high gear.

CHALLENGE 3: WE DO NOT PREPARE FOR INTERRUPTION

Unless we can find a way to isolate ourselves for an extended period, interruption is inevitable, but there are techniques to reduce the time it takes to recover and get back on track. When I was working on this chapter earlier today, I forgot to turn off my e-mail notifications. On a number of occasions I was alerted to a new e-mail in my inbox. The e-mail notification was an interruption of sorts; it made a sound and appeared in my field of vision. However, I can take advantage of the delay between my perception of the alert and my next action.

When we're interrupted, the temptation is to allow our attention to be drawn to our emotions, perhaps the annoyance we feel, but we can use the opportunity to remind ourselves of our higher-level goals and make a conscious decision about how we will respond to the interruption at a later time. Research suggests that these deliberate thoughts encode a higher-level goal in our brains, which our cognitive control processes reference when we return to our primary task [5]. It reduces the attentional demands of the interruption, and can help us to get back on track more quickly. It's important that you think clearly about how you will respond to the interruption. For example, when a notification arrived, I decided "I will continue to write this chapter, and delay checking my e-mail until lunchtime."

Do you find it more difficult to complete a task if someone is looking over your shoulder? What causes people to forget their well-rehearsed speech when they stand in front of an audience? What makes an entrepreneur lose their place in the middle of the most important pitch of their life?

This technique may sound contrived, but we need to adopt deliberate tactics to counter the influence of our overwhelming environment. Too often we operate on autopilot. As soon as an alert appears, we respond to it without any conscious thought. Our phone vibrates and we instantly pick it up and read the message without pausing to consider what we're doing or how we should respond.

STRESS & SWITCHING

There is also an emotional cost to interweaving tasks and switching. It seems that we can compensate for time-loss by working faster, but we pay for it. Switching increases stress, escalates frustration, increases our sense of time pressure and increases the amount of effort required to get work done [7].

Are you concerned by the research suggesting that up to 20% of a senior executive's role could be replaced by automation [10], or are you really happy about it? Either emotion could be competing for your working memory!

CHALLENGE 4: WORKING MEMORY COMPETES WITH OUR EMOTIONS

Most of us will have observed or experienced the interactions between cognition and emotion, but it's only in the last 25 years that neuroscience has begun to describe how network interactions are key to understanding our complex human behaviours. For example, when a subject is presented with an emotive word such as 'worthless', regions of the brain associated with emotion, behaviour, motivation and long-term memory are engaged.

Previously, emotion and cognition have been viewed as largely separate entities in the brain [8]. Presenting a subject with pictures that are designed to arouse an emotional reaction increases response times in tasks, regardless of the emotion that was conveyed by the images [48-50]. It takes time and shared cognitive resources for us to process emotion, and we experience competitive pressure in our working memory, even if the emotion is pleasant.

This effect is often most evident when we're carrying out a complex, novel task that requires us to use effortful, rather than automatic, thinking [9]. If an entrepreneur is excited about presenting a new pitch, this emotion will still compete for working memory, perhaps making it more challenging to remember what to say next. As part of this book, I interviewed Jyrki Törnwall, a face transplant surgeon. He described how the demanding nature of the microsurgery meant that it required more effort to maintain emotional control and interact pleasantly with the team in the operating room than it would normally. What emotions are competing for your cognitive resources?

The association between cognitive performance and emotion is clear, but too often we assume that we are immune to it. Simply recognising that our cognitive load and our emotional state can influence each other may help us to be more compassionate in our treatment of others and ourselves.

CHALLENGE 5: OUR VISUAL ENVIRONMENT IS TOO COMPETITIVE

Imagine you have just received a complex diagram from a colleague. It's gargantuan. Multiple boxes, connecting arrows and annotations fill the entire screen of your laptop and describe a detailed step-by-step process. Think about the following two scenarios:

Scenario 1:
The diagram arrives by e-mail and includes written instructions that explain the complex step-by-step processes and flows of information. You open the diagram on your laptop in full-screen. It's impossible to open your e-mail client at the same time, as it covers part of the diagram, so instead you read the written instructions from your smartphone display, while following each step of the diagram's process.

Scenario 2:
Your colleague invites you to a conference room where the diagram is displayed on a flip chart. You look at the diagram while your colleague uses the same written instructions you received by mail, but reads them out loud instead, so you can hear them as you follow each step.

Which scenario do you imagine to be easier in terms of cognitive load? Most people suggest that scenario 2 would be less demanding, but why should the experience be any different when the diagrams are identical, they are displayed at the same size and the instructions use matching words?

Cognitive load increases whenever our attention is divided between multiple pieces of information; the diagram and the instructions, for example. However, this effect is pronounced when information is presented in the same 'modality'. In scenario 1, all the information was presented visually, using the laptop and smartphone screens, and this increased competition for your working memory.

However, auditory information does not compete with visual items in the same way.

How do you interact with your colleagues? How often do they offer verbal instructions or provide spoken guidance? Most of the time, we receive e-mails with attachments. We rarely walk over to someone's desk, preferring to use instant messages to communicate across the office.

In scenario 2, the information was divided between visual and audio modalities, which reduced cognitive load [11].

MODALITY EFFECT AT WORK AND AT HOME

Consider your working environment. How many screens are visible at your desk? Many knowledge workers have one or two desktop screens, perhaps a tablet open beside them and almost certainly a smartphone somewhere visible, providing regular notifications and updates. Have a look at your laptop or desktop screen. How many windows and applications are open?

How about relationships outside of work? For most of human history, communication took place face-to-face, but we expanded our visual reach as we encoded thoughts in images, language in symbols and eventually created technologies to project our communication across the world. But is this the future we imagined?

BLADE RUNNER

In 1982, Blade Runner's movie audience watched Deckard, played by Harrison Ford, chase androids through Los Angeles' dystopian future. In one of many prophetic technological scenes, Deckard uses a videophone to contact Rachael, his 'replicant' muse, and invite her for a drink in a smoky bar. She turns him down, ends the call and the screen reveals that the interaction cost him $1.25 [12].

Science fiction writers have long imagined telepresence – providing the experience of being able to see and hear someone in another location – as the ultimate expression of human communication technology. But it appears that the futurists got it wrong. Blade Runner's storyline was set in 2019, and if communication trends continue, a more realistic depiction would have seen Deckard sending Rachael a WhatsApp message with at least three emoticons; an exchange that would have cost him nothing except for the telephone numbers and usage metrics he shared with the application's owner.

I used to call my friends at home. If they didn't pick up, I'd try to call them again later. Today, I'll send them a text message to see how they're doing and receive a notification to alert me that they've received and read it. The telephone call is a dying art and while 35% of people use their smartphones for video-calls, our appetite for text-based communication appears to be insatiable. This is having a significant impact on our cognitive load and attention:

1) Much of our communication is now presented in the same text-based modality, which increases cognitive load.

2) Ubiquitous, brief, asynchronous text-based communication encourages us to switch tasks regularly to check notifications, rather than enjoy dedicated or sustained communication time.

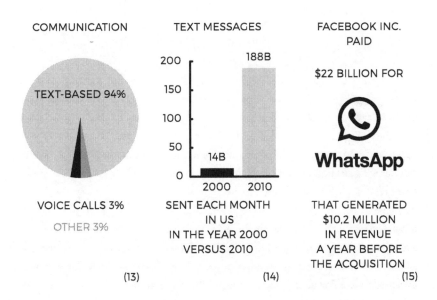

COMMUNICATION

TEXT-BASED 94%

VOICE CALLS 3%

OTHER 3%

(13)

TEXT MESSAGES

200
150
100
50
0

188B

14B

2000   2010

SENT EACH MONTH
IN US
IN THE YEAR 2000
VERSUS 2010

(14)

FACEBOOK INC.
PAID

$22 BILLION FOR

WhatsApp

THAT GENERATED
$10,2 MILLION
IN REVENUE
A YEAR BEFORE
THE ACQUISITION

(15)

Research from the UK suggests that just 3% of communication time is spent making voice calls, while 94% is text-based [13]. In the US, the number of SMS text messages sent each month grew from 14 billion in the year 2000, to 188 billion in 2010 [14].

Our dominant form of communication in and outside of work is visual and, more often than not, text-based. This trend is likely to increase, and we are not in the habit of applying any conscious controls to limit our exposure. Our limited working memory is filling and we're not doing anything about it.

Facebook inc. was confident enough in our enthusiasm for text-based messaging to pay $22 billion for WhatsApp; a startup that generated $10.2 million in revenue in the year before its acquisition [15].

CHALLENGE 6: THE HARDER WE WORK, THE MORE DIFFICULT IT IS TO RESIST DISTRACTION

'Pinging' notifications: likes, videos that play automatically and algorithmically curated content, all combine to stimulate our interests and provide intense and addictive sensations of reward. "Take a look at this!" says System 1. System 2 may, or may not, decide to help us make a good decision. The harder we work, the more difficult it is to resist distraction as working memory competes with self-control for cognitive resources.

It's inevitable that we'll be showered with temptation throughout the working day. Even if our workplace employs filtered internet access, smartphones provide continuous access to these delights. Research suggests that workplace policies may reduce social-media use during the day, but it's still very common [16].

The high cognitive load of our knowledge work makes us more vulnerable, and increases the likelihood that we'll give into temptation.

This makes it more important to assess cognitive load, find an optimal approach to distributing it through the day and develop tactics to help us to resist distraction; switching off WiFi, turning off our phones or leaving devices at home, are some examples.

CHALLENGE 7: OUR MENTAL BREAKS ARE NOT RESTFUL

It's tempting to believe that browsing social media represents a refreshing 'mini-vacation' for our mind – 34% of us admit to regularly using social media during the workday to take a mental break [16]. However, while it may activate our pleasure centres, these distractions are not restful. If we consider the CTL model, we can recognise that playing with our smartphones for a few minutes is simply another form of 'pseudo work' for our brains as we switch and engage in relatively complex tasks.

REST IS ESSENTIAL, BUT WE ARE NOT VERY GOOD AT IT

> *"Rest is not idleness."*
> John Lubbock, *The Use of Life* (1894)

Before I had a smartphone, I used to spend a lot of time letting my mind wander; standing in a queue in a shop, sitting on a plane. When we are in a state of wakeful rest and our attention is no longer focussed on the outside world, our brain enters the default mode (DM) of neural processing.

It appears that a form of neural network switching takes place when we move from maintaining focussed attention on our external environment and remain awake, but become internally reflective, such as during rest and daydreaming [17]. We can see the DM network engage when we shift attention inward, and decouple as we shift it outward.

Reviews of evidence associated with the default mode suggest that this internally focused mental processing is important for recalling personal memories, imagining the future, experiencing self-awareness, feeling emotions about the psychological impact of social situations on other people and constructing moral judgements [18].

DAYDREAMING GOOD FOR CREATIVITY

It also appears that those of us who are better at engaging this DM network at rest score higher on measures of cognitive abilities like divergent thinking, reading, comprehension and memory [18]. This would suggest that spending time in DM may help us to generate creative ideas, and offer the opportunity to explore many solutions and future possibilities in a way that demands little effort.

We could describe DM as the minimum intensity of low gear; when time pressure, task switching and information processing are at their lowest. This 'task-negative' state is a time for abstract thought and consolidation that seems to be essential to our optimum functioning, as individuals and with other people.

We will likely work better with others and also improve our capacity to learn new skills and generate the novel insights that set us apart as knowledge workers and will become increasingly valuable as automation replaces many productivity-based tasks. But how often do we allow our minds to wander in a state of constructive internal reflection? Generally, our hunt for novelty encourages us to spend every spare moment checking in on our devices.

CHALLENGE 8: OUR NERVOUS SYSTEM IS OVERSTIMULATED

Habitual checking on missed calls and messages can become an addictive behaviour pattern, increasing stress and disturbing sleep [19]. Even if our behaviour is not addictive, spending our days in a persisting state of moderate cognitive exertion, from morning until night, has a physiological impact.

We spend the majority of our days in cognitive middle gear. Not working particularly fast and not on anything too complex. Rather, we switch attention regularly, and engage with sufficiently demanding tasks to increase our cognitive load significantly above its resting state.

For endurance athletes, training in middle gear delays the recovery of the autonomic nervous system [20]. The effects of assiduous cognitive load are similar. After subjecting volunteers to a battery of cognitive tests for eight hours, which were designed to mimic the day of a knowledge worker, researchers identified increased activity in the 'fight or flight' sympathetic branch of the subject's autonomic nervous system that was consistent with fatigue [21]. Work can be stressful, but many of us are making our days more stressful than they need to be, and it's hampering our recovery.

SUPERCOMPENSATION

Organisms respond to stress, both physical and psychological, in a predictable way.

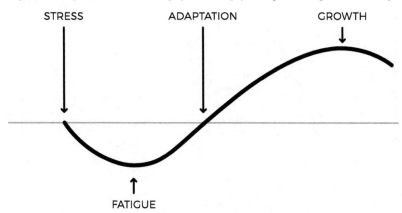

STRESS   ADAPTATION   GROWTH

FATIGUE

In the immediate aftermath of stress, performance is decreased, but then the organism recovers and performance bounces back. Hans Selye, in 1936, described this pattern as General Adaptation Syndrome. If sufficient resources and time for recovery are available, the organism will successfully recover, adapt to the stress and can even super compensate, to achieve a level higher than before.

However, the combination of too much stress and insufficient recovery results in the accumulation of fatigue over time that may be described as 'chronic fatigue'.

The fatigue we experience in each workday is acute. We engage in a variety of cognitive tasks that stress our nervous system. Even if these tasks are not optimally distributed, we should have time outside of work to recover. The challenge for most knowledge workers is that we fill our recovery time with more cognitively demanding work. We may not describe it as work, but the effect of our choices is indistinguishable for our brain and nervous system. We continue to check our phones every six minutes [22], combine watching TV with browsing the internet [23] and end our waking hours with a quick scan of our e-mail inbox before replying to a few 'urgent' messages.

If the stress on our nervous system is prolonged, we will struggle to maintain self-control in the face of the bottom-up competition for our attention and our work will suffer. In extreme cases, this accumulated fatigue may result in more serious fatigue-related health issues [21].

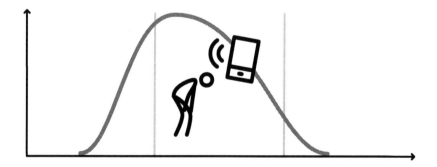

ATTENTION RESTORATION

Whenever we engage in an effortful mental task, we use our cognitive control resources – our attention, working memory and goal management. We direct our attention to form higher-level goals and inhibit our reflex responses so we can use our working memory and self-control to optimal effect. We can direct our attention in this way for some time, providing we win the battle between top-down goals and bottom-up pressures, but eventually, our attention will fatigue.

Ideally, we need to find a way to restore our focussed attention. I was speaking with Aki about this a couple of months ago, and he told me a story about how he trained drivers to be able to restore their focus and willpower, during a training camp in Switzerland.

"We were there by the cross-country ski track. The three drivers were quite good skiers. I was timing them over 300 metres. It was a little bit uphill. I said, "Now guys, today, with our training, you have to push maximum, three times." In between each sprint was good recovery, 10 minutes. After three times I said, "I will show that you can do it better, you didn't try to the maximum." They said, "No, absolutely we did the maximum." And then I took them 100 metres away, to sit in the nice sunshine, by the river. There were mountains, the Alps were in front. I said, "Now, look [at] this water, how beautiful it is, and this mountain, how it's reflecting the sun. Do this for 5 minutes. Try not to think about anything much, just think about what you feel and what you enjoy. We did that, then repeated the three sprints, this time, with 5 minutes recovery, but instead of hanging around the track, I said go back and look at the mountain and the birds. When they did that, they improved by 10%. They didn't believe it, but they said they felt so light, so full of energy. I think this can have even more effect when you have to work with your brain. This is why I always encourage people to take these 5 minute 'total breaks.'"

Aki had intuitively found a concept that is described in the literature as 'Attention Restoration Theory' (ART). ART distinguishes between voluntary attention, which requires direction and effort, and involuntary attention, which is 'effortless' [24]. It seems that natural scenes are a particularly abundant source for restoring us through effortless attention.

I used to make fun of the tacky mountain scenes that adorned offices at the turn of the millennium, but perhaps they were onto something.

Researchers tested this theory by instructing subjects to go for a 50-minute walk in two contrasting environments; one natural, the other urban. Walking in a natural environment had a strongly positive influence on restoring subjects' directed attention, where a walk in an urban environment did not.

Interestingly, the effect persisted even if the subjects went for a walk that was unpleasant, such as in the middle of a cold winter, providing the walk was through a natural setting. It even appeared that simply viewing pictures of nature could help to restore attention [25].

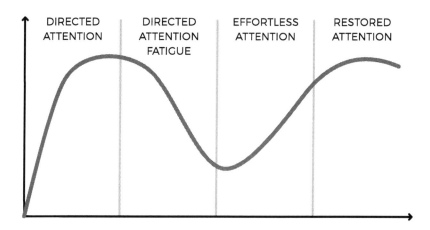

DIRECTED ATTENTION | DIRECTED ATTENTION FATIGUE | EFFORTLESS ATTENTION | RESTORED ATTENTION

CHALLENGE 9: LACK OF SLEEP IMPAIRS OUR COGNITIVE PERFORMANCE

How long do you sleep for, on average? According to data from the United States National Health Interview Survey, almost 30% of adults report that they get an average of less than six hours of sleep per night [26].

Simple reaction tests made on people after 19 hours of continuous wakefulness result in impairments comparable to having a blood alcohol concentration of 0.05%, which is the equivalent to being legally drunk in most EU countries [27]. Our reaction times slow, our quality of decision-making is reduced, the function of our working memory and long-term memory is impaired, our attention is eroded and we're more easily distracted [28, 29].

It's clear that our performance is diminished if we don't get enough sleep, but how much is 'enough'?

SIX HOURS SLEEP NOT ENOUGH

Surely six hours is plenty? It certainly feels like enough for many people. The problem is, it's not. Restricting sleep to six hours, for 14 nights, results in declines in cognitive performance equivalent to staying awake for 48 hours straight [30]. Perhaps the bigger problem is that we don't notice our performance is impaired.

In the initial days of the experiment that generated these findings, the subjects felt sleepy and rated their performance as diminished. However, this perception tapered as the experiment continued. After a few days, the subjects no longer felt tired and they didn't believe that their performance was getting any worse.

There's always one person at the party who gets progressively drunker, believing that their jokes are becoming increasingly hilarious, while everyone else wishes they would just go home. Sleep deprivation creeps up on us in a similar way.

Limiting sleep to six hours per night causes a progressive decline in cognitive function, but we are poor judges of our own performance. Our well-lit office spaces, lively conversations and monstrous caffeine intake can make us feel fully awake. Even if we're happy with our sleep-deprived performance levels, we are not performing optimally. And even if we're able to produce at a good level, we'll still be working much harder than we need to.

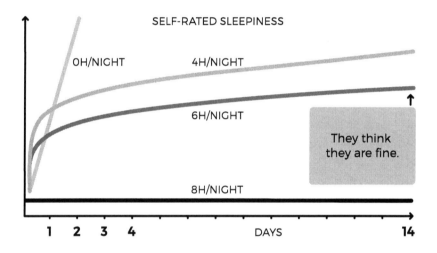

(30)

Knowledge workers are good at maintaining a continuous moderate level of cognitive work, but we are terrible at resting and sleeping. We need to re-learn to do and to 'be'.

CHALLENGE 10: OUR WORK HABITS ERODE OUR SENSE OF MEANING

For many knowledge workers, the day is dominated by 'shallow work'.

> *"Shallow work: Noncognitively demanding, logistical-style tasks, often performed while distracted. These efforts tend not to create much new value in the world and are easy to replicate."*
> Newport, C. 2016 [31]

You could equate shallow work with the cognitive middle gear. Whilst some middle-gear work is unavoidable and even necessary, a significant portion of it is likely self-imposed by our distracted work habits. The net effect is not just a reduction in the value we can create; we also miss out on the opportunity to enjoy a deeper sense of meaning in our work.

Where we focus our attention influences our actions, as well as our perception; it dictates what we ignore and what we see. If our attention is applied optimally, we can focus on what is most meaningful, important and valuable, but too often we end up perceiving a world that is out to hijack what we really want to achieve, and drag us into menial tasks. The challenge and question is this: are we doing anything proactive to counteract this view?

If you've ever eaten a burger and fries, only to return home and find yourself feeling hungry and a little guilty, you'll understand that junk food only offers fleeting satisfaction. Our daily diet of continuous inbox scans and status checks provides brief moments of hedonic pleasure at a neurological level, but this fragmented attention erodes our happiness and sense of meaning in our life and work.

FLOW

In 1990, psychologist Mihaly Csikszentmihalyi wrote a popular book in which he described a state of human consciousness defined as 'Flow'. If your cognitive workload is increasing as you try to figure out how to pronounce his name, please allow me to help. Apparently, "chick-sent-me-high" is the most accurate phonetic spelling.

Csikszentmihalyi asserted that:

> "The best moments in our lives are not the passive, receptive, relaxing times… The best moments usually occur if a person's body or mind is stretched to its limits in a voluntary effort to accomplish something difficult and worthwhile."
> (32)

Csikszentmihalyi went on to describe how humans can find genuine satisfaction when completely absorbed in an activity, especially an activity which involves their creative abilities, and that this experience is not a fixed state, but can be learned and developed. A key aspect is our exercising of control over the contents of our consciousness, as opposed to being passively determined by external forces.

POLARISE YOUR WORK

Athletes who follow a polarised approach to their training need to think carefully about whom they train with. Sometimes, they need to work alone, focussing their attention and cultivating their capacity to maintain the high-intensities required to reach their full potential. They carefully consider their training sessions, when to work hard and when to rest.

In the same way, knowledge workers would benefit from polarising their cognitive workload, re-learning to spend time in low cognitive gear and default mode. We need to create space in the day for constructive internal reflection, and be more assertive about who we work with and when. Our reflexive influences cannot always be trusted to guide our actions in the context of knowledge work. We need to switch off our smartphones, filter out the distractions from our environment, minimise and compartmentalise middle-gear work and build our capacity to tolerate high-gear efforts.

Athletes work hard and 'rest hard', and knowledge workers need to do the same. We can redistribute our cognitive workload and shift our cognitive curve to the right, doing more work, for the same effort, or the same work for less.

RESISTANCE

SPEED

COGNITIVE DRAG

The challenges faced by knowledge workers act like aerodynamic drag for a cyclist. If we don't find a way to cut through the 'wind-resistance' of sub-optimal working practises, we end up working harder simply to maintain the same speed.

THE PARADOX OF THE KNOWLEDGE WORKER

For the knowledge worker, in our increasingly automated, augmented, ageless and agile economy, the goal should be to nurture our capacity for learning new skills, create rare insights, generate novel approaches and do the high-quality focused work that is difficult to replicate by our competitors, be they robots or humans.

The same knowledge workers who need to nurture their capacity to learn are the most at risk of the fractured attention that destroys the pathway to value creation.

The people who need to pay attention the most, are most at risk of distraction.

We need to act top-down, consciously allocating our cognitive resources more effectively; bottom-up, proactively removing distractions that exert a powerful influence on us and also inside-out; addressing the habits and culture which can help us to stay on track. If we achieve this and reduce resistance, the effect on our performance can be exponential.

CONSIDER THIS

1) When we switch tasks frequently, it makes it harder to switch into low or high gear, when we really need to.

2) Are your breaks truly restful, or are you filling them with non-essential, but demanding' 'pseudo cognitive work'?

3) Did you recognise yourself in the study of people whose performance was impaired by 6 hours sleep, without realising it?

4) Do you need to adapt your environment to eliminate some distractions?

5) Can you create a more distinct, polarised rhythm, of high-gear and low-gear work, throughout the day?

7.
EFFICIENT & EFFECTIVE

In the coming chapters, I'll share some rules, productivity practises and principles to maintain wellbeing, maximise creativity and optimise knowledge work performance in some of the most demanding environments.

In this chapter specifically, we'll explore the following themes:

- The changing nature of work.

- The most important skills in the 4th Industrial Revolution.

- Creativity: who has it, and how to nurture it?

- Using mindset to release potential.

- Why self-control may not be as limited as we thought.

- Focus as the new IQ [26].

- Training your executive function.

- Priming your brain for high-performance.

- Hacking your environment.

- Polarising your work.

AUTOMOBILE CLUB DE FRANCE

In November 1895, Count Jules-Albert de Dion, Baron Etienne de Zuylen and a journalist, Paul Meyan, from Le Figaro, sat around a table for lunch at the Count's residence in Paris. A picture from the gathering shows Jules-Albert at the centre, his moustache waxed to perfection, as a waiter refills his glass with red wine. The three men had a vision for something that had never been imagined before. Their gastronomic meeting brought the birth of the Automobile Club de France (ACF): a private members club for motorcar enthusiasts [1].

In 1906, the ACF held the first Grand Prix for manufacturers on a 103-kilometre course near the quiet town of Le Mans [2]. The Renault test-driver, Ferenc Szisz, was victorious, powered by a 67kw, 8.5 litre engine, at an average speed of 101 kilometres per hour [3]. The engine required a huge capacity, as it was only able to operate at around 20% efficiency, and the majority of the energy provided by the fuel was dispensed as heat, so getting the job done required a brute force approach.

In the early days of motorsport, technical directives were limited, but as speed and power increased, rules were put in place to enforce safety and promote fair competition. The history of motorsport charts the parallel tracks of innovation and regulation, increasing efficiency and effectiveness.

While some motorsport voices continue to call for de-regulation as a means to promote development, the rules may actually be among the most important forces shaping motorsport's innovative landscape.

Efficient, productivity-orientated tasks are easy to reproduce by another human, or even a machine. Creativity is rare.

FROM EXTRACTION TO CREATION

The landscape of work has changed too, shaped by shifting needs and new requirements. Where the goal of work was once to extract the maximum amount of energy from a worker, and transform it into a tangible product, knowledge work turns this approach on its head. Knowledge work organisations should be mental energy factories, providing the fuel for cognitive athletes, energising teams and transforming mental energy into ideas and insights –

something that will become even more critical as automation replaces many repeatable, process-based tasks.

Humans are explorers, inquirers, and creators. The World Economic Forum identified complex problem solving, critical thinking and creativity as the top three skills required to thrive in the 4th industrial revolution [39]. Arguably, creativity is the foundation for all of them; complex problem solving and critical thinking require imagination, ideation, innovation and the ability to perceive multiple perspectives.

The challenges of knowledge work can make it difficult to create the conditions for creativity, but a lack of creative thought makes us less able to imagine a different future and overcome these challenges.

> Creativity is the antidote to the poison of efficiency over effectiveness. It's the solution to sending endless e-mails and making meaningless presentations, because it allows us to perceive the new opportunities that are unfolding in front of us, generate unique value and novel insight.

Creativity underpins effective knowledge work, but there is no perfect approach to producing ingenuity on demand. Exactly which individual and contextual factors provide the optimal circumstances for creativity is debated, but a brute force approach based on simply clocking the hours, is not one of them.

Creativity consists of at least four components:

1) The creative person

2) The creative process

3) The creative situation

4) The creative product

[4]

THE CREATIVE PERSON

All humans have the capacity to be creative and most of us could unlock more of our creative potential with the right process and conditions. We each have a unique 'cognitive style' that influences our creativity. For some people, this style may have a genetic basis, associated with a gene called COMT [5]. The COMT gene encodes the instructions to synthesise an enzyme that is critical for the function of the pre-frontal cortex. In particular, this enzyme helps to maintain appropriate concentrations of neurotransmitters such as dopamine and norepinephrine [6].

Dopamine concentrations in our brain play an important role in reward-motivated behaviour. Dopamine is associated with how attractive, motivating and pleasurable we perceive a behaviour to be [7]. This can influence how we plan, inhibit our urges and maintain effort. It also has a bearing on abstract thinking, emotion and working memory. Together, this can impact whether we choose to stay on track or look around at something new.

A particular variant of the COMT gene can result in some individuals exhibiting lower levels of dopamine in the prefrontal cortex. They may find task switching easier and demonstrate greater levels of creativity than average, perhaps as they search for dopamine 'hits' in new ways. People with an alternative COMT gene variant, which results in high dopamine levels, may display relatively less cognitive flexibility and more difficulty with switching tasks [5]. Genetic observations are generalisations, but it is clear that there is a wide variation in creative styles among individuals.

This is an important point to make in knowledge work, as I have heard many people label themselves as "not very creative." Creativity can be expressed in many different contexts. It may be manifested in the way that we can think of solutions to challenging situations at work, or resolve conflicts, not simply in a tangible creative output.

While many people assume that creativity declines with age, in domains that draw on knowledge and expertise, such as writing, philosophy and medicine, research suggests that creative achievement can peak in the early 40s, and declines quite gradually [8].

I encourage you to think of some examples of your own creativity in practice, perhaps in areas that you have not thought about before, and remind yourself that we can all be creative.

THE CREATIVE PROCESS

We crave new information. We are rewarded for searching out novelty and in the digital age, we have access to a fire hose of content to titillate the reward centres of our brain, but if we don't have rules and boundaries in place, we can easily become distracted and create little real value.

Contrary to popular belief, providing someone with a blank slate does not appear to optimise the creative process. Unbounded choice and opportunity can quickly overwhelm the limited resources of attention, executive function and working memory.

Creativity thrives when there is some pressure and limitation, but not too much. We could plot the creative process as an inverted-U.

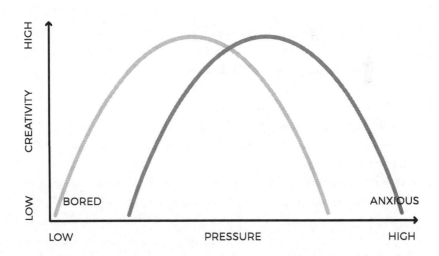

Too much time pressure impairs creative cognitive processing [9], but some pressure can fuel our creativity. Eliminating it can suffocate the process and create an inhospitable environment for innovation.

Our response to pressure is individual; some people thrive when their backs are against the wall, while others prefer a more relaxed approach. For certain individuals, a prize or honour can drive them to produce their most innovative work, whereas others are more motivated by intrinsic rewards. For most, it is a combination of the two.

CREATIVE DRIVING

I was speaking with Aki about creativity in motorsport, and he reminded me of Kimi Räikkönen, and his exceptional ability to "conceptualise three-dimensional space." This ability relates to 'spatial ability.' Individuals who score highly in this area tend to be very good at understanding and remembering how objects are positioned relative to each other. This ability can also relate to the skill of 'spatial navigation,' which involves the brain simulating and anticipating what it will see as it moves through a scene [10]. Theoretically, if a driver can simulate a circuit in their brain in 'higher-definition' relative to another driver, they could imagine more possible scenarios, and take advantage of them.

You may not think of driving a Formula One car as a creative process, but the drivers are continuously finding ways to take full advantage of every opportunity provided by their car, the conditions and their competitors.

Aki has worked with a lot of drivers, but Kimi stood out in this regard. Kimi has also shown an unconventional creative streak in driving, from a young age. A now legendary story tells how as a kid, in a karting race in Monaco, Kimi's kart was knocked over the barrier in a collision. Undeterred he continued driving alongside the circuit, on the wrong side of the barrier, until he ran out of road. At this point, he lifted his kart back onto the track then worked his way back through the pack, eventually finishing third.

We need enough space to let our imagination roam, but not too much that we lose sight of the objective. Something also needs to incentivise us to search out new information and ideas.

CONDITIONS FOR CREATIVITY

Creativity thrives in three conditions [11].

1) When we apply and combine old ideas in new ways.

Boundaries force us to look deeper within ourselves, to sift through our experiences for something that could be useful and pool our cognitive resources. Boundaries create the conditions that encourage us to combine what we already know, as well as the new ideas we can come up with.

2) When we feel enough pressure and incentive to encourage flexible thinking.

If we don't have any pressure or incentive, we can talk forever without actually creating anything. When a clock is ticking, or a reward is waiting and we need to find an answer, our minds open to new ways of looking at a problem and we become more cognitively flexible.

3) When we don't get too comfortable.

When we've finally developed an idea that we're proud of, it's easy to feel self-satisfied in the afterglow of creative breakthrough. This is one of the greatest risks in the creative process because we can easily become attached to an idea and miss further opportunities for improvement. One of the best ways to avoid this state is to regularly move boundaries and change rules. This creates a 'shelf-life' for your solutions and forces fresh rounds of innovation and creativity.

THE CREATIVE SITUATION

The development of a Formula One car is a good example of what can happen if you provide boundaries and creative conditions for knowledge workers. Team structures combine a breadth and depth of experience that promote the combining of old ideas in new ways. The World Championship competition provides pressure and incentives.

Rule changes on an annual basis prevent anyone from becoming too satisfied with their ideas.

A Formula One car has thousands of separate elements that must fit together perfectly. A race season could see 30,000 design changes being made to the car, 1,000 per week, as components are tweaked and improved to maximise performance [12].

The development of a Formula One car also illustrates one of the myths of the 10,000 hours rule. Achieving excellence is not the result of countless cycles of mechanical repetition. It works more like the neural network I described in Chapter 3. Processes are repeated, but parameters are deliberately adjusted after each cycle of learning, to get closer to the desired result.

DEFAULT MODE AND CREATIVITY

Crafting a 'creative situation' isn't just about setting up boundaries for work; it can also involve allocating space for creative reflection. Our brains have a distinct network of interacting brain regions that become active in periods of wakeful rest, such as when we daydream or let our minds wander. This default mode network (DMN) activates whenever we are not involved in a task. Consequently, it's sometimes described as a 'task-negative' state.

Entering 'default mode' has strong associations with creative and divergent thinking, comprehension, remembering the past and planning for the future [13, 14]. Some evidence has also observed a positive correlation between creative performance, across all measures of creativity, and the physical volume of the grey matter that makes up the default mode network [15].

THE CREATIVE PRODUCT

The technical story of Formula One describes the importance of quality over quantity, of efficiency over brute force. The 1906 Grand Prix may have been won by Renault, but Mercedes also fielded a car in the race. A company called 'Maybach' designed Mercedes' first 6-cylinder engine for Mercedes. Its 11-litre capacity produced 78kW of power. Now, 110 years later, Mercedes is still competing, and winning. In the 2016 Formula One season, Mercedes' F1 W07 Hybrid cars were piloted by long-time Hintsa client Lewis Hamilton, and his team mate Nico Rosberg to a third consecutive Formula One constructor's championship.

Formula One cars don't have engines anymore, they have 'power-units' and the performance characteristics are quite different to those of their predecessors.

The power unit system is designed and engineered by a team based in the English countryside in Brixworth, Northamptonshire, who have over 25 years of knowledge in supplying Formula One engines.

Working to the limit of the technical regulations, Mercedes AMG High Performance Powertrains have been able to create a system that can produce nearly 10 times the power, with 1/7th of the capacity of its Maybach ancestor. Brains have replaced brawn with precision, sophistication and efficiency.

The development of a Formula One car also illustrates one of the myths of the 10,000 hours rule.

Achieving excellence is not the result of countless cycles of mechanical repetition. It works more like the neural network. Processes are repeated, but parameters are deliberately adjusted after each cycle of learning, to get closer to the desired result.

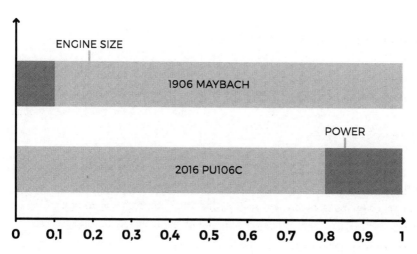

(16,17)

Boundaries, pressures and changing conditions can inspire the creative process, but we also need to develop the cognitive flexibility to take advantage of every centimetre of space and all the resources we have available to us.

Endless cycles of development, testing and refinement, with a hefty dose of ingenuity, mean that today's Mercedes PU106C power unit delivers at least 47% efficiency, versus 29% in 2013 and around 20% in 1906. There have been greater improvements in the efficiency of internal combustion engines in the last three years than in the last century.

When you provide boundaries, resources, and a clear objective, then release people to do their best work, great things are possible.

BOUNDARIES AND OUR BEST WORK

For a knowledge worker, our creative space is represented by our conscious hours. Our resources are the capabilities of our brain. How can we make the best use of them?

We've defined the rules and limitations of our cognitive capabilities in previous chapters. We can now begin our own process of testing and development, experimenting, trying new approaches, and adjusting after each cycle of learning, to get closer to the desired result.

FORM A FLEXIBLE MINDSET

I enjoyed school. Teachers praised me for my innate ability, but I struggled when I reached advanced Maths. My parents offered to get me extra tutoring, but I declined. I was too proud. I decided that, if it didn't come easy, maybe I just wasn't good at maths. I dropped the class.

Stanford professor, Carol Dweck, would have described my mindset as 'fixed.' I believed that intelligence was innate, that it couldn't be changed. In 2006, Dweck popularised her research in a best-selling book Mindset, which was my first encounter with her research. Dweck describes how our beliefs about the sources of success and accomplishment can have a profound influence on our performance [18]. I recognised myself and I was challenged.

The idea of a growth versus fixed mindset fascinated me. Even if you don't have the VO_2 max. to be an Olympic medallist in cross-country skiing, many people can double their aerobic capacity with training. By replacing brute force and the daily grind with a more precise and thoughtful approach, we can revolutionise our approach to knowledge work, too.

A growth mindset suggests that our potential may be exponentially greater than we imagine and that the efficient, effective and sustained allocation of our cognitive resources is the most important determinant of what we can achieve.

SELF-CONTROL

I once had a temporary job, doing administration work in an office. There was a poster on the wall featuring an eagle soaring over a mountain. The image had a large black border around it and the phrase "Believe in yourself" was typed in bold, white lettering. When I first saw it, I laughed. We Brits are cynical and a phrase like this was an easy target. But I may have been wrong to dismiss it so quickly.

The prevailing view used to be that self-control was a limited resource [19]. For some, this can be a disempowering message, leading us to resign ourselves to raiding the cookie jar after a tough day in the office. However, more recent research has challenged some aspects of this view [20].

BELIEVE IN YOURSELF

When I started to work with Hintsa, I began coaching a number of young drivers in various single-seat racing series. All of them aspired to reach the Formula One World Championship.

Most drivers start in karting before graduating to an open-wheel series such as Formula 4, then perhaps Formula 3, GP3 or even GP2, before they have a shot at a Formula One seat. Along the way, they learn the skills they need to succeed, progressively training their cognitive and physical capabilities and learning to survive and thrive in motorsport.

This process is characterised by learning and development, but there comes a point when drivers need to show their 'killer instinct' or risk getting left behind. It's not enough to simply keep improving. To succeed at the top of the sport, drivers can't just think they have a chance of victory, they have to believe it. In fact, Aki used to say that the best drivers didn't believe that they could win. When they got in the car, the best drivers knew that they would win.

Aki had a famous question that he's asked many young drivers. I remember the first time I heard it, when I was sitting-in on one of his consultations. He looked the young driver straight in the eye and said:

"Are you here to win, or just do your best?"

His client was startled. Aki spoke with so much authority, and he cut straight to the point.

IS WILLPOWER LIMITED?

Some people believe that willpower is a limited resource. Others do not, and this seems to have an impact on how we perform after difficult experiences that make demands of us. Specifically, a recent study explored the influence of our beliefs about willpower on performance at work, after experiencing a demanding day.

It seems that people who believe that willpower is limited, and therefore that a demanding day will have 'emptied' their 'willpower tank,' expect to make less progress in unpleasant tasks, anticipate that they will be more exhausted and are less effective and motivated as they work towards their goals. After similarly demanding experiences, people who believe that willpower can actually be stimulated by demanding tasks seemed to experience fewer negative effects from the demanding day, and kept striving towards their goals more effectively.

This study supports the notion that self-control and willpower can be influenced by our beliefs, and that our motivation, rather than the resources we have available, may be the more important influence on whether we keep pushing towards our goals, or instead decide to save our energy [21].

EXTREME LANGUAGE

As we explored in earlier chapters, our perceptions are an interpretation of reality that is strongly influenced by our goals and expectations, rather than being an entirely truthful representation. The language we use can reveal where our perception may be biased and direct us toward areas for improvement in our thinking and performance.

What do the words you use say about your beliefs? Are you in the habit of using extreme language? I don't mean swearing. I mean phrases such as "I can't change," "This is just the way I am" and "There's nothing I can do. These extreme statements are often indications that we may have 'primed' our implicit cognitive capabilities with faulty information, and that we may need to pause and take the opportunity to use some effortful and more effective thinking, to imagine a new future.

Negative words can prompt automated System 1 responses that may represent a very skewed version of reality. Next time you notice yourself using extreme, negative words, consider it as a prompt to engage effortful System 2 thinking. What other factors can you take into account? Remind yourself that change is possible, that you are capable of much more than you think and that your beliefs play a significant role in this.

NEUROPLASTICITY

If you need some ammunition to blow System 1's negative suggestions out of the water, try this: our brains are always changing. We can change and improve throughout our lives. In fact, our brain changes itself at every level in response to interaction with our environment.

'Activity-dependent plasticity' describes how using our cognitive functions, and personal experience, changes the structure of our brain in specific ways. It is the biological basis for learning and the formation of new memories [22].

Myelin is a tissue that wraps around the neurons in our brain and is crucial for the speed and fluidity of our thoughts and actions. Researchers have described how patterns in the growth of myelin (a process called myelination) are related to the particular activities we engage in [23]. It seems that in our brains, specific skills relate to specific 'circuits' – collections of neurons. When we act and experience the world, cells called oligodendrocytes and astrocytes sense the nerve firing and respond by wrapping more myelin around that neuron, which improves the neuron's performance. When we practise and work in an effortful and deliberate way, we can improve our brain at a neurological level.

BACK TO SCHOOL

We can train our brains to improve our cognitive control through developing our executive functions; the supervision, coordination and control of our cognitive processes, but the evidence on how to achieve this still requires a lot more investigation [24].

Before I started to be more intentional about eliminating distraction and improving my focus, I used to wonder whether my brain was in a better state during my time at school and university. If I had to go back to school, would my brain be ready? Sure, I know a lot more now, but has my cognitive control degraded in the last 10+ years?

When I was at school, I didn't have a smartphone and my internet connection was so slow, I'd get bored with waiting before I got the chance to be distracted.

Also, consider the creative output of kids in school, and their rate of development and learning. At the end of every day, I had something to show for it. Perhaps a new concept I had learned, or piece of work I'd produced. It's something I see repeated in my eldest son today and the evidence is stuck all over our refrigerator. Education systems may not be perfect, but kids are great knowledge workers.

Often, we assume that there is something magical about children's brains that help them to learn at such a fast rate, but our brain is capable of incredible feats for the majority of our lives.

As we get older, our learning processes are increasingly governed by our conscious executive control. At an anatomical level, this shift is associated with maturation of the prefrontal cortex in our brain [25]. This means that we become more aware of, and engaged in, the learning process. We can improve our self-control and our will to persist at learning tasks. We can use our executive functions to draw on more mature and developed cognitive control resources and reflect on our accumulated experience to enhance our learning and apply it in practise.

Perhaps you're not happy with the way you're living and working now, but you can still learn, grow develop and improve.

FOCUS IS THE NEW IQ

Some studies suggest that cognitive control capabilities can be improved through programmes designed to develop executive function. A number of areas have been singled out for training including inhibitory control (resisting habits, temptations or distractions), working memory (mentally holding and using information), and cognitive flexibility (adjusting to change). A number of these studies have been conducted among children [26], but relatively few in healthy adults.

Cal Newport has recently popularised the phrase "Focus is the new IQ" and research suggests that he's right. Executive function, which includes focus, is more strongly associated with school readiness than intelligence quotient (IQ) [26]. I'd argue that Executive functions are more important for adult knowledge workers than IQ, too. Self-discipline and attentional control in particular are critical. IQ and knowledge are the fuel, but our executive function enables us to unlock the potential of these intangible assets; allowing us to do our best work, rather than chase digital squirrels all

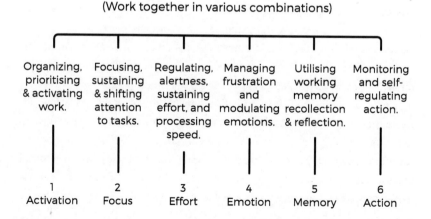

EXECUTIVE FUNCTIONS
(Work together in various combinations)

Organizing, prioritising & activating work.	Focusing, sustaining & shifting attention to tasks.	Regulating, alertness, sustaining effort, and processing speed.	Managing frustration and modulating emotions.	Utilising working memory recollection & reflection.	Monitoring and self-regulating action.
1 Activation	2 Focus	3 Effort	4 Emotion	5 Memory	6 Action

Without effective executive functioning, we can have the highest IQ in the world, but we'll function like a 1906 Maybach engine: producing a hell of a lot of heat and sound, without getting much useful work done.

day. Executive functions set the rules within which our creativity can flourish.

In theory, as adult knowledge workers, our prefrontal cortex is developed enough to apply our executive functions effectively, to do great work. However, our working practises often impair our cognitive control. We switch tasks, succumb to distraction and create unnecessary competition for our attention, but what can we do about it?

The evidence to support executive function strengthening programmes is still mixed, in both children and adults, but there are some indications to suggest how we can create an environment conducive to repairing our cognitive control, improving our knowledge work performance, reducing stress and enhancing enjoyment.

PREPARATION

Making a good start is critical in Formula One. Each race usually lasts between 90 minutes and 2 hours, but the drivers need to be ready to perform at their best from the beginning.

All media and non-essential personnel must leave the grid 10 minutes before the start. Then the drivers sit in their cars as engineers and mechanics work through specific procedures to prepare the vehicle. The cars are only started in the last minutes before the race, as the majority of the cooling for the power units comes from airflow over the moving car and the units become vulnerable to overheating if they're left standing for too long. The one-minute signal is issued and mechanics must clear the grid within 45 seconds. Fifteen seconds later, the gantry lights turn green, indicating the start of a single formation lap. This is no warm-up for the drivers, as they must precisely execute the hard accelerations, braking, weaving back and forth that is carefully planned to bring the brakes and tires up to optimal operating temperature.

After completing the formation lap, the cars resume their positions on the grid and the race director initiates the start sequence. This transfers timing control to an automated system and a sequence of five red lights is illuminated, followed by a pause.

The system dictates the duration of this pause at random. The drivers concentrate on the strip of bright LEDs with a laser focus. As soon as the lights go out, the race is on. We encourage the drivers we work with to create their own 'pre-performance routine.' This is a set of behaviours designed to prepare their body and mind to 'switch on' peak performance, whenever they need it.

THE PRIME METHOD

When I was writing this book, I tried to work in 90-minute blocks, focussed on a particular task, before taking a short break. At the start of each block, I got into the habit of doing a 30-second priming exercise, to prepare my brain and increase the likelihood that I would start well and follow the right track. I asked myself three priming questions – I call it the 'PriME' method.

1) **Priority:**
   What is the most important thing I must achieve
   in the next 90 minutes?

2) **Mindset:**
   How can I perceive the challenges in these
   90 minutes with a growth mindset?

3) **Elimination:**
   Is there anything I can get rid of
   to reduce the likelihood that I'll be
   distracted?

I used to have the bad habit of starting a 90-minute block with a 'warm-up' of browsing through websites and articles that I thought could be relevant, but more often than not, this process resulted in a lot of wasted time and mental energy. Adopting the PriME method has helped me to engage with my most important tasks more quickly and retain a state of focused attention, for longer.

Before starting work, I emptied my working memory of any irrelevant information by writing a list of the tasks and ideas that were hanging around. This included a quote I'd remembered, that I may use later in the chapter, and a note that I need to buy some milk later.

For example, my priority in the 90-minute block I'm working in now, is to flesh out bullet-point notes from yesterday on the themes of expectation, biases and performance, and write approximately 1500 words. With regard to my mindset, I don't have all the information I need yet, and that's a challenge, but I've reminded myself that I've already identified the research papers that will provide the insights I'm looking for. For elimination, I started this session by switching my phone into 'do not disturb' and locking the door to my office, as the kids are at home.

HACK YOUR ENVIRONMENT AND RETRAIN YOUR BRAIN

Rather than being a limited capacity, relying on a single resource, self-control appears to be a combination of executive functions and working memory, tied closely to our motivation. Our attention attempts to allocate our cognitive resources efficiently and effectively [27] but we can also be proactive, putting systems and processes in place to modify our environment and take some of the workload away from our brain.

The word "hack" used to refer specifically to unauthorized access to data in a system or computer. However, it's been appropriated as a verb to describe a range of quick fixes and clever solutions to problems. There are countless ways to hack your environment to improve focus, productivity and creativity. Here are 10 recommendations to help you begin your own testing and development process – training your brain and modifying your environment to improve efficiency and effectiveness.

1. PHYSICAL EXERCISE

A physical exercise class may be one of the most effective brain hacks for improving cognitive control, in children and adults. Across age-groups, regular aerobic exercise can provide a simple way for healthy people to optimise a range of executive functions such as task switching, selective attention, response inhibition and working memory capacity [28]. Studies using electroencephalogram (EEG) to monitor brain activity during behavioural tasks have demonstrated that higher fitness is also associated with increased cognitive flexibility [29].

Some of the largest fitness-induced benefits for our brain are associated with executive-control processes [30]. This is a great incentive to move more during your work day and to include more physical activity in your week – something we will explore in more detail in later chapters.

2.   PLAN 'CLASSES'

We can learn something from our school days. The idea of breaking your time down into 'classes,' which focus on certain subjects, is actually a pretty good one for all of us. As I explained previously, many of us unnecessarily increase our cognitive load and reduce our effectiveness by spending too much time in cognitive 'middle gear.' We don't create time boundaries, we switch tasks regularly and we are drawn towards activities that offer instant gratification, but result in little value generation.

Try to plan at least four hours of your day and break it up into designated 'classes' where you focus on a particular project or task. Plan times with a specific goal in mind and estimate the cognitive load associated with the tasks, so that you can polarise the distribution through the day. During these four hours, alternate between working very hard for focussed periods, or take it very easy and allow your attention to recover.

When we work with young drivers, we often encourage them to focus on the next corner, rather than allowing thoughts about the entire lap, or race, to distract them. They need to learn to put a good lap together – but it's overwhelming to think about everything. Breaking tasks down into achievable and specific chunks reduces the load on our working memory and decreases switching cost, as we can focus on a discrete task, rather than switching back to the 'big picture' constantly, in order to stay on track.

As I wrote this chapter, I broke my day into 90-minute blocks and scheduled the time between 5:30am and 9:30am with the following activities and clear goals:

- *05:30 – 07:00:* Flesh out bullet-point notes from yesterday on the themes of expectation, biases and performance (High gear). Aim for 1500 words in this 90-minute block.

- *07:00 – 07:30:* Breakfast with my wife and kids, without looking at any digital devices (low gear).

- *07:30 – 09:00:* Write 10 bullet points on 'hacking your environment' (high gear).

- *09:00-09:30:* Re-read 'Leadership' themed research papers in preparation for next section (middle gear – as I'm switching among a few different papers).

I've actually scheduled my whole day, as I'm in the middle of a 'sprint' period of this book project, but on a typical work day, I try to ensure that I get four good hours, so I can achieve some prioritized high-value, high-focus, high-gear work, before the chaos of the day begins!

You may find that four hours, including 2 x 90-minute high-gear periods, is too much for your executive control to handle at the beginning. In a similar way to when we started school, many of us need to go back to basics, start with short days and re-learn self-discipline and attentional control. If that means starting with 30 minutes of focus, that's fine! Start somewhere and build it up.

You will make your life easier by scheduling your 'classes' at the time you know you can get your best work done. For me, this is early morning, but it varies by individual preference and lifestyle. In time, you may find that you're able to schedule progressively more of your day, but I suggest you aim to get to the point where you can schedule four hours of personal 'classes', focussed on particular subjects, perhaps broken up into 2 x 90-minute 'high-gear' blocks and 2 x 30-minute low-gear recovery periods.

3.   EMBRACE BOREDOM

We discussed the common temptations for knowledge workers previously. When we feel bored,
arousal is often low, we feel dissatisfied with our
environment [31] and we often view the things we
are tempted by as a means to improve our situation,
even if experience tells us otherwise.

*I don't need to accept bore-
dom anymore because I
have my smartphone! I
can quickly enter the re-
warding cycle of trigger,
action, investment and
variable reward.*

I can remember many days at school when I was
bored, but I had to accept the boredom. I looked
out the window at the trees and restored my attention, though I didn't realise I was
doing that at the time. I let my imagination flow in some idle-time, simulated a more
interesting future, or I accepted the tedious nature of the task and kept grinding
through the work, so I could get to the end as quickly as possible. Learning to cope
with boredom taught me tactics to restore my attention, use time creatively and develop my ability to inhibit my responses.

THE TOP-THREE REASONS FOR USING SMARTPHONE APPS

Next time you're waiting in a queue, count how many people are using their phones.
Many of us have lost the ability to stand and wait without using an electronic device.

A recent study suggests that some of the main reasons we use our smartphones are for
'connectedness,' 'excitement,' 'curiosity' and 'productivity' [32]. However, another study
published in the same year investigated the reasons we use the apps on our devices.
Their findings suggest that our main motivations for pulling out our phones are more
likely to be associated with being alone, being bored, or waiting for something [33].

These motivations all relate to some form of under stimulation. When we are under
stimulated, often in low-cognitive gear and particularly if we are not used to the
sensation, we are likely to start foraging for new information. The smartphone means
that we never need to be bored again, but when we give in to the temptation of distraction to fulfill this 'need' we degrade our response inhibition and cognitive control
abilities. We need to embrace boredom again and use it to teach us something. Next

time you are waiting in line and bored, stay bored, and use it as an opportunity to train your brain.

However, sometimes willpower is not enough, and we need a helping hand.

4.   LESS IS MORE

Our visual environment is too competitive. The laptops, smartphones and tablets on our desk have become symbols of the hyper-productive knowledge worker, but it's likely a folly that is compromising the effectiveness of our work, our relaxation and our recovery.

There are good cases for using multiple screens and it can enhance performance in a given task such as writing an article and referencing a source from a different device, for example.

The problem of multiple screens is that it can encourage task-switching and it can increase demands on our attention unnecessarily, compromising our performance and recovery. We should also consider what we are doing in these switches. How much value are these 'sub-tasks' creating? It's a good opportunity to apply a Pareto analysis. You may find that, during a period of frequent screen hopping, 80% of your output is being generated by 20% of the work you are doing. Could you get rid of this wasted work by eliminating some screens, open apps or programmes?

The average Brit switches between their mobile phone, tablet and laptop 21 times an hour during an evening as they snack on bite-size chunks of digital content [34]. If you can avoid using multiple screens, you will eliminate a lot temptation and increase your likelihood of staying focussed and relaxed.

5.   PUT IT AWAY

It was easy at school; I didn't even have a smartphone. If I'd had one, I would have been told to put it away. Today, I try not to waste my limited cognitive control resources on self-control, if I don't have to. Often it's easier to eliminate distraction, as in step 3 of the PriME method, than have to make the effort to avoid it.

For me, this involves minimising the number of screens I'm using and leaving my phone, and any other unnecessary devices, set on 'flight mode'. I may be tempted to look at my phone, but during the time I'm considering whether I'm tempted enough to walk all the way over to find it, System 2 has usually had a chance to modify System 1's suggestion and redirect me towards my higher-level goals.

SHUT DOWN, DON'T MINIMIZE, AT THE END OF THE DAY

I shut down applications on my desktop, rather than simply minimizing them. Most importantly, I do this at the end of the day. Shutting down, rather than minimising, means that the notifications disappear, and this way I can avoid being distracted by them automatically appearing, when I open my computer in the morning.

The cost associated with being aware of an unread e-mail sitting in your inbox is equivalent to losing 10 IQ points [35]. Shutting applications down at the end of the day and switching my phone to airplane mode means that I'm not bombarded with notifications of unread messages when I open my computer or check the time on my phone in the morning.

I have to admit, this was tougher than I thought it would be. Like 79% of smartphone owners, I used to always look at my device within 15 minutes of waking and instantly entered a reactive, distracted state of mind. I had a Pavlovian response to picking up my phone or opening my computer. My brain would drool dopamine with the expectation that new information was on its way.

Breaking this habit took effort, as I knew that there were messages waiting for me even if I couldn't see the notification, but I also knew that checking them would lead me down a rabbit hole of distraction if I started reading and replying. Perhaps worse, if I only read the titles or the first few lines, as I often did, the new thoughts would hijack some of my attention and working memory for the rest of the day.

I had to create a new 2-step habit to replace the old habit. Step 1 started the night before, with the shut down and airplane mode process I've just described. Step 2 was to start my day with a new coffee-making ritual. Even then, I still try not to touch my phone until the first 90-minute pro-active block of activity is complete.

In time, the absence of the visual trigger of notifications from my phone and computer degraded the stimulus-response. The power my phone had over me weakened and I felt able to start my day with more clarity, tranquility and more easily enter a state of focus and productivity.

6. 'ASYNCHRONISE' YOURSELF

If we had to design a digital information shovel for the 4th Industrial Revolution, it probably would not look like e-mail. The average inbox is an exercise in visual competition and e-mail threads can become so long and convoluted that it's easy to surpass the limits of working memory long before you find the message you're looking for.

One of the best things about text-based communication, whether it's e-mail, an instant message or a post on a collaborative working platform, is that the message may arrive instantly, but we don't have to respond straight away; it offers efficient asynchronous information exchange. I don't have to be there to receive the message and I can batch my responses at a later time.

For some reason, knowledge workers have made the unconscious decision that electronic messages should be treated the same way as a red-telephone. We've become hyper-responsive. When it rings, we leap across the room.

Quarantining e-mail within shorter periods, rather than interweaving it throughout the day, is associated with a number of benefits. A recent study found that checking e-mail three times per day, as opposed to as often as we can, is associated with less stress and improved physical and psychological wellbeing [36].

I believe that one of the greatest failures of modern e-mail and messaging applications is that instant notifications are set 'on' as a default. We need to reclaim the asynchronisity of electronic communication. Who is with me! Maybe I'll print that manifesto on a very wide t-shirt.

7 TIPS TO IMPROVE YOUR EMAIL

1) Do not give your email address for marketing purposes.

2) Turn off email notifications.

3) Do not start your day with email.

4) Set time for email processing, a maximum of three times per day. Try to empty your inbox during these times.

5) Process every email: delete, archive, delegate, do, do later. For bigger activities, schedule a future time.

6) Respect others, and only forward or copy e-mails when there is a good reason.

7) Keep your emails short and subject lines descriptive.

7. UPGRADE YOUR MEETINGS

According to the World Economic Forum, complex problem solving, critical thinking and creativity are the top three skills we will need in 2020. People management, and coordinating with others, are numbers four and five [39]. Meetings will continue to be an essential part of our working life, perhaps even more important than they are today.

Many of our current meeting practises offer a lot of room for improvement. Meetings often lack clear direction and leave us feeling that they could have been replaced with a single, well-worded e-mail. However, with a few simple changes, they can become a great opportunity to be creative and to collaborate effectively.

10 WAYS TO UPGRADE YOUR MEETINGS

1) Use the PriME method (Priority, Mindset and Elimination), before you begin a meeting, to establish a clear purpose, target and agenda.

2) Only invite the relevant people.

3) Ensure meetings start on time.

4) Send materials early and expect people to come prepared.

5) Do not use the meeting time to go through the sent material: focus on discussion and decision-making.

6) Consider standing and walking meetings.

7) Consider limiting meetings to either 10, 20, 45 minutes, or 1 hour 45 minutes. Most people schedule meetings to start on the hour, or at half-past, so planning meetings for these durations should provide a 10-20 minute break before the next scheduled meeting. Any meetings expected to last longer than 1 hour 45 minutes should be broken down into smaller 'chunks.'

8) Consider prohibiting the use of smart phones and reading emails during meetings.

9) Consider daily or weekly short update meetings with your team. This can help to keep people informed and eliminate many other meetings.

10) Also schedule unstructured meetings, for more informal, social and 'unforced' creative interactions, but be clear about the distinction between these meetings and those with a defined purpose, target and agenda.

8.   ASAP OR VIP?

At school, a fellow pupil couldn't simply walk into the room and start talking to you in the middle of a class. Another teacher would never wander in and ask you about a different subject, while you were learning from another member of the faculty. They had to wait. Students are VIPs – very important people – and their learning and creative time is sacrosanct.

Limited access is the essence of a VIP experience; it's turning left when you board the plane, it's the roped off area in the nightclub. We need to create our own VIP bubble of knowledge work to get our most meaningful and valuable work done.

1)   **Step 1:** You are a VIP

The first step in this process is to set expectations with co-workers and customers that access is limited – you are a very important person with a unique contribution to make and the value you deliver to your company and clients will be enhanced if you're able to focus. Set the expectation that you need to create space and time to do this. If you're a leader, help your team to create this limited access for themselves as well.

2)   **Step 2:** Schedule time for work and time-off

A well-known global consulting group conducted a four-year-experiment with a radical approach to work. Consultants in this firm generally worked in teams of four. One of the interventions in the experiment required every team member to take a complete day off each week, sometime between Monday and Friday, and to schedule this day off in advance. This meant they only worked four days out of seven.

In addition, they had to take a complete evening off work and also pre-schedule the time for this. The study leaders added another consultant to the teams, to ensure each client had four full-time equivalents working on the project.

In the early stages of the study, they deliberately chose a team of consultants who were working with a new client that the firm wanted to cultivate intensively. The project involved a lot of interaction with the client. The study report notes that the consultants were anxious about this new approach, but after five months of employees experimenting with deliberate periodic rest and work periods, the consultants reported increased satisfaction with their jobs, that they were more likely to envision a long-term future at the company, that they were more content with work–life balance and they were prouder of their accomplishments. In addition, they also reported enhanced value delivery to the client [37].

Proactively scheduling work and rest can improve life and performance.

9. SCHEDULE, DON'T 'TO-DO'

Jotting down a 'to-do' list is the usual response as we try to move from being reactive to proactive. However, we often write tasks with vague descriptions and our lists can quickly become an unwieldy distraction of ill-defined, uncompleted items. Also, when we finally sit down to complete some tasks on our lists, we waste time and mental energy thinking about how we need to approach them.

In contrast, scheduling tasks to be completed at specific times, with specific instructions, can have a positive impact on productivity and cognition.

> If you schedule a task and use a verb to describe what you need to do, it's more likely turn into 'done,' than remain as 'to-do' and it will free valuable cognitive resources.

For example, rather than writing: "Kilda e-mail"

I can add an event in my schedule at 9:30am that says: "Look at layout options, choose preferred option and let Kilda know by e-mail."

This small amount of extra time and detail means that I stop worrying about what I need to do and I don't need to waste any cognitive resources remembering what the task involves or when I need to do it. It's more likely to be completed and, by being specific, it makes it much easier to delegate to someone else.

10. DON'T BE A PERFECTIONIST

It's impossible to do everything. As Tim Ferriss says, "Oftentimes, in order to do the big things, you have to let the small bad things happen [38]." This challenge has a number of levels:

1) Limiting attention can release your creativity, but you need to think carefully about who and what you give your attention to.

2) Accepting that attention is limited and following its 'rules' means that you also must accept that some things will pass you by and go unnoticed.

3) Letting things pass by means that you will annoy some people who are used to being able to make themselves appear on your radar anytime, but this group of people is likely much smaller than you think.

POLARISE YOUR WORK

When people apply the methods described here, their days are characterised by more distinct periods of hard work, followed by effective recovery and reflection – a polarised model of work.

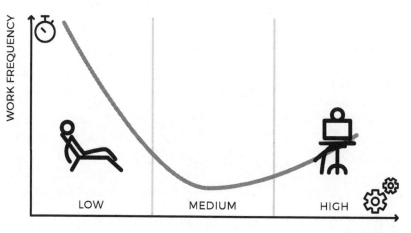

Low: Relaxation and recovery (low complexity, low switching)

Protect this time by avoiding distractions (switching) and pseudo-work (social media, etc.) Possible in brief periods through the day, but should also take place over longer periods, usually during the evening.

Medium: Routine and quick tasks (medium complexity, higher switching)

Some switching is inevitable, as you are likely to be able to complete the medium-gear tasks, such reading and replying most e-mails, quite quickly as the work is not too complex. Complex issues should actually be avoided when working in this way (fast and switching) as it's much easier to make mistakes. Schedule separate time for the complex issues you discover while working in this gear.

High: Focussed and demanding tasks (High complexity, low switching)

Reserve longer periods for deep focus, to allocate cognitive resources to the complexity of the task, rather than in switching or time pressure. Switching tasks should be avoided to maintain focus and reduce unnecessary cognitive load.

When you reflect on the ideas presented in this chapter, how do you think your 'attention matrix' would look if you applied them?

COGNITIVE GEAR	REACTIVE	PROACTIVE
HIGH	TACTICAL PROBLEM SOLVING CRISIS MANAGEMENT	COMPLEX & IMPORTANT STRATEGIC & LONG-TERM
MEDIUM	ADMINISTRATION E-MAIL PHONE CALLS	
LOW	'DEFAULT-MODE' TIME	READING A BOOK
ZERO	NAPS	NIGHT-TIME SLEEP

We find that people 'rescue' time, thanks to reduced task-switching and cutting down on the frequency with which they check e-mail. As a result of this extra time, gained from more proactivity and 'time-boxing' discipline, they are able to make better progress on tasks with strategic and long-term significance. In addition, stress is reduced due to minimised switching, they enjoy more creative down-time, and better recovery.

Try out some new ideas, measure the results, adjust the parameters and repeat. You can be efficient and effective. "Believe in yourself."

TRY THIS AT HOME (AND AT WORK)

1) Next time you notice yourself using extreme negative words, consider it as a prompt to engage effortful System 2 thinking. What other factors can you take into account? Remind yourself that change is possible, that you are capable of much more than you think and that your beliefs play a significant role in this.

2) Try to plan at least four hours of your day and break it up into designated 'classes' where you focus on a particular project or task.

3) We've become hyper-responsive to electronic communication, but could you change your approach? Checking e-mail three times per day, as opposed to as often as we can, is associated with less stress and improved predictions of physical and psychological wellbeing. Next time you are waiting in line and bored, stay bored, and use the time as an opportunity to relax and train your brain to resist the urge to look at your devices.

4)   Set expectations with clients and co-workers and limit your email and electronic communication to deliberately scheduled blocks of time. It can be helpful to set up an auto-responder, to inform senders when you are likely to check your messages and get back to them.

5)   Try the 'PriME' method:

    Priority: What is the most important thing I must achieve in the next 90 minutes?

    Mindset: How can I perceive the challenges in these 90 minutes with a growth mindset?

    Elimination: Is there anything I can get rid of to reduce the likelihood that I'll be distracted?

JÜRG ZELTNER: PRESIDENT, UBS WEALTH MANAGEMENT

Jürg Zeltner is speaking to me from his office in Zurich, where he leads UBS's Wealth Management division. He's worked for the firm for more than 30 years; joining the Swiss Bank Corporation in 1987, which merged with the Union Bank of Switzerland in 1998 to become UBS. Jürg begins by reflecting on three of the major shifts that he's seen during this time.

"We've seen more macro changes than ever over the last 30 years. We've witnessed the biggest ever wealth creation, part of it on the back of huge leverage, part of it because economies, such as China, were growing. The world saw more people move out of poverty than ever before. These changes are another step of evolution; some would even call it revolution. The real question is: have we seen the peak of it?"

Secondly, Jürg has seen a major shift in the way we access and consume information.

"The way information is delivered to people is very different now. For a long time, especially in our industry, we benefited from information arbitrage, but today everyone has so much information to hand. We've also seen a massive increase in the use of 'big data'. Previously, we had it, but nobody used it. Now there is a 'war' to maximize the use of data."

CHANGE IN WAYS OF WORKING

The third shift Jürg has identified is in the way people communicate with each other in the business environment.

"We've moved away from purely hierarchical systems to team approaches. We need new ways of engaging with clients and employees. We need to think about the way we inform ourselves and gather information before we make decisions. We need ways to grasp these changes and determine what it means for society and for our industry."

Problem solving among diverse, inter-disciplinary teams, not only in terms of gender, but also in terms of what people have lived through, where they have been, and what they have seen, will grow in importance.

CHANGES IN WHAT PEOPLE WANT AT WORK

"The workforce is changing fast," says Jürg. The Future of the Workforce, a report commissioned by UBS Wealth Management, identifies critical ways in which the workforce is set to change in the coming years.

"Tomorrow's workforce will expect their employers to counteract a new wave of automation and digital disruption by creating work – and places to work – that optimise their mental, physical and emotional health, and performance."

This trend is in stark contrast to historic perspectives on wellbeing in the workplace, something that Jürg identifies in his own life. "If you'd asked me 10 years ago. I would've told you that I had no time for that. I thought 'I have a big runway, I feel good.' Then you realise that time is limited, and that you need to take some personal responsibility, find your own purpose, your own drive, your own balance. The more you're in synch with yourself, the more efficient you are as a leader."

Jürg's observation is supported by UBS's research, which has identified that staff productivity rises by an average of 13% in businesses that introduce strategies to boost levels of wellbeing. UBS's report also identifies that working with a purpose, shaped by clear and shared principles, will become increasingly significant for employees.

"People want their values and principles to be in place at work and at home. The more we say 'change is the only constant,' the more important purpose and values become."

RECIPES FOR WELLBEING AND PERFORMANCE

On a personal level, Jürg has implemented a number of tactics of his own to optimise his efficiency and effectiveness. He shares three of the behaviours that have helped him step off "the hamster wheel that we often fall on to."

1) "Acknowledging that you need sleep is the first 'big one.' You need to recognise that you need quality recovery time."

2) "Acknowledging your own physique. That does not just mean doing sport, it means having good nutrition and balance. Importantly, it means addressing socially expected behaviours. You have to create a line and say 'this is what I do!'"

3) "Try to organise each day by following a rhythm. Have shorter meetings, allow more time in-between for yourself. Try to have a more balanced day."

LEADERS MAKE FOCUS ON WELLBEING 'ACCEPTABLE'

Jürg is also keen to emphasise the role of leaders in helping people to invest time and energy in their wellbeing.

"People often struggle to talk about what they need, and I think leaders have a role to play, to say 'This is something you need to focus on and it is something that you should make a personal priority.'"

Continuing the theme of 'three,' Jürg offers the following timely reflections on leadership:

1) "You need to be a 'pro'. That's expected of you in today's world. Regardless of whether you're a lawyer, a client advisor, a financial expert, you need to be professional in what you do."

2) "You need to be in control of yourself. You need to be able to manage yourself with your interests, your ego, and your aspirations. You can't be perfect, but you need to manage this dimension if you want to be qualified to lead other people."

3) "Your institutional leverage only comes if you're able to lead other people. Because you might be a great person on your own, but the question is, 'can you institutionalise?' Can you take people on a journey? Can we make that journey better together?"

In some circles, there can be a tendency to focus on the potentially negative effects of change, but Jürg encourages us to see the future as a source of opportunity.

"The world is a complex place, and sometimes you might see more risks and challenges. While it's very true that a lot is demanded of us as leaders, we should never lose sight that this can create opportunities for the ones who try to embrace it. I would say people who are willing to learn and adapt are going to be happier people. People who try to fight against reality are going to struggle to deal with it. The notion that we all learn, we all change, we all adapt, is a good thing and a very relevant learning for all of us."

Jürg concludes by looking back at his time at UBS once again: "I feel as excited to be here today, as I did on day one."

8.

ON A NEW TRAJECTORY

"Driving an F1 car is not a particularly healthy thing to do [...] I want to live a quality life when I'm old, and not suffer from horribly degenerated discs."
Four-Time Formula One World Champion, Sebastian Vettel

When I first heard this quote, I was surprised. It's rare that a professional athlete considers life after sport, but Sebastian Vettel is clearly thinking in the long-term. We often use this quote in our presentations, to highlight the importance of looking after our body, throughout our lives.

In this chapter, we'll explore a number of key themes in relation to our health, well-being and performance including:

- Why we can't separate the body from the mind.

- What does healthy aging look like?

- Are masters athletes 'freaks,' or can we learn something from them?

- What type of exercise is most beneficial?

- Why recovery is about more than sleep.

- The three metrics you should try to measure.

It's too easy to forget about our physical selves, until it's too late. This was a point that Aki was always eager to make when a client came to see us. "What path are you on? How does this fit with big-picture?" He'd often pull out a marker pen and draw a graph to illustrate what this path could look like, something like the one below, but much less neat, on the flip-chart in his office.

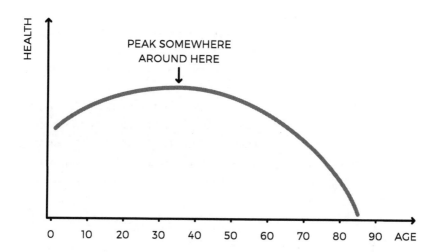

During the time that I've been writing this book, I've used an alarm to remind myself to stand up, move around, and stretch at regular intervals. It's a practice I recommend to many of my clients, but have rarely followed myself – until recently.

I was flying back from the West Coast of the United States, earlier this year, and decided that the 11-hour flight would be a great opportunity for an

When I deconstruct it, the idea of setting a digital alarm to remind me that I have a body that needs to move, is a little strange. Perhaps I need a more fundamental wakeup call.

epic, uninterrupted work session. I got a lot of work done, but woke up the next day and found that I was unable to move my neck. The hours hunched over my laptop caught up with me. I received some treatment and followed a rehabilitation process, which resolved the issue, but it made me realise that I needed to pay more attention to my body while working. I direct so much attention to my cognitive work, I sometimes forget about my physical self.

For most of our history, regular movement has been an incidental and essential part of life. Everyday tasks required exertion and, even in the industrial age, many forms of employment were physically demanding.

However, we've created a world that has made us less reliant on our bodies. In more industrially established nations, labour-saving home appliances became common

The decoupling of physical capacity from many of our daily activities means that we're often only aware of our body when something starts to go wrong.

in the 1950s. Global car ownership grew fourfold between 1950 and 1999 [1]. The service economy developed and separated physical effort from value creation for many people. Today, we may feel that our physical presence seems less important than ever. Our thoughts and ideas create value and influence. I can sit at a computer, work and can connect remotely with almost anyone, anywhere in the world. The importance of being physically fit and present, at home and at work, seems to have diminished. We can easily become convinced that it is our minds that are primary influence on the trajectory of our lives.

WE CAN'T SEPARATE THE BODY FROM THE MIND

Viewing cognition as formal logic, which we do through the information processing model, may encourage us to detach our perception of the world from our body. Much of our thinking is still influenced by our old friend Descartes. His 17th Century theory of the mind claimed that "there is a great difference between mind and body [...] the mind or soul of man is entirely different from the body [2]."

But evidence suggests that we cannot separate mind and body. Our experience of the world is 'embodied' and this reality even leaks into our everyday language. We use metaphors to make sense of abstract concepts, by describing them as being positioned and active in a physical space [3]. We say things like: "He's at the height of his powers" or "I was under their control" and "I gravitated towards the idea."

Whatever you do, whether it's thinking, moving, recovering or simply staying alive, one molecule supplies the energy: Adenosine triphosphate (ATP). It's been described as 'the energy currency of life'.

Our emotions and experiences have a distinctive physiology, expressed as patterns in our body and brain [4]. We use our mind and our physical bodies to help us make sense of ourselves, other people and interact with the wider systems we are part of.

THE ENERGY CURRENCY OF LIFE

Within our brains, research suggests that regions associated with cognitive and physical tasks may share a common motivational system [5]. In addition, whether an activity takes place in the body or the brain, a single 'energy currency' facilitates every transaction.

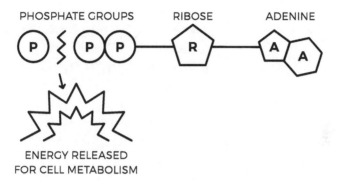

When ATP is broken down, energy is released. The energy in the food we eat, combined with the oxygen we breathe, rebuilds ATP once it's done its job, so it can be used again throughout the body and brain.

The average human body only contains about 250 grams of ATP [6]. Consequently, it has to be continuously recycled after it has been broken down. Each day, the average person turns over an amount of ATP equivalent to their own body weight [7].

What we pay attention to influences the effort and energy we allocate to a task. Whether a task is cognitive or physical, our attention ultimately determines where and how we invest our ATP [8]. To ensure that we invest our ATP in a way that fits our short-term and long-term goals, we need to pay attention to the right things.

WHAT WILL YOUR LIFE LOOK LIKE?

When I spend time with clients and drill-down to the core of what they're looking for in life, the most common motivation seems to be the desire to have enough energy, time and the capability to invest in the things they feel are important. Achieving these aims has a significant cognitive attentional component, but there is also an important physical aspect, which is easy to overlook. It doesn't matter how well-trained our attention is if we don't have the energy or the physical capability to do what we want to do.

We only have one body to get us through life. If we are going to stay functional and capable, for as long as possible, we need to pay more attention to it.

It sounds obvious, but our physical selves are essential, even as we spend increasing amounts of time interacting with each other through digital representations of ourselves. If we need to set an alarm to remind ourselves about our physical body, this message probably needs emphasising.

LIVING AND WORKING LONGER

The 20th century was a time of profound change socially, technologically and economically. Science and engineering overcame a number of fundamental challenges, which critics had previously deemed unsolvable [9], and global average lifespan doubled in the space of 100 years [10].

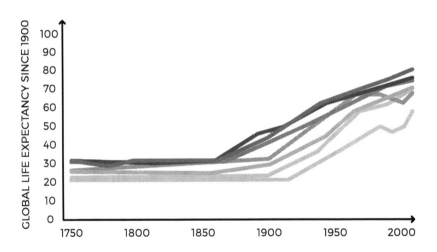

Global lifespan has doubled since 1900 [10].

Changes in lifespan have continued into the 21st century. Someone who is 50 today could expect to live until they are 83 [10]. A baby born in 2007 in the US, UK, Japan, Italy, Germany, France or Canada has a 50% chance of living until they are over 100 [11].

It's likely that we will work for more years than any generation before us. For many, this will be a necessity as much as a choice, as the increasing social costs of an ageing population are pushing back retirement age in many countries. These trends will have significant economic, social and psychological impacts, but one of the key questions we need to ask in relation to these topics is 'do you want an increased lifespan, or an extended health-span?'

LIFESPAN OR 'HEALTH-SPAN'

Different parts of our body and brain mature at different rates, so it's very difficult to say what a human 'peak age' might be. However, it's clear that the first phase of life is dominated by growth, while declines become more apparent in the second half.

Many of us assume that the ageing process is a fixed process, that we reach our peak then begin an irreversible decline. This hasn't stopped an entire industry from trying to make an impact, though. The global market for anti-aging products, technologies and services is expected to grow from $282 billion in 2015, to $331 billion in 2020 [12].

We're living longer, but we're living 'sicker.' The problem is more than skin-deep. The top three global killers are associated with cardiovascular disease [13] while physical inactivity is a primary cause of most chronic ailments [14].

In 1949, a 39-year old epidemiologist called Jerry Morris made the observation that London's double-decker bus drivers, who spent their days behind the wheel, had significantly higher rates of cardiovascular disease relative to the conductors, who spent their days climbing up and down the bus stairs. Morris extended the study to the postal service, and noted that postal workers who made their deliveries using a bike or on foot had fewer heart attacks than employees who served at the counters in post-office branches [15].

In 1958, he published a paper in the British Medical Journal, which woke many people up to the idea that we need to pay more attention to physical activity and that if we do, we may be able to reduce the risk and delay the onset of chronic disease [16].

This early work eventually gave rise to the notion of lifespan verses health-span: that we could 'compress morbidity' and delay the development of chronic diseases, squeezing them into as brief a period as possible at the end of life.

It seems that many of us would prefer to 'die young as late as possible.' We can start making active decisions that can likely influence this outcome, today, but we need to reconnect with our physical selves and reframe our perspective on what the human body is capable of, at all stages in life.

WHAT'S POSSIBLE?

One of my great inspirations was my first cycling coach, Geoff Cooke. I spent a lot of time working with him to develop my strength, power and speed, but he also taught me a number of valuable life lessons. In particular, it became clear to me that the human body and mind is capable of great feats throughout life. When I was 18, Geoff regularly out-lifted me in the gym, and beat me in sprints in the velodrome, despite our 40-year age gap.

Before his coaching career, Geoff was an accomplished cyclist, winning a gold medal at the 1974 Commonwealth Games. He held multiple National Championship titles in track cycling events, and represented Great Britain in the 1972 Munich Olympics. Geoff retired from competitive cycling at age 34. The following year, he became the National Coach for the 'British Cycling Federation'; a position he held for the next 10 years.

During this time, the popularity of masters competitions, featuring a number of age categories, increased significantly. The Sydney World Masters Games attracted double the number of competitors that took part in the Sydney 2000 Olympics.

In 1995, aged 51, Geoff decided to make a comeback to competitive cycling. Soon after his return to the sport as a rider, he won a bronze medal at the World Masters Track Cycling Championship. The following year, he won two gold medals. His successes now includes 61 National Championship titles, nine European Masters Championships and 31 gold medals in the World Masters Championships.

At age 72, 21 years on, Geoff is still racing. In August 2016, he was in the final stages of his preparation for the World Masters Championships. Geoff was taking part in a training session at his local velodrome. He was riding in a group, 40-laps into a 50-lap warm-up. Each rider was taking turns to ride on the front, before peeling off, and the pace was starting to increase.

"We were really legging it round," says Geoff, which means they were probably riding at around 45-50 km/hr. "I felt comfortable, because I had the most terrific form [fitness]".

Geoff was counting down the laps, calculating that he would be at the front, ready to contest the sprint, in the closing metres of the session.

"That's where I wanted to be, but then somebody punctured. They fell off, and they were lying in front of me, across the top of the track. I dived for the inside-line, to try to avoid the crash, but one of the bikes slid down the track, in front of me. I hit the bike, went over the top of the handlebars, and I don't remember anything until I came to [regained consciousness]."

Geoff fractured five ribs, broke his collarbone, his scapula and punctured a lung. He was admitted to intensive care, where he stayed for a few days, before being moved to a conventional ward. With the World Championships just nine weeks away, his dream of defending his multiple titles was in tatters.

After eight days in hospital, Geoff was discharged to continue his recovery at home. He spent a few days doing some basic rehabilitation, trips to the sauna and some short rides on an indoor trainer, until he couldn't stay away from the track any longer. Though he could barely carry his bike and bag, he dragged himself back, set up his bike, and began to ride around. He gradually increased his speed, lifting himself in and out of the saddle, as he would have to in his sprint and time-trial events. He continued to test his body and mind, to see how they responded to the effort. After 30 laps, Geoff had made a decision: "I've got eight weeks until the World Masters Championships. It's on!"

On 4 October, two months and three days after he smashed into the track and landed in intensive care, Geoff had the opportunity to defend his world title in the Men's Time-Trial; a gruelling event requiring competitors to ride as fast as possible over 500-metres. Geoff's closest competitor at the event was David Rowe, a former teammate from the 1972 Munich Olympics, who'd also returned to compete as a masters cyclist. In the time-trial, riders set off individually and race against the clock. Geoff needed to better Dave's time of 39.906 seconds to secure the goal medal.

Geoff's bike is fitted into the automated start gate on the wooden 250-metre track. A metal frame holds the bike in place, keeping it upright with two pneumatic actuators that grip the back-wheel. They will only release the rider at the end of an automated sequence of 5 loud 'beeps'.

Beep! 5 seconds. Take a big breath in.

Beep! 4 seconds. Breathe out.

Beep! 3 seconds. Breathe in again. Your lungs are working well now.

Beep! 2 seconds. Out again.

Beep! 1 second. Rock back, fill your lungs, extend your arms.

BANG!!!! Drive from the hips. Keep your body square. Power down – forcing yourself over the handlebars – pushing as much energy into the pedals to accelerate the bike as fast as possible.

Geoff sprints hard out of the gate, out of the saddle, before quickly assuming an aerodynamic position. He hits the first bend on the track. The g-force generated by the steep banking forces his arms into the handlebars and stresses his freshly healed scapula and collarbone. He's wrestling the bike, driving as much force as he can into the machine, compelling it to keep accelerating.

He's 20 seconds in – one-lap to go. Geoff's face is a mask of pain. It looks like he's slowing. His mouth is wide open, his lungs are being stretched to their limit and his five fractured ribs bend with the effort. The final corner. The final few metres, and he throws the bike at the line. The time flashes up on the giant timing-board that hangs inside the velodrome – 39.052 seconds. He's the World Champion once again!

"When I was on the podium and they were playing the national anthem, I've got to tell you, I was a little bit emotional, and I'm not really an emotional character. I'd dug myself out of this big hole, and I'd won it."

Nine weeks between intensive care and a World Championship Gold medal, at the age of 72, is an inspiring example of what the human body and mind can achieve.

STUDYING MASTERS ATHLETES

I didn't simply include Geoff's story as an entertaining example of what's possible if you pursue a lifetime of physical training. Every one of us can learn something from masters athletes.

Sport provides a laboratory for studying what human beings are capable of. In athletic competition, cardiovascular, respiratory, neuromuscular as well as cognitive systems must all work well individually, and as a system, making it one of the best testing grounds for how our body and brain should work together at their best [17].

Studying ageing is a challenge. As we get older, the number of confounding factors in observational research increases. The longer we live, the more choices we make, the wider variety of environments, stimuli and stresses we are exposed to. This can distort results, making it difficult to discern the difference between natural declines in health and performance, and deteriorations that occur as a result of lifestyle factors and poor choices.

However, the high levels of physical activity among masters athletes mean that they should be free from many of the negative effects of sedentary behaviour [18].

Any declines in athletic performance therefore mirror the changes in the body and mind that occur as we age, rather than being a result of inactivity or other intervening lifestyle factors.

The performance of masters athletes can provide us with a biological model to understand what healthy, optimum aging looks like [19, 20, 21].

COMPRESSED AGEING

The performance changes in masters sporting events display a 'curvilinear,' rather than linear, pattern. Instead of reaching a peak in their 30s, before experiencing an inexorable and linear decline, masters athletes retain close-to-peak performance for much longer, experiencing a gentler decline, followed by a rapid drop-off, much later in life..

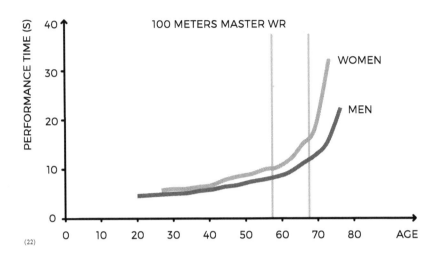

These findings reflect the aim that many of us have in life: maintain our health, physical and cognitive capacities for as long as we can, and compress ill health into as short a period as possible.

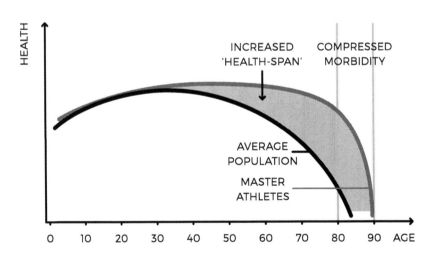

WE ARE ALWAYS GROWING OR DECAYING

Whether we are aware of it or not, our body is always changing. It's either growing or decaying. If you're alive, you are either investing energy in growth, or liberating energy through decay. Our metabolism includes all the chemical reactions involved in these processes, and it can be summarised in two routes:

- Catabolism (decay) - breakdown of molecules to obtain energy.

- Anabolism (growth) - manufacture of the compounds required by our cells.

Our body strives to maintain a balance, monitoring and controlling critical parameters within specific ranges. This state of balance is known as homeostasis, but it's a moving target. The body and brain try to be as efficient as possible with the resources available. If you don't use it, you lose it. The body 'decides' what capacities it needs to upgrade, and what it can get rid of, depending on where we direct our attention and ultimately on the decisions and actions we take.

Human life is dominated by these patterns, but our decisions can make a significant difference to the trajectory of our life. When we are young, the body sends a lot of 'growth signals' involuntarily. We don't have to make active decisions to encourage our body to grow fitter and stronger – a cascade of hormones does that for us. As we get older, we need to be more intentional to offset the 'decay' signals that begin to dominate. However, the signals don't need to include a lifetime of athletic training. Significant benefits are possible from relatively small 'doses' of physical activity combined with sufficient quality rest and recovery.

MAXIMISE GROWTH, MINIMISE DECAY

If you're younger than 35, there is still time to maximise 'peak' health and fitness. Ideally, you should aim to start from as high a point as possible, before the influence of decay becomes more pronounced. However, if you're older than 35, significant improvements, and even reversals in some areas, are still possible.

It's never too late to reconnect with your physical self and change your trajectory for the better. Studies have demonstrated that even 90 year- olds can improve their strength and power, with the appropriate training regimen [23].

Where should you be directing your attention, time and energy? In the context of your body, the most effective decisions you can make to change your trajectory can be grouped in two areas:

1) Upgrade your chassis: Improve the function of your musculoskeletal system.

2) Upgrade you engine: Increase your capacity to supply energy (ATP) for all of life's activities.

MOVEMENT IS MEDICINE

If I told you there was a pill you could take to enjoy all of the benefits listed below, you'd take it wouldn't you?

- Improves strength
- Improves endurance
- Supports bone health
- Reduces risk of diabetes
- Reduces risk of cardiovascular disease
- Reduces risk of diabetes
- Improves muscle quality and function
- Helps with weight control
- Reduces anxiety and stress
- Increases self esteem
- Improves concentration and attention

(24-28)

All of these benefits are associated with simply moving our bodies, which sets off a cascade of positive 'growth' signals. If we are moving, our body is incentivised to adapt and increase its supply of energy, and improve the function of our body and brain.

Increasing your levels of physical activity is one of the few interventions that has been demonstrated as beneficial across age-ranges, ethnic groups, and spectrums of physical ability. The benefits of physical activity far outweigh the possibility of adverse outcomes in almost every population [31].

However, as with the distribution of our cognitive work, these periods of physical work need to be interspersed with periods of rest and recovery. While physical work sends growth 'signals', the actual growing takes place when we rest. We can imagine our decisions about when to move, physically work or rest, as a selection of levers we can 'pull' to alter the trajectory of our lives. In the context of this chapter, we're going to focus on five levers:

1) Move more

2) Move slow

3) Move fast

4) Move heavy

5) Recover well

MOVE MORE: TAKE YOUR MEDICINE

Physical activity levels in our leisure time have remained relatively constant over the past few decades [29]. However, sedentary activities at home, such as watching TV or consuming other media, coupled with technological advances in the workplace, mean that we spend a lot more time sitting over the course of an average week than we used to. This change has a number of significant metabolic consequences [30] that encourage our bodies to enter a 'decay state'.

As our weekly minutes of physical activity decreases, risk of premature death significantly increases [31].

Simply moving more, and moving more regularly, even if we have to set an alarm to remind ourselves to stand up and walk around now and again, has a powerful influence on reducing the risk of disease, death and improving quality of life [32].

There seems to be a dose-response association between total sitting time and the risk of dying from anything.

BUT I GO TO THE GYM…

One of the reasons I fell into the trap of sitting for long periods during the day, was that I thought my regular daily exercise habit made me immune from the impact of sedentary behaviour. I convinced myself that, if I went to the gym, or rode my bike, and worked-out hard for an hour, surely this was enough to offset the static hours spent at my keyboard. This was a view shared by many of my clients, a number of whom still competed in endurance sports at a relatively high level. Unfortunately, we can't 'out-exercise' our desk-jockey lifestyle.

In 2009, researchers studied 17,013 people aged between 18-90 years old. They found a dose-response relationship between sitting time and dying from anything. More significantly, they also found that this risk was independent of overall physical activity levels [33]. It doesn't matter how active you are. If you sit down for long periods, you are increasing your risk for chronic disease.

These findings have been supported by a number of other studies. Those of us sitting for 11 hours or more, per day, are at the greatest risk, regardless of how much physical activity we do [34]. Sitting for six hours per day, versus three hours, significantly elevates our risk of death, especially from cardiovascular disease, in both men and women [30].

MOVE SLOW: INCREASE THE 'SIZE' OF YOUR ENGINE

Back in Chapter 3, we discussed how the human body can perform over a wide range of intensities and durations. When we move relatively slowly for extended periods, our 'aerobic system' supplies the majority of the energy we need.

Finding ways to increase our volume of low-intensity aerobic activity – meaning an intensity that still allows us to speak in full sentences – is a powerful way to 'upgrade our engine,' the body's capacity to regenerate ATP and supply energy for all of life's activities. Physiologically, these efforts are in the low-gear range. The sustained elevated heart rate, breathing and repeated low-intensity muscle contractions set off a torrent of beneficial signals in our body. In particular, they stimulate the body to increase the number of mitochondrial 'energy factories' in the muscle cells and improve the structure and function of our heart, lungs and blood vessels. Effectively, by working at low-intensity, for extended periods, you can increase your 'energy budget.'

Aiming to accumulate 10,000 steps each day has become a common means to increase daily physical activity. It's often the default 'benchmark' set by many activity trackers and platforms, and represents approximately 8km of walking. Programs designed to accumulate 10,000 steps a day have been shown to positively influence many variables that are indicators of health, such as fitness and psychological well-being [35]. This makes sense, as most health benefits occur with at least 150 minutes a week of moderate-intensity physical activity [31], which it is possible to achieve with 10,000 brisk steps each day. While some studies have not been supportive, many have demonstrated that increasing step count, and trying to integrate additional steps into your day to reach the 10,000 target, can be beneficial in terms of increasing physical activity and health [36].

FROM 30 TO 90 MINUTES PER WEEK

It seems that the most important aspect is to have a goal, and try to improve the amount of daily activity we engage in with small increments. The most dramatic difference in risk occurs between people who are inactive (less than 30 minutes of physical activity per week) and those with low levels of activity (around 90 minutes per week). While additional benefits occur as the amount of physical activity increases, through higher intensity, greater frequency, and/or longer duration, the research is clear that some physical activity is better than none [31]. Here are some practical ways to upgrade your physiological engine:

ACTIONS:

1) Create a goal of increasing the amount of moderate-intensity physical activity you do each week – that's extended periods where you feel that your heart rate and breathing is elevated, but you can still speak. A goal of increasing by 10 minutes per week is a good place to start. If you can reach 150 minutes of this kind of activity per week, that's great.

2) Track your daily steps for a period of time, using a wrist-worn wearable, and try to increase your average step count by 500 steps per day, until you reach 10,000.

3) Try to divide your physical activity across the week, rather than binge-ing at the weekend. A good target to work towards is 30 minutes of moderate-intensity physical activity (working hard enough to break a sweat, but still able to carry on a conversation) five days per week.

4) Don't get too hung up on the goals of 10,000 steps, 150 minutes or 30 minutes five times per week. The key is to start doing something and try to improve from where you are now, with small, achievable targets.

(37)

MOVE FAST: UPGRADE THE 'FUNCTION' OF YOUR ENGINE

The metabolic reactions that keep us alive and facilitate all of our activities take place in structures within our cells called 'mitochondria.' You can imagine them as your body's engine; the 'energy factories' of your cells.

Some research suggests that a number of ageing and age-related disorders, ranging from Type II diabetes to Alzheimer's, may be related to a crisis of 'energy supply,' as these conditions are so strongly associated with the 'high-energy' tissues of the brain, liver, and heart [38].

The more mitochondria we have, and the better they work, the more activities we can do before we become exhausted. We all need to find ways to maintain and improve the function of our mitochondria, whether we're elite athletes or simply aiming to improve health and wellbeing.

Moving relatively slowly, for extended periods, sends signals to increase the number of 'mitochondrial energy factories' in our cells. However, moving fast, when we get really out of breath, creates high-energy demands that send signals to encourage the mitochondria to work even better [39, 40].

When I talk about 'moving fast,' I'm referring to vigorous aerobic exercise. You feel like you are working hard, and would struggle to complete a sentence without needing to take a breath. This kind of exertion is commonly referred to in the context of 'high-intensity interval training' (HIIT), which involves repeated bouts of high-intensity effort, followed by varied recovery times.

HIIT training has been criticised by some people, due to the potentially unpleasant nature of high-intensity efforts. However, while the high intensity periods are demanding, the 'built-in' recovery periods seem to produce more favourable responses than would be expected. These findings seem to be relatively stable across age-groups, from young, to middle-aged adults [41] and many people find HIIT sessions very enjoyable [42].

HIIT TRAINING

In 2015, a systematic review and meta-analysis concluded that traditional moderate intensity training and HIIT could both elicit large improvements in the VO_2 max. (the measure of the maximum function of our cardiovascular system) of healthy, young to middle-aged adults. However, HIIT training improvements in VO_2 max. were greater following HIIT, compared with endurance training [43].

Each 'high-intensity interval' may last from five seconds to eight minutes, performed at 80% to 95% of a person's maximum heart rate. The recovery periods are usually performed at 40-50% of maximum heart rate. The duration of recovery periods may be less than, equal to, or more than, the length of the work interval, depending on fitness levels and objectives.

A typical HIIT session could last between 20 and 60 minutes, but even shorter sessions have been demonstrated to be beneficial. In a 2012 study, participants took part in 10-minute high-intensity cycling sessions, three times per week, for six weeks. Each session involved a series of 10-20 second all-out sprints. This brief activity was sufficient to significantly improve health and fitness markers in the healthy, but sedentary, men and women who took part. Insulin sensitivity increased by 28% and VO_2 max. increased by 12-15% [44].

ACTIONS:

1) Just six weeks of HIIT training may be a time-efficient way to 'upgrade' your energy metabolism [40]. A practical way to try this would be to sign-up for a series of HIIT training sessions, perhaps in a group context such as a cycling spinning class, with a qualified instructor.

2) You can still experience many positive benefits from engaging in moderate to vigorous exercise, where you feel out of breath, but do not follow a HIIT protocol. For example, you could run, cycle or swim at low intensity, and integrate a few sprint efforts of 10-60 seconds.

3) Many people seem to feel like it's only worth exercising if they have a free hour. Research suggests that even 10-minute sessions can be beneficial, if they're repeated a few times per week. Speak to a qualified coach or fitness instructor about how you could design a short session to fit into your day.

4) The most 'pleasurable' high-intensity intervals appear to be 60 seconds or less at near maximal effort – approximately 90% of maximum aerobic capacity [41]. You might mention that to your fitness instructor, too!

5) We strongly recommend that you consult with your physician before beginning any exercise program.

MOVE HEAVY: UPGRADE YOUR CHASSIS

Aki often speaks about conversations that he's had with his friend and colleague, Dr. Smith L. Johnston. Dr. Johnston was one of NASA's top flight surgeons, specialising in Aerospace Medicine, and has been practising for over 35 years. Medical teams have been concerned about astronauts' loss of muscle mass during space flight for some time. Even regular exercise is not enough to stop reductions in muscle mass and strength, following prolonged periods in micro-gravity.

Dr. Johnston reinforced a message with Aki, which he has passed on to me and the rest of the Hintsa team – hold on to your muscle. During the time that we've been writing this book, Aki has been battling cancer, but he hasn't given up going to the gym. In fact, over the last year, he's even taken part in a friendly bench-press competition with a very well-known Formula One driver.

Investigations that have been conducted in space have helped to provide us with a better understanding of muscle atrophy as we age here on Earth [45].

While moving more, slow and fast are primarily associated with upgrading our 'engine,' 'moving heavy' is about upgrading our 'chassis.' Lifting weights is often associated with high-performance sport, or vanity, but our muscle mass and strength is vital for determining the trajectory of our lives. As we age, if we don't send the appropriate 'growth signals,' our muscle mass decreases but our skeletal structure can remain relatively unchanged.

If we don't make active decisions to build and maintain our muscle mass, we could end up with an adult size skeleton, and the muscle mass of a five-year-old, increasing our risk of poor health, musculoskeletal problems and falls.

After turning 50, muscle mass begins to decrease at a rate of 1-2% per year, and muscle strength declines at 1.5–5% per year [46].

In addition to helping us move, our muscle mass has a profound impact on the function of our metabolism. Building and maintaining muscle is associated with a range of health benefits and holds the promise of improving our health span, as well as our lifespan.

- Having more functional muscle may be associated with a 'whole-body neuro-protective effect,' leading to better function of the nervous system [47].

- While more research is required, muscular strength appears to play an important and independent role in the prevention of cardiovascular heart disease [48].

- Being in the top 25% of muscle mass for your age-group appears to be a significant positive predictor of longevity [49].

- Peak muscle power is an important predictor of how well we'll function in old-age [50].

ACTIONS:

- Resistance exercise, involving specific training for the major muscle groups of the body, is an effective way to increase muscle mass as we get older. It also seems that when it comes to changing our trajectory, the earlier we start the better [51]. However, it's never too late; strength-training programmes conducted with participants over 90 years old have been shown to improve function and movement, lower risk of falling and improve muscular power [23].

The evidence strongly suggests that it would be a good idea for many of us to start lifting heavier loads that we are used to.

ACTIONS:

1) Try to include resistance training as part of your life, at least two-times per week. This could involve completing 8-12 repetitions of 8-10 different exercises that target all major muscle groups [37].

2) You could use body weight, resistance bands, free weights, medicine balls or weight machines. However, there is a risk of injury if you are not familiar with the movement patterns of these exercises. We recommend that you work with a qualified coach or fitness trainer, who can create a suitable, progressive programme for you.

3) Before the age of 50 is the ideal time to build and reach peak muscle mass, but improvements are possible at almost every stage of life.

RECOVER WELL: WHERE IT ALL HAPPENS

Moving more, moving slow, moving fast and moving heavy all send powerful signals to our body. However, these signals are actually a form of stress. Often, when we think about resilience, we imagine bouncing back to where we were before. However, if you gradually increase stress over time, enough to encourage the body to keep adapting, but not too much that it cannot recover, growth signals dominate, and you become stronger and fitter.

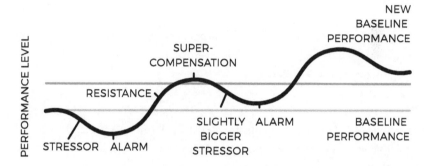

Applied to various forms of training, you can lift heavier weights, run for longer and produce more power. In fact, you can upgrade your body's capacity to supply energy for all activities. This is a process known as super-compensation, which I mentioned in Chapter 5. We can apply it to our cognitive skills, too. The learning process is stressful. It takes effort, time and it's actually only afterwards that we consolidate our learning.

When we work, we stress our body and mind. When we rest and recover, we provide the opportunity for our system to absorb and respond to the stress, and get stronger.

COGNITIVE BIAS AND RECOVERY

"'Could you work 130 hours in a week?' The answer is yes."
Marissa Mayer, Yahoo CEO [52]

Marissa Mayer, the current CEO of Yahoo, describes how she believes that the capacity to tolerate extreme work schedules was an essential ingredient in Google's early success, and other startup companies she's been involved in since. This schedule would be equivalent to working up to 18.6 hours per day and only sleeping 5.4 hours per night.

Lack of sleep is a serious issue for health and performance, but 'bottom-up' influences on our thinking can lead us astray, through an over-reliance on cognitive 'shortcuts' that degrade our decision making.

If we prime System 1 with faulty information about what the human body and mind is capable of and requires for optimum functioning, it's easy to celebrate long hours and little sleep as examples of what it takes to succeed. However, being surrounded with these messages makes us more likely to fall prey to the 'bandwagon effect'; the probability that we believe something increases, based on the number of people we know who hold that belief. We may also be completely unaware of declines in our own performance as a result of poor recovery.

Walking through a natural setting, or even just viewing pictures of nature, can help us restore attention. It also appears to be very important for mental processing, recalling personal memories, imagining the future, and feeling social emotions.

In 1960, a survey study conducted by the American Cancer Society found that most people slept between 8.0 to 8.9 hours. In 1995, this dropped to 7 hours. Recent analyses indicate that a greater percentage of adults report sleeping six hours or less than ever before. Today, more than 30% of adult men and women, between the ages of 30 and 64, report sleeping less than 6 hours per night [53].

Perhaps you fall into this category and think you're fine. In Chapter 5, we looked at the study demonstrating that sleeping for 6 hours per night, for two weeks, resulted in decreases in cognitive performance equivalent to staying awake for two days straight. Perhaps worse, is that after a couple of days, the participants didn't notice their own performance declines. In reality, they were continuing to get worse each day.

Sleep also seems to play an important role in learning and the formation of memories. Through a process called 'long-term potentiation,' signals between neurons are strengthened [54] as we sleep. Sleeping may also help us with 'relearning' and improve our capacity to re-acquire forgotten information [55]. Both learning and re-learning are essential for performance today, and enhancing these capacities could significantly improve our productivity and quality of life as we age.

We should try to work in blocks of focussed time, interspersed with periods of deliberate rest to maximise productivity and creativity. This day-time recovery, when our brain enters 'default mode' also appears to be very important for mental processing, recalling personal memories, imagining the future, and feeling social emotions [56].

Sleep and lack of recovery isn't only an issue in relation to cognitive performance. Sleep disruption is associated with negative impacts on metabolic health, insulin resistance, incidence of obesity, diabetes and potentially some forms of cancer [57, 58, 59].

CORPORATE FATIGUE

Physicians report that fatigue is one of the commonly reported complaints by patients. It's a nonspecific symptom, but is often characterised by reduced capacity or motivation for work, and subjective feelings of lethargy and sleepiness [60]. In our experience, the top 10 reasons for knowledge workers experiencing excessive or prolonged fatigue include at least one item from the following list: *

1) Too much work (high volume)

2) Poor time, energy and cognitive load management (creating the illusion of too much work)

3) 'Workaholism' (self-induced excessive, obsessive behaviour)

4) Chronic stress

5) Monotony (boredom due to repetitive tasks) and/or boredom (a generally disinterested state)

6) Poor nutrition

7) Insufficient sleep quantity and/or quality

8) Insufficient exercise

9) Insufficient rest

10) Excessive exercise with insufficient recovery

Fatigue can be associated with a number of medical conditions, so it's a good idea to check with your doctor, if you have any questions about it.

SLEEP AND RECOVERY IS THE MISSING PIECE

For years, we've been bombarded with messages about physical activity and movement, but it's during sleep and recovery that our body can recover from the stress and grow in response to the good decisions we make. Many of our clients have found it helpful to spend a period of time tracking a few basic metrics about themselves, to improve their awareness of activity, sleep and recovery patterns.

SELF-QUANTIFICATION

Wearable technology is forecast to become the most popular global fitness trend in 2017 [61], but the evidence to support the use of wearables in changing health related behaviours is mixed [62].

One of the challenges in wearable devices is the lack of a feedback loop [63]. They provide information but then, so what? To address this challenge, you need to start by measuring metrics that are genuinely useful, accurate enough to draw some insight, provide clear actions and follow-up and a progressive pathway, so improvement continues. At Hintsa, we are working on a number of digital solutions to meet these needs.

Wearable devices are facilitators, not drivers of behaviour change [63], but we have found that encouraging people to monitor some key metrics for a period of time can help to draw valuable attention to key areas of their lives; it improves communication with coaches (including 'peer' coaches); and seeing improvement can be rewarding and seems to reinforce helpful behaviour patterns.

Following are three of the most useful metrics to provide insight into what's going on in our body, as well as signals about how we are responding to physical and psychological stress:

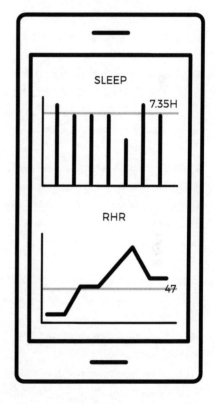

- Daily activity

- Resting heart rate

- Sleep

Both heart rate and sleep feature a high degree of inter-individual variability, i.e. we shouldn't try to compare our results with each other. Also, the accuracy of the measures varies between devices, but they can be useful to track longitudinal trends.

As I've been writing this book, I've noticed a number of interesting trends in my activity, sleep and heart rate. In particular, during the closing weeks of the project, I've noted how daily steps have decreased, average sleep hours have decreased, and resting heart rate has increased, likely indicating that physiological and psychological stress is increasing. This is not a way I would like to live in the long term...

MEASURING SLEEP

There are many different sleep-tracking devices on the market, with a high degree of variability in the quality of the results. No commercially available device is yet able to provide the accuracy of clinical assessment, but some are able to provide 'directional accuracy', i.e. they can demonstrate if trends in sleep duration are getting better or worse. Again, simply starting to track sleep can be a helpful way to draw attention to the activity, and encourage us to prioritise it.

SLEEP, BLUE-LIGHT AND ALCOHOL

We often encourage clients to try experiments on themselves, to observe the impact of recommendations our coaches make. For example, research has described how blue light from electronic screens can suppress melatonin production by 22% [64], which may have a negative impact on sleep.

In addition, studies have demonstrated that alcohol intake before sleep inhibits our parasympathetic (rest and digest) activity and encourages sympathetic (fight or flight) activity to dominate [65]; exactly the opposite effect that we are hoping for. Alcohol interferes with sleep quality, even if we feel like we go to sleep quickly, and a sleep tracker and heart rate monitoring may draw our attention to this reality.

As an experiment, try to avoid electronic screens and alcohol for two evenings in a week, to see if you can measure any changes, both objectively and subjectively.

MEASURING HEART RATE

Some devices measure sophisticated heart rate metrics, such as heart rate variability, but the evidence to support the use of HRV to assess recovery and fatigue, using consumer devices, is still emerging.

By simply measuring how often our heart beats each minute, at rest and during exercise, we can gain useful information, particularly if it is tracked over an extended period of time. The first consumer wearable to measure heart rate 24/7, without using a chest strap, came to market in 2013 [66]. Since then, many heart rate measurement options have become available using optical sensors, on a wrist-worn device. This has made heart rate monitoring a much more practical and easy to apply solution, for many people.

The heart responds to both physical and psychological stimuli via our sympathetic (fight or flight) and parasympathetic (rest and digest) autonomic nervous system. You can see this in practice in everyday life; heart rate increases when we physically exert ourselves, and most people experience significant increases in heart rate before they have to do something that they find psychologically stressful, a public speaking exercise, for example.

Heart rate can offer some useful insights into what is going on in our body and mind. You can even measure your heart rate without a device, by taking your pulse, using two fingers.

RESTING HEART RATE

Resting heart rate, a measure of how many times your heart beats every minute while you are awake, but restful, is usually between 60-90 beats per minute [67]. A lower resting heart rate may be associated with longevity, but it appears that one of the main things to look out for, as a signal that your health may be heading in the wrong direction, is a resting heart rate that is gradually increasing over time [68]. In contrast, as our physical fitness increases, we will often observe that our resting heart rate decreases.

Tracking resting heart rate offers a simple 'inferred signal' to provide some insight into your levels of fitness, physical and psychological stress, and an indication of the direction your health is taking. However, there are two important caveats; not all heart rate monitoring devices are accurate, and the information from them should not be considered a substitute for the advice of a qualified medical professional.

You could try an experiment for a few weeks, to see if you can see connections between changes in resting heart rate and patterns in sleep, stress and physical activity.

IT'S NEVER TOO LATE

We all have the potential to change the trajectory of our lives. If we pay attention to the right things, and make good choices, this can make a profound impact.

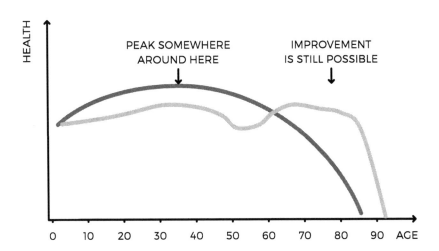

The most important point to keep in mind is that no one needs to be perfect. Don't let perfect be the enemy of 'good enough.' It's never too late to get started, and even small changes can create a big difference in the end.

What we pay attention to influences the effort and energy we allocate to a task. What do you need to pay attention to now, and how can you put this into action? We will explore this question, and more, in the next chapter.

ACTIONS:

1) We're going to be living and working for longer than ever, so we need healthy, high-functioning bodies. Increase your awareness of your daily sedentary time and physical activity patterns. Use a wrist-worn tracker for a 'sample period,' and you may be surprised to learn how much time you spend sitting during an average week. Take a short movement break at least once per hour [32], whatever you are doing.

2) Consider tracking resting heart rate and sleep, for a period of time. While the data from consumer wearables varies in quality, combined with your own subjective rating, you may be able to begin to establish some personal trends in your recovery.

3) It's particularly important to proactively plan exercise and rest periods during busy times, but remember that doing something is better than doing nothing. A nine-year longitudinal study observed exercise once per week reduced the risk of developing cardiovascular disease and diabetes [69].

4) Plan to 'peak' at the right time. In the same way that athletes choose important competitions where they aim for peak performance, knowledge workers should plan to be well-rested before and leading up to important events, so that they can give their best performance.

5) Have at least one day off per week, where you do not do any work.

ALEX STUBB: FORMER PRIME MINISTER, PARLIAMENTARIAN AND IRON MAN

It's a rainy late afternoon in Helsinki. Alex Stubb is delivering his interview from a high-performance 'WattBike' indoor trainer, so our phone conversation is accompanied by the steady whirring sound of Alex's pedalling.

"Exercise is the only way to get through the dark, Nordic November," jokes Alex, who began his day with a yoga class, before going to work. Now he's at the gym, combining both exercise and work, although he's quick to clarify that this is unusual. His motto is: "one hour of exercise gives you two hours of extra energy each day".

> "When I'm training it's about creating space for myself; switching everything off, no Twitter feeds or e-mail alerts, no texting. It's my time – my personal time."

In addition to serving as Finland's Prime Minister, Alex has held a number of ministerial portfolios, including Minister of Foreign Affairs and Minister of Finance, so he knows a lot about the stress that comes with high intensity work. He also understands the importance of getting enough rest.

ALWAYS HAVE AN OFFICE WITH A BED

> "Even as PM, which was 24/7, I had to schedule short breaks for myself, just to switch off and read a glossy magazine, watch the Tour de France on TV, or just hang out on Instagram."

Alex also taught himself to switch off completely using the Winston Churchill power nap as a way to reboot the mind.

> "It's 15-20 minutes in a horizontal position. It could be on the floor or on a bed – but I totally shut down."

He applies the same principle to endurance sport. "People think endurance means going flat out all the time! But if you're constantly on, you're performance is going to deteriorate." As a regular competitor in marathons and triathlons, including Ironman, Alex admits to being results-oriented, "but only to compete with myself." In his training regime, he opts for a ratio of 20% high intensity and 80% slower or less intense activities.

EVERYTHING BEGINS WITH THE CALENDAR

For Alex, the calendar represents the skeleton for the body of the day. "If the skeleton is off, then everything is off. If there's too much work, too much stress, then I won't be able to perform." Alex has tried to adopt an 8: 8: 8 work, play, sleep philosophy. While he'll often mix the ratios on work and play, to be with his family or fulfil work commitments, what he won't do is compromise on the 8 hours of sleep.

At the office, Alex sees a lot of low energy, including colleagues falling asleep at meetings. "During most all-night negotiations, it's quite easy for me to be the last man standing, just because I've trained for it," says Alex.

But this only works if he has advanced warning that an intense period at work is coming so he can prepare for it. "If I've been training hard then I'll be just as tired as the next man."

WHEN IS EXTREME TOO EXTREME?

As the 'sports nut' of Finnish politics, Alex's approach to extreme training has not been without its controversies – some say he goes too far.

On this, Alex is willing to be introspective, analysing the risk of getting too excited about exercise and losing focus on something else important. The advice he gives himself is to always be aware of his overall stress load at work and training. According to the experts our brains can't differentiate between mental and physical stress," says Alex, "so if there's a very intense time at the office, I know that the exercise has to be toned down."

PRIORITISING EXERCISE IN THE WORK PLACE

Having said that, Alex believes a balanced exercise regime can improve performance at work. He's seen how endurance training can boost his own creative input. "Running consolidates my thinking. I get ideas for speeches, columns. It's like a chemical reaction," he laughs.

One of the first things Alex did as Foreign Minister was to renovate the building's gym. He also told staff they were free to exercise during work hours. Some welcomed the move while others took exception to it, including eyebrow-raising media articles about wasting tax-payer money.

Alex sticks to his view that investing in wellbeing is the right way to go. "We need to dispel this idea that exercise should be illegal at work." In the same way, Alex wants to get rid of the macho myth that we can all go without sleep. "When colleagues brag about working late and only getting four hours sleep, I just see it as unprofessional. A top athlete would never brag about that."

YOU CAN'T PREACH WELLBEING TO PEOPLE

But change has to come from the inside. Alex believes showing an example and sharing experiences is the right way to reach people. As a proponent of the theory that 'sitting kills,' Alex takes initiatives like organising standing up meetings or scheduling outdoor walking meetings.

"But more leadership is needed," Alex insists. He'd like to see more senior leaders coming to the office with their gym bags.

FINISHING WELL

For now his low-intensity session is whirring down and Alex has to go and pick up his son. In closing, we take a look at Alex's life trajectory so far:

- **0-20** was playtime and game time, where he competed in a number of fast moving, interval focussed, sports like ice hockey, handball and football. "They suited my short attention span." Then came golf, which won him a scholarship to a US college. "Golf was against my nature really, I had to learn patience, out there alone with my thoughts and every part of the performance coming first from stillness."

- **20-40** was about general fitness, going to the gym and for an occasional run, while he focussed on a young family and developing his career.

- **40-60** is where he is now, almost halfway through. With not too much left to prove in his career, Alex talks about going deeper into reading and deeper into writing. He has already published 16 books. It's also a chance to go deeper into endurance sports for his overall wellbeing, including watching his weight. "At this age, it's easy to fall into the trap of relaxing over a bottle of wine instead of going for a one hour run and then before you know it, you're 15 kilos overweight." It's also about being social, and the immense joy that comes from finding a new family of sporting friends. "We come in all ages and all sizes."

- **60-80** is too far out to know for sure, though Alex has already set himself one major goal for his 80th year. "I'm going to complete the Hawaii Ironman!"

9.
INSPIRED & IN CONTROL

Aki and I are at a Hintsa team workshop in Helsinki. Part way through the day's programme, in his inimitable style, Aki poses a question to everyone in the group.

"What do people want?" he asks.

He's not just asking about us, he's asking about all of humanity. I dread and love these moments in equal measure, because I know we will learn something, but he will not put the answer on a plate for us. We take turns in responding with increasingly complex and convoluted answers. Finally, after a few attempts, Aki puts us out of our

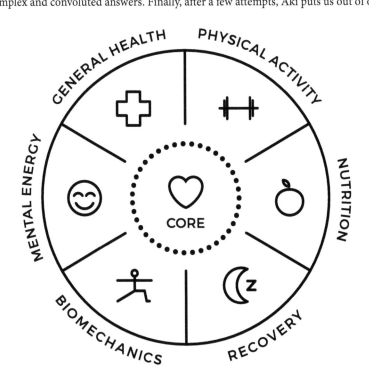

misery with a surprisingly straightforward response.

"People want happiness and success."

Simple, right?

Managing our attention and our actions to achieve this aim is not as easy as programming a computer with a set of instructions. It's more like embarking on a journey. We need to think about what happiness and success means for us, which means that we need to draw our attention to who we are and the impact we want to have. We need to train our attention, discover a sustained source of motivation and inspiration, and use this to keep investing our energy and time in the right places. Also, life doesn't always turn out as we expect, and we're not on this journey on our own, so we need to consider other people and the complex systems we are part of.

In this chapter, we return to the circle of better life, which provides a context for putting all of these elements together; moving from perception to action and into sustainable change. We'll consider:

- The best starting points for our journey.
- Why attention is the key to achieving our aims.
- Why we work 'inside-out.'
- Why knowing what to do is not enough.
- How attention relates to emotional intelligence.
- Why emotional intelligence is a crucial skill for wellbeing and performance.
- How inspiration can be a 'multiplier.'
- Why people are so important when things don't work out as we expect.

Once again, we'll view these aspects of the human experience through the lens of our cognitive abilities.

LOOKING TO THE FUTURE

"What are you here for?"

Aki puts the question to a new client. We're in Aki's office in Geneva. It's January, but the weather outside is clearing. It's still freezing cold, but the sky is a cloudless, iridescent blue. I look out of the large glass window, over the buildings at the snow-capped trees on the mountainous ridge, on Geneva's west side.

I've only been working at Hintsa for a couple of weeks. I'm trying to understand more about the Hintsa method and how Aki works, by sitting in on some of his consultations.

Our client is a successful business leader and fiercely intelligent, but he looks a little puzzled. "What am I here for?" he repeats the question to himself.

He explains that he always feels tired, that he used to be very fit, but he's let himself go, that life has got in the way and that he feels lost.

Aki nods and listens. When the client stops talking, Aki sits patiently, but doesn't speak. By now, I've realised that this is part of Aki's style – he knows what questions to ask to find the story behind the story. He also knows when to provide answers, and when it's best to keep listening.

The client is silent for a moment then begins speaking again.

I realise that Aki's pause has challenged the client to re-focus his attention from the problem to the solution. He started by focussing on the negative; his fatigue, his lack of direction and the decline in his health and fitness. Then the conversation was quickly redirected to the vision of what a better future could look like.

"I want to feel good in my body, like I used to. I want the freedom to use my strengths and pursue my interests, not be controlled by the 'system.' I want to feel like what I'm doing has a purpose, spend more time with my friends and family. I'm here because I want more energy," he says heavily.

"Exact!" Replies Aki. He gets up from his chair and begins drawing on the flip-chart. He writes "Goal" at the top, underlines it enthusiastically, and scrawls the words "more energy."

Over the next hour, Aki asks questions and draws out the client's vision of his better future. He asks him about where he came from, how he views himself, what he thinks of his body, his character strengths, how much energy he has now, where this energy is being invested, he asks what he thinks is most important, who are the most significant people in his life, where he would like to have an impact, what is helping him achieve his goals and what is holding him back. He asks what he would like to be doing with his life in 10 years' time.

In time, Aki populates a table with the targets, measures, resources and assumptions that will become the basis for his programme. Aki highlights a number of issues, but keeps the focus on the goal and vision the client had in mind.

ONE YEAR LATER

One year after his first meeting, the same client returned to Geneva after completing his programme. In the intervening period, he'd worked with a Hintsa Performance Coach, various specialists and continued to meet with Aki, but the most significant changes were the result of his own decisions and small things, done consistently well. He experienced some substantial changes in his life. The highlights were as follows:

Objective measures:

- Dropped 18kg of body fat.

- 13% improvement in VO_2 max.

- 8% improvement in Peak Power output.

- 42% improvement in trunk (core) strength and stability.

Subjective measures:

- 33% improvement in ability to take time for his own interests.

- 50% improvement in relationships with friends.

- 33% improvement in rating of quality of life.

- 33% improvement in sense of purpose in life.

The results of the programme for this client are clear, but initially I found some people sceptical about the solution-focused approach. They were often surprised when we started by asking them about their vision and goals. They were eager to tell us about what was wrong, to start fixing things straight away, rather than exploring what was really driving them, and what they were hoping for.

Some people said that it was overly optimistic and even expressed a feeling that, if the medical tests results found something worrying, this may be the motivation they'd need to change. You do need to consider problems, address root causes and create plans to solve them. But beginning with the problem in mind, rather than the positive vision, is not the better way forward.

If you were diagnosed with a chronic health condition such as heart disease, cancer, stroke, respiratory disease or diabetes, this should be sufficient motivation to change your behaviour, right?

In 2012, researchers posed this question based on longitudinal data from 17,276 individuals. The primary focus was to compare pre- and post-diagnosis health behaviour, during the 12 years covered by the study. Basically, did people change anything after they were diagnosed?

The study concluded that people rarely made positive changes in lifestyle behaviours, even after they had been diagnosed with a chronic condition. This is despite strong evidence to suggest that adopting a healthier lifestyle, such as stopping smoking, increasing physical activity, eliminating heavy alcohol consumption and improving diet, can extend longevity, reduce the likelihood of the condition recurring and enhance quality of life [1].

Even when our problems are described in crystal clear terms and the consequences of ignoring them are grave, fear of an early death and the perceived obligation to improve our lifestyles based on a health diagnosis is not sufficient to motivate sustained behavioural change.

The aim of avoiding ill-health, or even death, does not seem to be sufficiently motivating to shift our attention and effort to behaviours that may help us. It seems that we're more likely to be inspired to change by a more substantial positive vision of the future, than scared into altering our lifestyle.

WHY DOES IT WORK?

Dr. Richard Boyatzis is an expert in the field of emotional intelligence and behaviour change. In 2013, he and his fellow researcher, Dr. Anthony Jack, collaborated on a study [2] to assess the difference between these two types of approaches. They divided a group of volunteers into two. Each volunteer was interviewed for 30 minutes on themes relating to 'life coaching' and performance, but the coaches who conducted the interviews used two contrasting approaches.

> *Group one (NEA):*
> Coaches asked questions that focussed on the problems and challenges the volunteers were facing. The coaches emphasised problem-solving techniques to try to identify solutions, but it tended to bring up issues associated with other people's expectations, weaknesses, obligations, and fears.

> *Group two (PEA):*
> Coaches asked questions designed to encourage the volunteers to imagine a positive future, such as how they'd like their lives to look in 10 years' time. The questions drew out the volunteer's vision in more detail.

Dr. Boyatzis describes the coaching approach in group two, which emphasised vision, hopes and dreams, as "coaching and mentoring to the Positive Emotional Attractor (PEA)." This contrasts with coaching in group one where the approach is characterised as coaching to the "Negative Emotional Attractor (NEA)."

After a period of five to seven days, both groups of volunteers were asked a series of follow-up questions by the same coaches, using the same approaches as in the first interview. During this second round of questioning, the student's brains were scanned using fMRI, to measure blood flow. The results demonstrated that the two contrasting interview approaches activated different and distinct regions in the brain.

A PLAUSIBLE MECHANISM

The difference in blood flow points to an underlying mechanism, backing the notion that PEA can support behaviour change, and help to explain why this form of coaching and mentoring may be a more effective way to achieve our goals.

The PEA, positive goal-focussed coaching, resulted in activation of regions in the brain associated with developing a plan or vision for the future. In addition, when we focus our attention on the positive, reward circuits in our brain are activated [2]. Areas related to parasympathetic nervous system activation also 'lit up,' along with those associated with the experience of positive moods. When our parasympathetic nervous system takes the lead, heart rate and blood pressure goes down and our field of attention widens. When we do not feel threatened, our mind considers that it's safe to take time over decisions and think more deeply. We become more cognitively flexible, able to simulate multiple future possibilities and consider new ideas, as well as taking into account how other people think and feel. We are engaging System 2 and therefore more likely to consider multiple factors, our higher-level goals and direct our attention on what really matters.

Coaching and mentoring that encourages people to imagine a positive vision of the future, focussing their attention on characteristics and virtues such as their possibilities and dreams, vision and strengths, compassion, curiosity, experimentation and learning, has been shown to enhance behavioural change. Perhaps unsurprisingly, coaching to the NEA is associated with worse outcomes.

These patterns of activity are vital for motivation, cognitive flexibility, sustaining positive feeling and keeping going when we experience challenges – characteristics that are crucial if we are trying to change our behaviour and work towards a goal [2].

In contrast, the NEA approach, which emphasised the problem over the vision, activated brain regions associated with activation of the sympathetic 'fight or flight' nervous system and regions of the brain related to blaming ourselves, and experiencing negative moods. When we experience NEA, our sympathetic nervous system becomes more dominant. Physiologically, heart rate and blood pressure increase, but we are also more likely to make decisions based on fast, instinctive, but sometimes faulty, System 1 thinking. Even if System 1 has been

POSITIVE EMOTIONAL ATTRACTOR

NEGATIVE EMOTIONAL ATTRACTOR

primed with good information, our attention narrows during NEA, so we do not consider as many options or ideas. We are more likely to be fixed, rather than flexible. When we contextualise our goals in the context of the problem, we are less likely to be effective in planning or execution.

It seems that if a coaching or mentoring process begins by encouraging the client to imagine a vision of a better life, brain activity is stimulated that makes it more likely the client will achieve the changes they are hoping for.

Dan Goleman quotes Dr. Boyatzis as saying:

> "You need the negative focus to survive, but a positive one to thrive" [3].
> Dr. R.E. Boyatzis

A negative approach is ideal if you are about to be run over by a car. You need the 'bottom-up' pressure and sympathetic nervous system activity to avoid danger. In this context, you should forget your higher-level goal of getting to the other side of the road. It would also not be the time to consider the driver's motivation or ponder the wider systemic issues of road safety. You just need to recognise the danger as quickly as possible, and get out of the way. But this is not a great approach when we are considering our long-term future.

Consider the implications of this for your life and work. When you encounter a challenge do you see problems and threats, or do you step back and imagine what a more positive future could look like, then start working on a plan from there?

BUILDING A BETTER FUTURE

One of the drivers Hintsa works with has a large quote, painted on the wall of his gym. It says "build yourself your happiness" and it's a reminder that we need to take an active role in achieving our dreams.

In Chapters Seven and Eight, I emphasised how our attention plays a powerful role in the way we allocate effort and energy to our tasks. Coaching to the Positive Emotional Attractor is another example of this. We need to train our executive functions and be aware of where our mind is leading us. What do we need to pay attention to and what should we ignore? Keeping a clear, positive goal in mind goes a long way to helping us achieve this.

Too often, our distracted world means that we can fixate on what we do not have, or what others have, rather than our own path. This is exacerbated as many of our social-media profiles are curated to show only the best filter-enhanced moments of the people around us.

One of the criticisms of the positive approach to coaching and mentoring is that it would presume to ignore any problems or negatives. This is not the case. The key is to choose your entry point and priorities and create a positive, vision-orientated context for the process of working towards your goals.

WORKING INSIDE-OUT

The Hintsa approach starts inside out, with the client's vision and their core, as opposed to outside in, driven by external forces and surface level problems.

Consequently, we increase the likelihood that clients reduce their feelings of being threatened by what is going wrong, or what is happening now. Instead, when they imagine and simulate a positive future, they enjoy a more relaxed state and apply their executive functioning capabilities to their full capacity. Their attention will be broad, they will be cognitively flexible enough to imagine a better future and benefit from the 'top-down' influence of higher-level goals to improve their active decision making. With a positive vision, they are also more likely to simulate the sense of reward they will feel from achieving their goal, which should in turn strengthen their resolve.

For example, in the context of the client I mentioned earlier, we needed to design a programme to address the problem of his excess body fat, poor biomechanics and low-level cardiovascular fitness, but the context for his efforts to change these metrics was his vision to live a life full of energy and purpose, with the people he cares about. This was a much more powerful motivator, at a deep cognitive and emotional level, than the superficial idea of fixing his aching back, even though that was an important by-product of the programme.

Coaching and mentoring to the Positive Emotional Attractor still involves problem solving, but the positive entry-point reframes the process and helps us make the best use of our brain.

When people speak about Aki, they often talk about the encouragement and inspiration he gave them. He helped them to imagine a dream and believe that they could achieve it.

WHY KNOWING WHAT TO DO IS NOT ENOUGH

If you provide a robot with a clear set of instructions, you can be reasonably confident that the task will be carried out effectively. However, human cognition is much more complex. It is not enough to simply tell people what they need to do. If it was, no one would be writing self-help books anymore.

We need to address our sometimes messy and intricate emotions. We need to develop emotional competency to thrive in life and achieve peak performance. For this, we need to develop an expertise in shifting our attention from ourselves, to others and the system we are part of, while considering and simulating multiple possibilities.

ROGER THE ROBOT?

Roger Federer is widely regarded as one of the greatest tennis players of all time. The Swiss champion, who's been ranked in the world's top-10 since October 2002, is known for his cool-head and 'robotic consistency.' However, this external reliability belies a deep expertise in maintaining focussed attention and emotional self-control combined with a high degree of task-based skill.

While we may never be able to match Roger Federer's backhand slice, we can all improve our cognitive capabilities and emotional intelligence.

Federer has not always been so calm and collected on court. As a junior player, he was known as a 'hot-head', but he clearly cultivated his capacity for emotional control as his career progressed. Roger Federer is not a robot, he has spent time learning how to be aware of what is going on inside him, how this will impact others and how to manage his emotions and his interactions with other people, to achieve his goals.

A FRAMEWORK OF EMOTIONAL INTELLIGENCE

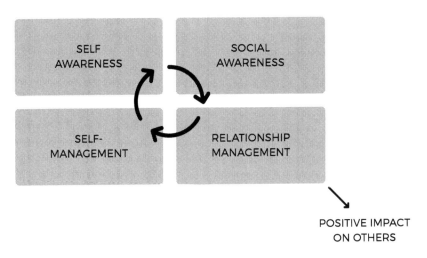

(4)

We can describe a framework of emotional intelligence (EI) including self-awareness, social awareness, self-management and relationship management. Emotional intelligence helps us to plan and sustain energy and enthusiasm as we try to achieve our goals, and work more effectively and peacefully with each other [4, 5]. Emotional intelligence has always been important, but cultivating the competencies that underpin emotional intelligence will be increasingly significant as automation and robotics replaces all, or part of many jobs, and humans in the workplace become increasingly differentiated by their unique human characteristics and skills.

2020 SKILLS

'People management,' 'co-ordinating with others' and 'emotional intelligence' are all in the WEF's 'top-10 skills for the 4th Industrial Revolution (6)' but we could see all of them as related to the skills and competencies of emotional intelligence.

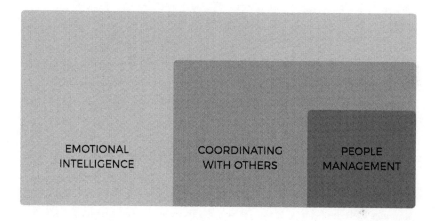

Organisational leadership began to be formally studied and documented in the last Industrial Revolution. During this time, leadership was based on the principles of top-down command and control, production and tangible assets.

Little thought was given to the idea that subordinates could play any role in the leadership process [14]. If you were not a manager, you may as well have been a robot.

However, the world of work has changed. Today, knowledge workers still have boundaries, but we are no longer fixed to a production line that moves at a set speed, overseen by a foreman. Knowledge work is complex, dynamic, less hierarchical and team-based. We need to nurture human assets and consider how skills and competencies such as emotional intelligence, management, leadership, operating culture, skills and processes work individually and together to generate value.

The ability to influence ourselves and others is fundamental at all levels of a knowledge work organization, and the ability to influence is strongly associated with how well we know ourselves, and how we can manage our attention.

To be efficient and effective, to enhance our wellbeing and our performance, we need to learn to use our attention to focus our time and energy, but also develop the capacity to move our attention from ourselves, to the impact we want to have on other people and in the wider systems we are part of.

EMOTIONAL INTELLIGENCE, COGNITIVE INTELLIGENCE & ATTENTION

Emotional intelligence closely relates to attention and the executive functions of our brain. Essentially, emotional intelligence is a set of competencies and skills that we use to shift our attention between self-focus, other focus and beyond. We can use these skills to accurately judge our own and other people's emotional expressions, to regulate our own emotions and discern their impact on others. If success and happiness is the goal, these skills are fundamental.

In previous chapters, we've explored how processing emotion shares 'circuits' and competes with other cognitive processes in our brain [7-8]. For example, presenting a subject with pictures that are designed to arouse an emotional response increases their response times in tasks [9]. Emotional intelligence and attention share some of the same 'circuits' in our brain. The circuits related to emotional, social intelligence and decision making also overlap, but these circuits are independent of the neural system supporting our cognitive intelligence [10].

It's possible to have a high cognitive intellect, but lack emotional intelligence. This means that we can have highly developed task-based skills – we know what to do – but fail to be able to apply these skills effectively in the real world.

While fMRI scans have been able to reveal the independent nature of our emotional and cognitive intelligence circuits, there are plenty of examples of this estrangement occurring in practise.

There is no doubt that Steve Jobs was a successful businessperson and by all accounts he possessed a very high level of cognitive intelligence. However, it seems that he was lacking in some emotional competencies and skills. In 2011, Walter Isaacson wrote Steve Jobs' bestselling, authorised biography. Isaacson recounts a story that took place shortly after Jobs had been made chief executive of Apple, for the second time. Apple needed an existing supplier to improve their performance. Specifically, they needed them to deliver spare parts more quickly. The supplier was fast enough to meet the terms of its contract, but was asked to work faster still. They were struggling to meet demand. Jobs instructed the manager who was in charge of the supplier to break the contract. His manager warned him that this could lead to legal action, but Jobs simply replied:

> "Just tell them if they f*!k with us, they'll never get another f*!$ing dime from this company, ever." [11]

The manager complied with Job's directive, broke the contract then promptly resigned from the company, before Jobs had the opportunity to fire him, apparently.

EI AND IQ

Sometimes, top-performers' weaknesses can be masked by their exceptional abilities in one area. Perhaps Jobs' inspirational leadership and extraordinary aptitude for motivating himself and others is an example, but who is to say that the best cannot get even better? Most of us need to cultivate both cognitive and emotional intelligence.

Emotional intelligence and executive functioning are critical components in improving life and performance, individually and collectively. In Chapter 7, we explored how 'focus is the new IQ' and that we may not be able to fully use our cognitive intelligence, without sufficient attentional control.

Popular culture has acclaimed many leaders' low 'EQ to IQ' ratio as the secret to their success. However, we should be aware of cognitive bias in our thinking. This could simply be an example of availability bias: perhaps we are overestimating the importance of the low EQ 'killer-instinct.' Most of us would struggle to get away with Jobs' approach without losing our own jobs.

Managing our attention is the key that unlocks both EI and IQ.

Similarly, if we're not able to shift and sustain attention, focussing on ourselves, considering others and the wider systems we operate within, we may be intellectually very capable, but find ourselves unable to function optimally in our own lives and in our interactions with people.

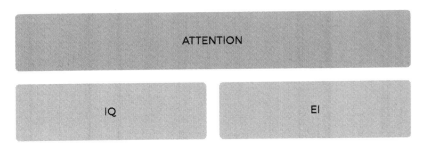

Being emotionally intelligent requires us to be able to pay attention to what we are thinking and feeling (self-awareness) as well as direct our attention to what others may be thinking and feeling (empathy). The evidence is strong that a high level of emotional intelligence is a key differentiator in many successful businesspeople [13]. We could build on the framework of emotional intelligence I introduced earlier by describing some specific competencies:

- Self-awareness: Knowing your emotions, your competences, your capacity, what you are thinking, and how you are able to listen to the signals your body is sending.

- Self-management: Emotional self-control, adaptability, achievement & positive outlook.

- Social awareness: Empathy & organisational awareness.

- Relationship management: Inspiring leadership, influence, conflict management, teamwork and collaboration. [4, 5]

LEADING OURSELVES AND OTHERS

Finding the balance between self-awareness and self-management, social awareness and relationship management is a skill. We can develop it through practise, simply by finding opportunities to apply these competencies regularly. You could even assign yourself a goal of finding ways to use these specific competencies in your everyday life.

Too much or too little attention in any one area can result in suboptimal performance and negative outcomes – either we become fixated on the organisation and forget about the people, as in the earlier Steve Jobs example, or we can focus on the wrong areas and lose sight of the big picture.

Developing these skills requires a high degree of self-leadership. Leadership is our capacity to change, influence and inspire. This applies equally to the changes we want to see in ourselves, as well as others.

ATTENTION JOURNEY

As we explored throughout this book, the processes that are taking place in our brain have a profound influence on what we perceive and how we act. Attention determines what we think is important and worthwhile, directing our cognitive resources and regulating our investments of time and energy. This influences how we perceive ourselves, what we change, how we influence others and where we make an impact in the world.

What we pay attention to will limit or increase our potential for wellbeing and performance. Attention connects our Core with our active decisions and every other element in the circle of better life. Ultimately, attention connects 'being' and 'thinking' with 'doing'.

IDENTITY, PURPOSE & CONTROL

When I first began to work with Aki, he asked me three questions:

- Do you know who you are?

- Do you know what you want?

- Are you in control of your life?

The questions were designed to help me to explore my Core – my sense of identity, purpose and control. They were also a means to practice attention management, think deeply about my goals and vision for the future, and to act accordingly.

IDENTITY: DO YOU KNOW WHO YOU ARE?

Our identity is a self-concept that develops over time. It includes our physical identity, our character and sense of spirituality. The origin of the word 'spirit' can be traced back to the Latin word 'spiritus.' This was translated from the Greek word 'pneuma' which means 'breath.' The word 'spiritual' has picked up various connotations over thousands of years, but one way to view the concept of spirituality is as beliefs and practises that promote a sense of 'connectedness.' Whether or not this has a religious connotation, it seems that some form of spirituality is central to the human experience.

Some aspects of our identity are within our control, influenced by the choices that we make; how we spend our time, or what we believe, for example. Others are outside of it, such as where we grew up. These two aspects are closely interrelated and difficult, perhaps impossible, to tease apart.

Often, when we turn our attention to ourselves and think about who we are, we gravitate towards external, more tangible aspects of our identity; a job-title or the names we use to describe our relationships to other people. I have a job title, I'm a husband and a father. We also have a physical component to our identity. It influences how we perceive ourselves and how we interact with the world.

These aspects are important, but we can go deeper still. We can use our attention to reflect on our previous experience, consider our characteristics and virtues such as their strengths, compassion, curiosity, experimentation, and learning, for example. Individual 'signature strengths,' which can be identified using validated psychometric instruments, are regarded as essential to a person's identity. Having the opportunity to use our strengths, such as hope, enthusiasm and energy, gratitude, curiosity and love, has a strong influence on our life satisfaction [15-17].

This internal reflection can be a conscious process. There are tools available to help us, but it's crucial that we learn to 'be' as well as 'do.' Time spent in 'default mode,' the network of regions that is activated when we are not focussed on a task, plays an important role in self-reflection, feeling social emotions, recalling personal memories, planning for the future and forming our identity [27, 28].

Often, when we ask people to reflect on their identity, their greatest revelations have come at unexpected times, when they've gone for a relaxing walk in nature, for example, rather than during a time of focussed attention.

PURPOSE: DO YOU KNOW WHAT YOU WANT?

Aki's second question drew my attention to how I can have an impact beyond myself. When we shift our attention from ourselves on to the influence we want to have, we take the next step towards action.

Our character, attitudes, beliefs and values have a deep influence on our sense of purpose, so we still need to pay attention to what we are thinking and feeling (self-awareness), but then we need to shift our attention and simulate what others may be thinking and feeling (empathy) and think about how this relates to our relationships, organisations and society.

The extent to which our sense of who we are matches up with how we act has been shown to positively predict our sense of meaning in life, positive feelings and moods [29]. Identity and purpose must be connected.

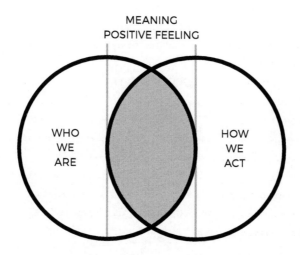

Even if people describe themselves as unhealthy, continuing to work still seems to be positively associated with longevity [18].

For many people, their primary sense of purpose comes from their work and the external aspects of identity I described before, but this may come with some risks. For example, many people experience a rapid decline in health following retirement [18].

However, for healthy adults, retiring just one year after the age of 65 is associated with an 11% reduced risk of death from all causes. Previously, studies such as this have been criticised on the basis that healthier people may be more likely to retire later. However, even when taking into account demographic, lifestyle and health issues, the results in this recent study support the relationship between later retirement and longer life [19].

Another recent study [19] explored the association between being a member of social groups and risk of death. If people had two group memberships before they retired, the risk of death in the first six years of retirement was 2%, providing they maintained membership in these groups.

The study concluded that the effect of social group memberships on mortality was comparable to that of physical exercise [19]. *Our sense of purpose, living for something greater than ourselves and connecting with other people, is crucial to our wellbeing and even for our survival!*

If they failed to maintain membership of one of the two groups after retiring, risk of death increased to 5%. If they lost both groups, the risk leaped to 12%. For every group membership lost in the year following retirement, quality of life, as reported six years later, dropped by 10%. Comparison with a control group confirmed that these effects were specific to the transition from work to retirement.

CORE PEOPLE

I'm indebted to my colleagues, who have provided so much invaluable feedback during the process of writing this book. I spent quite a lot of time speaking to Juha Äkräs about this chapter, in particular. I introduced Juha in Chapter 4. He is the person who suggested that we go cross-country skiing in Davos. Juha spent a significant portion of his working life at Nokia. He joined the company in 1993 as a Project Manager and held a number of increasingly influential roles culminating in the position of Executive Vice President of Human Resources. He also served on the Nokia Leadership Team, a position he held until he joined Hintsa. Juha has seen a lot of people join and leave the workplace. Some survive, others thrive, and he has made a number of observations that are worth sharing.

Recently, we were speaking about the importance of 'core people' in relation to identity and purpose, as well as for our wellbeing and performance. He summed up the definition of 'core people' as:

1)   People who give you unconditional love.

2)   People who encourage you.

3)   People who challenge you and help you to learn in a constructive and balanced way.

Juha also spoke about 'mentors' and 'sponsors'. Too often, we can get hung-up on the idea of needing to find someone to help us get life 'sorted' or to guide our career, but if the starting point is based around these aims, we may not find the person we need.

It's important to start working with someone and cultivate a connection with them, so you are both invested in each other, and you actively nurture the relationship.

GIVING AND RECEIVING

Social relationships are as much about what we give, as what we get. Considering other people, particularly when we feel empathy for them, triggers the release of a hormone called oxytocin. Oxytocin seems to make us more generous [20], but the release of oxytocin may also be beneficial for our own feelings of 'connectedness,' psychological, physical wellbeing and positive health outcomes [21].

Rather than one person, we need a group of core people with interdependent relationships based on mutual trust. We particularly need these people when hard times come, because life rarely turns out as we expect.
When we're struggling to believe in ourselves; when there is a massive challenge ahead; when we are scared about tomorrow; if we are hit by sickness; we need people

who can help us step away from the problem, people who can remind us that we can adopt a growth mindset, that change is possible, and that it's never too late. At that moment in time, you need to have people to talk to and share the challenge, so you can excel in the face of it.

HOW CAN YOU FIND YOUR PURPOSE AND KEY PEOPLE?

Aki is famous for asking clients to write letters to themselves. He once told me a story from back when he was working with a young race driver. Like almost all of our young drivers, he was aiming to be a Formula One World Champion. Aki asked him to write a 'core letter' about who the most important people in his life were, and why. The driver didn't really understand the importance of writing this letter, until much later.

I've become increasingly interested in this letter-writing approach. It's a method that we regularly use as part of Hintsa programmes.

> *"How do I know what I think, until I see what I say?"*
> (Attributed to E.M. Forster)

Writing is an important component of 'meaning-making' in human cognition. The act of expressing our thoughts as written words can be a helpful process to develop our executive function and attention. Meaning-making is not a simple procedure where we extract information from our memory and translate it into symbols. It's an active process that requires effort. It nearly always involves System 2. We need to consider multiple factors, direct and sustain our attention. We have to struggle to generate and shape our ideas [22].

For many of our clients, writing a 'core letter' is the first opportunity they have taken to produce long-form prose, for some time. We communicate with text a lot, but it's often in short, poorly-constructed 'snippets'. Writing engages our attention, information processing, retention and retrieval in a structured and sustained way that we may find unusual, at first.

My conversation with Juha continued during the days that I was writing this chapter. When we were speaking about the 'core letter' task, Juha made the observation that, during his time working at Nokia, a radical change in workplace communication took place. When he began his career, people still wrote letters, memorandums and long-form business plans. They gradually transitioned to more abbreviated PowerPoints and e-mail, which initially made some people feel like they were missing the full story. Now we are used to it, and continue the trend of abbreviation with increasingly 'Twitter-like' short messages. We reflected on the impact this may be having on our thinking and what we are paying attention to. Are we priming System 1 with good 'data' and equipping System 2 with sufficient information to consider what is really important, or are we reinforcing our tendency to use cognitive shortcuts?

Asking deeper questions about our sense of purpose can be a helpful way to draw our attention to the real impact we want to have beyond ourselves. It's part of the 'visioning' process I described in the PEA (Positive Emotional Attractor) approach to coaching and mentoring. Writing down our thoughts encourages us to clarify our thinking and it can move our focus outward and into the future.

Sometimes we simply ask people to write down what they would like their impact to be in the next 10 years, but one of my colleagues recently led us through a hard-hitting exercise. He asked us to write our own obituary (!) and provided a series of questions to prompt our thinking:

- What and/or who did you impact or change?

- How did you impact or change this person/these people?

- What were the major accomplishments in your life?

The 'obituary exercise' is popular in coaching, but I still found it to be a sobering experience. I don't think about dying very often and I experienced some powerful emotions in the process. It's up to you if you choose to try it, but personally I've found it to be a useful, inspirational and positive tool, in the right context.

WHAT IS INSPIRATION?

Your purpose should be the reason that you get out of bed in the morning and feel excited about the day. It's a source of inspiration and intrinsic motivation that sustains our effort and evokes our creativity. I've often heard people talk about being 'inspired' by their sense of purpose, but what does that actually mean?

Inspiration is a motivational state that compels individuals to bring ideas into fruition [23]. We can describe inspiration as being composed of three components:

1) Evocation: a stimulus object, such as a person, an idea, or a work of art, evokes and sustains inspiration.

2) Transcendence: we gain awareness of new possibilities that transcend ordinary or mundane concerns.

3) Approach motivation: we feel compelled to transmit, realise, or express the new vision.

[23]

Inspiration can be measured objectively, and it is a good predictor of creativity [23]. Inspiration also appears to have a significant influence on productivity in knowledge work [24].

While inspiration is a distinct state, it is associated with positive moods and experience. Being inspired with a positive vision for the future has a powerful influence on our own brain and body: our heart rate and blood pressure decreases and our attention broadens. We can measure increases in activity in regions of the brain associated with becoming more cognitively flexible, open to new ideas and can consider how other people think and feel more effectively.

LEADERS WHO INSPIRE

The 21st century has seen the acceleration of four workplace trends:

1)   Customer experience as a major source of competitive advantage, even in product-focused companies.

2)   More collaboration with less direct supervision.

3)   An increasing reliance on intrinsic motivation.

4)   Growing importance of belief in the company's mission and values.

Inspiration, with its potential for compelling individuals to bring ideas into fruition, being associated with positive feelings, cognitive flexibility and creativity, will be increasingly valuable and useful in light of these developments.

INSPIRATION IS A MULTIPLIER

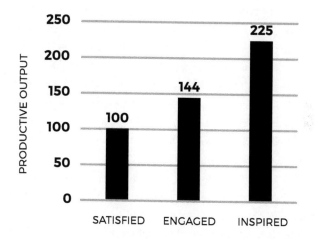

Bain & Company conducted a research project among 300 executives, asking them to rate their impressions of employee productivity [25]. Employees were divided into three groups: Satisfied, Engaged and Inspired, based on a classification of how well the employees' needs were met. The hierarchical scale was inspired by Maslow's research and ranged from basic needs for the satisfied employees, up to deriving meaning and inspiration from the company's mission and their leaders, for the inspired employees.

Findings suggest that it would require 2.25 satisfied employees to produce the same output as a single inspired employee [25]. Inspiration has a multiplier effect on productivity in knowledge work, but you cannot extract it, you must evoke it.

The researchers defined a 'relative productivity index,' calibrated against the satisfied employee group. The value for productivity in the satisfied group was set at an index level of 100, and the engaged and inspired groups were compared against this.

The results of the study concluded that engaged employees produce at an index level of 144, while inspired employees scored 225 on their productivity index scale.

[25]

WHAT MAKES AN INSPIRATIONAL LEADER?

Inspiration is closely related to the skills and competencies of emotional intelligence. The capacity to inspire relates to our capability to shift attention between self-awareness and self-management, social awareness and relationship management. We need an awareness of our own strengths, how they impact other people and how we can use them within the system we are part of, as well as an awareness of the shared goals we are trying to achieve. We need to combine this knowledge to paint a picture of a positive future, drawing people's attention, evoking the 'visioning' response in them, and the good feelings, cognitive flexibility and sustained motivation that will inspire our teams to bring ideas into fruition.

It doesn't appear that any particular combination of strengths provides a 'magic inspirational potion' [24], but it seems that many of the best leaders exhibit a high degree of emotional intelligence, cognitive flexibility and the ability to quickly shift their focus among themselves, other people and their strategy [3, 12, 13].

PURPOSE AND INSPIRATION GO HAND-IN-HAND

Inspiration is a state that we can nurture and improve. As we train our executive function through better decision making and habits; nurture the skills of emotional intelligence; build our cognitive intelligence; and reflect on our identity consciously, and in 'default mode', we sow the seeds for inspiration.

We can cultivate these seeds by:

- Finding our 'core people' and investing in interdependent relationships so we can support and inspire each other.

- Thinking deeply about our sense of purpose and the impact we want to have beyond ourselves.

- Sharing a vision in the context of a positive future, rather than focussing on problems.

CONTROL: ARE YOU IN CONTROL OF YOUR LIFE?

As our attention moves from our identity, to our sense of purpose, we eventually need to consider the final element in our core: our sense of 'control.' Control plays a significant role in connecting our perception of the world, what we think is important, with what we actually do.

As we discussed at the end of Chapter 4, attention and motivation are so closely linked that you could almost see attention as a 'master regulator.' The apparent common motivational 'node' for both mental and physical effort [30] means that what we pay attention to influences how effectively our brain prepares itself for action, our motivation and how much effort we apply to a task [31].

Our attention helps us make 'cost-benefit' decisions, weighing the investment of effort against the potential gains [32]. We will only direct physical or mental energy towards what we think is important enough to pay attention to.

We live and work as part of large and increasingly complex systems. We need attention to unlock the full potential of our emotional and cognitive intelligence; combining our knowledge-based competences with self-awareness, self-management, social awareness and relationship management.

We will be in control of our lives to the extent that we can manage our attention.

Are you making decisions based on good information and thoughtful consideration, taking into account multiple factors including what you are really aiming for? Are you taking advantage of the pause between perception and action, to make active decisions about where you focus your attention?

We can develop our sense of control by finding and developing ways to regularly use our strengths in the service of our vision. We can also look for ways to practise emotional intelligence – self-awareness, self-management, social awareness and relationship management – in everyday interactions. We can also make coaching to the 'positive emotional attractor' a habit, by focussing on our positive vision of the future in our internal reflection as well as our interactions with others. This will trigger the reward circuitry that's vital for motivation, cognitive flexibility, sustaining positive feeling and help us to keep going, despite inevitable setbacks [2].

Exploring these core questions is an ongoing process, but when we have established our vision, our priorities and our high-level goals, our brain will be well prepared to commit resources to live in a way that is consistent with our identity, purpose and vision for the future.

ACTIVE DECISIONS

Moving our attention among our identity, sense of purpose and control can be challenging, but this is the fundamental skill that will help us navigate through our complex, rapidly changing and competitive environment, and manage our time and energy more effectively, in line with what we feel is most important.

Our active decisions are where we translate perception into action. The elements in our core work together to help us make consistent good decisions, which impact the elements in the outside of the circle of better life: physical activity, nutrition, sleep and recovery, biomechanics, mental energy and general health.

One of most distinctive aspects of Aki's philosophy, which the Hintsa programmes have 'operationalised', is the 'inside-out' approach. If you start by trying to improve an element in the outside of the circle, before you've considered your core, your attention may not be prepared to make the automatic or conscious decisions that will allocate the resources you need to help achieve your goal. By starting inside-out, we learn to pay attention to

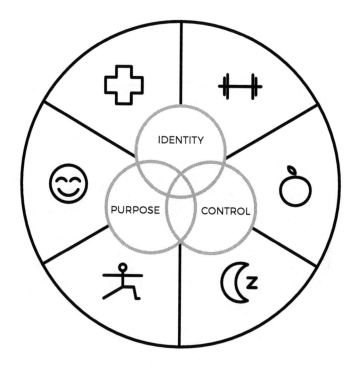

what is most important in our conscious and our automatic thought processes.

If you start by considering your core, you can find ways to make the outer elements in the circle fit with the road you have chosen as well as train your brain to make decisions and invest physical and cognitive efforts in ways that fit with this. In time, the small decisions become habitual and the tiny alterations in trajectory help to keep you on the path towards your goals.

There is more competition than ever for our cognitive resources, but we have unparalleled opportunities to help us develop ourselves, work with each other, imagine and realise a better future.

We can become experts in navigating through life, deciding what we need to pay attention to, and what we should ignore. Our cognitive capabilities may be limited, but most of us are only using a fraction of our potential. Our attention, emotional intelligence and executive functions can be developed and improved [3]. If we allocate and pool our cognitive resources efficiently and effectively and invest our energy where it matters, we can have an exponential impact on our life and our performance.

ASK YOURSELF

1) Can you describe your overarching goal?

2) What would you like your life to look like in 10 years?

3) Can you relate to the idea of coaching to the 'positive emotional attractor' versus the 'negative emotional attractor' in your own 'self-talk'?

4) Can you relate to the idea of coaching to the 'positive emotional attractor' versus the 'negative emotional attractor' in your conversations with other people?

5) Can you see the connection between attention and making best use of your cognitive and emotional intelligence, in your own life?

6) When was the last time you took a step back to consider your identity; your physical self, your character and spirituality?

7) Who are the 'core people' in your life?

8) Do you have a vision that inspires you?

9) How does your vision fit into the wider system you are part of?

10) What active decisions are you inspired to make?

RALPH BRAUN: CANCER SPECIALIST, SPORTS DOCTOR

Professor Ralph Braun holds up a paper 100 cm tape measure to his patient. It's the kind of tape you might find at IKEA for measuring furniture.

"How old are you?" he asks, "forty-five? Ok." Ralph cuts off 45 cm from the tape

"Did you ever smoke? Yes." He cuts off another 10 cm.

"Now you have cancer, hmm, maybe 40cm, maybe 2cm." He does some more cutting.

Ralph hands the tape measure to his patient.

"Here's your piece of paper, here's your life, now what do you want to do with it?"

For his patients, cancer can often be the cue to thinking about what really matters. "This kind of exercise with the tape measure helps tremendously," says Ralph. "It's a crude truth that forces people to the root of their thinking."

LIFE DOESN'T ALWAYS TURN OUT AS WE EXPECT

We are sitting in Ralph's consultation room in the department of Dermatology at the University of Zürich. The patients Ralph meets here are typically people who've led busy lives and put all of their efforts and savings into the future. All of a sudden they've got a cancer diagnosis. The future they've been planning may never happen.

"That destroys people: it turns their lives upside down" says Ralph. "Everything that has been true in the past is no longer."

Ralph's background is in dermatology and dermato-oncology, with a specialty in the non-invasive diagnosis of melanoma. In his field, cancer doesn't mean a patient has to die. "But they are dealing with the unknown."

ARE YOU IN CONTROL?

Ralph, who is a Hintsa Science Board member and long-time associate of Aki and the Hintsa group, shares the philosophy of helping people regain control, or "putting patients back into the driver's seat of their lives," as key to success.

Ralph points out that people will only direct physical or mental energy towards what they think is important enough to pay attention to: "We all take around 60-70 thousand decisions a day," he says, "should I scratch my head, should I use the stairs or the elevator, should I eat healthy or junk food?"

A SENSE OF PERSONAL AGENCY HELPS ENORMOUSLY

Even something as simple as getting patients to manage diet can help them step up and feel more in control. "Simple things like seeking out organic food, adding more nutrition, or using less sugar." Ralph also encourages patients to start exercising or to continue with existing programmes: "I say do your 10 thousand steps a day but maybe just reduce the amount during chemotherapy."

While diet and exercise in themselves, don't always help in the treatment of cancer, Ralph is convinced it's the sense of personal agency that can yield such enormously positive results. "They rediscover their power instead of just floating around like flotsam on the ocean."

PEOPLE WITH A STRONG SENSE OF LIFE PURPOSE ALSO FARE BETTER

Ralph admits he has no solid research to support this conviction. "There's no funding for this stuff because the research would involve a huge number of patients over a very long time and is very expensive." But Ralph feels he has a sense of which patients might fare better than others. They don't fight against the diagnosis but are ready to accept it and start moving forward. These people usually also have a strong sense of life purpose and they fit into Ralph's metaphor of the ballistic missile, which we mentioned in Chapter 9.

"A ballistic missile," Ralph explains, "is always off course, making constant adjustments, but it's only able to make these adjustments because it knows exactly where it is going."

HEAL THE WHOLE PERSON NOT JUST THE DIAGNOSIS

Like Aki, Ralph believes in pro-active healthcare and treating the whole person, not just the diagnosis. "Today's medicine has lost its soul!" Ralph laments. "You have 15 minutes in the chair to cover everything. There's not enough time to go deeper."

THE SKIN IS THE MIRROR OF THE SOUL

Ralph has co-edited several books and authored many medical publications on dermoscopy and skin cancers. He talks about the skin, the largest organ in our bodies, as the mirror of the soul.

"We can't separate the mind from the body," he says.

As an ice-hockey fan, Ralph supports of the Zurich ZSC Lions Ice Hockey Team in a medical capacity. If a player or another individual has a skin problem, Ralph senses immediately when things are going on below the surface. "They have to come out somewhere."

To extend the ice hockey metaphor, Ralph claims that "every person has a place for them where the ice is the thinnest. An Achilles heel if you like: Some people will have chronic lower back pain, some others headaches or stomach pain. For people I see it's the skin."

LIVING IN 'THE WORRIED WORLD'

How do we treat this? "Anxiety is a feeling that cannot be explained away rationally."

Again Ralph comes back to attention management.

"Attention is the gatekeeper for what we perceive and how we're going to react."

He might ask his patients to look around the room and focus only on the colour blue.

"Suddenly their mind engages only on things that are blue. They start to see the room in a very different way even though nothing has change in the room apart from their perception." Another test is to ask a patient to focus only on the act of swallowing.

"It's about bringing your attention to a point, says Ralph. "Think about all those times in your life you've swallowed and never realised what a terrible noise it makes." He laughs: "People are so surprised...it's all about perception"

"IF IT WAS EASY WE WOULD'VE DONE IT ALREADY."

Ralph asserts that we can all be in control of our lives to the extent that we can manage our attention – including the difficult decisions. We all have at least one thing in our lives that we simply don't want to go to because we know it will be so hard to change." It might be an economic problem, a marriage issue; we're aware of what it is but we don't want to touch it because we know it's going to be painful or it puts our entire lives in question.

"I get a lot of tears in my practice because we take on a lot of hard subjects," he says. But with a conviction derived from years of experience in his field, Ralph tells people:

> "As long as you know who you are and where you want to go, you're going to make it. Never forget that!"

10
RUN & FINISH WELL

Why is it that the most challenging moments in our lives offer the greatest clarity? Why do we have to encounter the possibility of everything being stripped away before we can see what really matters?

It's summer, 2015. Aki asks me to meet him in his office. He has something to tell me. Not unusual. We've had an ongoing conversation for the last two years. I share an idea with him and he shares another with me. We go our separate ways and think about it for a while, then arrange a time to meet up and talk about what we've found.

I make us each an espresso, and we sit down in the lounge.

"I have cancer. It is serious, but I will fight it."

Aki drops the bombshell. I don't see it coming. Neither did Aki, but despite the fact that he has just found out he has a grave medical condition, he only manages to dedicate 11 words to it, before he switches back to focus on his mission.

"Now… we need to start the book."

Aki wasn't trying to be brave, though he was. He wasn't trying to keep anything from me; he simply had his eyes firmly fixed on what was most important to him. He could see it clearly. It was about his family – his wife and children – and his mission.

"Take this down." He instructs me. I grab my laptop, position it on the table between us and hit 'record'.

PART 1: COFFEE FARMING

Aki sips his coffee and thinks for a moment. The coffee reminds him of a story from his time in Ethiopia. After the collapse of the Ethiopian communist government in 1991, the long task of demobilising and reintegrating the regime's soldiers fell to non-governmental organisations, such as the one Aki was working with.

There were health, social and economic problems to deal with. Fundamental issues needed to be addressed. The men needed money, but there was a deeper problem.

Aki seems, as always, to have considered the whole person. These men had lost their way, and needed to find a route to a new future. This was the priority.

> "They had lost their sense of identity. They used to belong to families, in a village society, but they didn't know who they were anymore. As men in the community, their purpose was to bring bread home, but they had no path to achieve this. They were not in control."
> Aki Hintsa

CONTROL

When Aki talks about control, he always talks about looking ahead to what is coming, into infinity, even. The importance of looking ahead is starting to be supported by some fresh perspectives in psychology, too. Marty Seligman, one of the founding fathers of positive psychology, has suggested that his field has placed too much value on the past and present, and undervalued the future [1].

With a future-orientated framework, we metabolise the past [1] and simulate future possibilities to evaluate what is most meaningful, important and valuable. It helps us to direct our attention and connect our goals with our actions, today.

It seems that one of the most important aspects of human cognition is our capacity for 'prospection:' the mental representation and evaluation of possible futures.

This future-orientated view is liberating. We can see memories as a source of experience for simulating alternative future paths, rather than simply a storehouse for what has already occurred. Instead

238

of our memories holding us back, locking us into patterns of cause and effect based on previous experience, we can use memories selectively to craft new narratives and simulate multiple possibilities.

Humans grow and develop by 'mastering the present and pre-empting the future' [2].

IN THE RIGHT PLACE, DOING THE RIGHT THINGS

I sat back and was silent, finishing my coffee and thinking about what Aki had just said. "They were not in control." What does someone who has just been diagnosed with a life-threatening disease think about control? I used to struggle with the notion of 'control' in the Hintsa model. Control is a powerful word and it's obvious that we can't control everything. We can't engineer-out the unexpected from life. I decide now's the time to ask him what he meant.

> "Control does not mean calculating everything 100%, it means that you have chosen the way you want to go. You own that road.
>
> I felt fit, I felt strong. Everything was good. But you can have the wrong card in your hand; you can get some disease. This is what we can't choose.
>
> The right kind of control, it means that you know you are in the right place, and that you are doing the right things."
> Aki Hintsa

Control is the natural successor to our reflections on our sense of identity and purpose. Control is as much about choosing a mindset as it is about selecting an action.

Control is the 'gear-box' between who we are, what we want and how we choose to act, regardless of the external circumstances.

A CLEAR VISION

Aki wants to continue his story. We're back in Ethiopia. Someone donates a plot of land for the ex-soldiers and gives them the opportunity to start growing coffee, one of Ethiopia's largest exports. Aki and the development organisation begin a project with about 60 men.

"I was criticised when we started this programme. People said that there was no way it would succeed. I told them, 'perhaps that is true, but these men do not have clear vision of what they want and they have lost their identity and purpose, we need to give them the chance to find it.'"
Aki Hintsa

Growing coffee is a hard, slow process. Seedlings of the coffee plant are raised in 'nurseries,' before being planted out six to twelve months later. The manual labour to dig the holes for the coffee plants is tiring and time-consuming. Once the mature plants are bedded in the ground, it takes three to four years to produce a harvest that is commercially viable.

"Everyone wanted to be the big coffee maker," Aki recalls. But while many of the new farmers dreamed about owning large plantations, one man in the group took matters into his own hands. His peers became distracted, letting their attention drift from idea to idea, but he continued to focus on his vision, and move closer to his goal. He also saw an opportunity in his comrades' impatience, and began offering to buy up their shares in the land.

> "He worked so hard on his own plot, and then he bought a share from the next guy. Then he started to produce a little coffee, because it takes years to produce the first harvest, and he started to buy up the other guys' shares one-by-one. Then after some years, he set up a coffee mill, to process the coffee. This one guy initiated it and it transformed this little village. Suddenly, he had achieved his dream."

The ex-soldier's vision was years away when he first began to dig holes in the ground and raise the seedlings. Perhaps it would result in success, perhaps not. He didn't know. He couldn't control everything, but he could choose to make the right decisions today, in line with who he was, who he wanted to be, and the impact he wanted to make.

> "He had a clear sense of identity and purpose, a commitment to make the active decisions he needed to, to work hard. Dreaming is not enough. You have to make your journey step-by-step."
> Aki Hintsa

CHOOSING YOUR ATTITUDE

One of Aki's fundamental messages is that we can't control everything that happens to us, but we can choose our actions and attitudes, which are key to building a better life.

In time, many of the soldiers reintegrated into the community, regaining respect for themselves and others. Aki and his team's resources were limited, but they made a significant impact with what they had because they worked from the inside out, helping people to imagine a new vision of their future and supporting them step-by-step along the way.

"I really liked this guy, because he proved to me that I was right!" Aki concludes the story of his favourite Ethiopian entrepreneur with a hearty laugh. He grabs a piece of fruit from the table and bites into it. "This is good," he says with a smile.

Even in the hardest circumstances, being thankful for the simplest things can have a profound effect. Try it for yourself. Every night for the next week, before you go to sleep, write down three things that went well that day, and describe why they went well. They could be really small things, or big things, it doesn't matter.

The effects of this exercise have been studied, and it turns out that they persist. Even though the volunteers were only instructed to do the exercise for one week, it seems that it had a positive 'addictive' quality and people continued with it [3]. People who are asked to record 'three good things' at the end of each day for one week report significantly higher positive emotion six months later. We feel pleasure when we remember good things. This reinforces the practice.

One of the most powerful predictors of life satisfaction is gratitude [4]. Imagining a positive future can be powerful and effective, but practising gratitude, by paying attention to the good things we already have, can also have a significant impact on our wellbeing, today.

PART 2: ATTENTION EVERYONE

Is attention the 'new oil?' It's limited, we've learnt to exploit it more effectively in the last 100 years, and it's certainly valuable, both to us and other people. Early in 2016,

Facebook, a company that has built its business on harvesting attention, overtook Exxon to become the world's fourth most valuable company.

We are hardwired to search for novelty, but we now have access to a firehose of distracting content. At worse, this simply wastes time, but it may have deeper consequences, if we don't use the tools we have carefully.

What we pay attention to determines where we invest our energy and our time. Attention is a limited resource. It is the key that unlocks, or limits, our potential.

What are the implications of directing our attention towards other people's perfectly presented lives? Is this having an impact on our ability to be grateful for what we already have? How are our own curated digital experiences influencing the memories we are constructing? How is the content we are consuming influencing our perception of what's important – our identity and our sense of purpose?

There's more competition for our attention than ever before, but how jealously are we protecting it and developing our capacity to focus our attention?

MANAGING ATTENTION

Research has demonstrated that, over time, we develop the capacity to manage our attention in favour of positive, over negative, material [6]. This seems to occur at the level of our attention processing. As we age, we learn to dedicate more of our working memory to positive, rather than negative, emotional stimuli. Basically, we get better at looking for and thinking about the good things in life. I sometimes wonder whether these findings would be replicated, if we repeated the study in 30 years, time, after a lifetime of media consumption.

Our perception and our memory are actively constructed. What we see and remember can be influenced. Where we choose to direct our attention creates an interpretation of reality, rather than an entirely truthful representation. Similarly, memory is not simply a retrieval mechanism. It's a deliberative attention process, where our goals influence how we construct and remember the past [5].

In the previous chapter, we explored how the experience of positive emotions can increase the breadth of our attention and our cognitive flexibility [5]. Research has also described how positive moods improve creative and holistic thinking [6]. Our attention has a profound influence on our perception, which has a powerful influence on our decisions and, ultimately, our actions.

The ability to manage our attention, and influence how we shape our perception of reality – past, present and future – has a deep impact on our wellbeing and the impact we can create in the world.

What are you paying attention to? Our favourite Ethiopian entrepreneur could have focussed on the tiring nature of the holes he was digging, but he instead concentrated on his vision for the future – the bigger impact he wanted to make.

The management of our attention underpins our control – our agency to choose how we respond, how we spend, restore and increase the energy we have available.

Are your perceiving threats or challenges in your life? Are you directing your attention towards your mission, or your social-media feed? Are you looking around at what other people have, or appreciating what you have already? Managing our attention is one of the most important skills that we can develop. Your attention is valuable, and you need to direct it carefully.

Wellbeing is not the absence of sickness or dysfunction. There are actually plenty of people in the world who are physically healthy, but still don't feel satisfied. There are also people with illnesses who manage to live with passion, meaning and purpose. Wellbeing is a presence, not an absence. It's a capacity we can increase and build and a skill that we can develop [3] through the choices we make.

Humans are fantastic at adapting. We eventually get used to almost any change.

Wellbeing is not simply the pursuit of pleasure and happiness, either. There are 'hedonic feel good' components in human wellbeing, but these pleasurable feelings are generally short-lived. A famous study among lottery winners has been cited extensively in this context. The researchers found that, while the lottery winners experienced an initial 'burst' of happiness, they soon got used to the new experience. Before long, they resumed their pre-lottery win state and were not found to be any happier than non-winners [7]. 'Habituation' is sometimes used to describe this phenomenon.

We can 'upgrade' our happiness. For example, it would be foolish to think that, if someone was living in oppressive circumstances, they would not be substantially happier if their situation improved [8], but research suggests that an improvement in their situation would eventually become a new 'set-point.' They wouldn't notice the improvement any more, and they would need a new 'hit' of pleasure to boost their happiness again.

The 'eudemonic' perspective contrasts the hedonic pursuit of pleasure. Aristotle is believed to be one of the first people to describe eudaimonia, a philosophy rooted in the belief that leading a virtuous life, and doing what we feel is worthwhile, is the route to lasting happiness. It also asserts that realising our potential is the ultimate human goal [9], and that humans have a fundamental motivation towards growth.

SELF-DETERMINATION

For many knowledge workers in established economies, basic needs have been met, but it's still common to experience a sense of being unfulfilled. Self-determination theory, a eudemonic perspective that also has its roots in Aristotle's thinking, may shed some light on this.

Self-determination theory contends that, throughout different cultures and times, humans have exhibited three inherent and fundamental needs:

1. Competence

The need to feel confident and effective in our actions. We are motivated to seek challenges that fit our competencies, and have a desire to enhance our skills and capabilities. Our sense of competence has an intrinsic component, but external validation of our competence is also important.

2. Relatedness

The need to feel connected with others, being cared for ourselves, and caring for other people; the need to have human connections that are close and secure, while still respecting autonomy and facilitating competence.

3. Autonomy

The need to choose what we are doing and be able to 'self-govern'. It's important to note that self-determination theory distinguishes autonomy from independence. For example we could make a choice to be autonomously dependent. Alternatively, someone may be forced into independence, if they lost their job for example. This would not represent autonomy. Research suggests that people are more likely to depend of people who support their autonomy, perhaps reflecting the importance of 'interdependence'.

(19, 20, 21)

In large organisations, it's easy for these basic needs to be compromised. Feelings of competence can be undermined by performance reviews which mean that only employees judged to be in the top percentiles feel confident and effective. We can feel increasingly disconnected from each other as a consequence of some work practices and distracted habits; people sending e-mails while talking to you, for example. Rigid job-descriptions and processes can reduce our sense of autonomy. Emerging trends, such as automation, may leave some workers fearful of being made independent, forcibly.

One of the reasons that 'startup culture' feels so attractive is that it seems to offer the potential to fulfill some of the needs described by self-determination theory. However, regardless of our context, we can make choices, in terms of how we lead ourselves and others, to meet our desire for competence, relatedness and autonomy inside and outside of work.

These choices relate to our sense of 'control'. Can you identify and find opportunities to use your strengths, inside or outside of work? Who are your 'core people' as we explored in the previous chapter; people who give you unconditional love, people who encourage you and people who challenge you and help you to learn in a constructive and balanced way? Can you choose your mindset, even if you can't control everything that is happening around you?

WE CAN CHOOSE OUR MINDSET AND ATTITUDE

I had an outstanding conversation with Formula One champion, Mika Häkkinen, while I was writing this book. I've known Mika for a couple of years, and nearly every time I meet him, he comes out with a great phrase or comment that's worth writing down.

> "You can choose your reactions to things and you can also choose who you spend time with. I always try to surround myself with positive people."
> Mika Häkkinen

One of the reasons I love Mika Häkkinen's story is that it speaks of so much passion and perseverance. It took him nearly 100 races before he reached the podium in Formula One. The stress and 'failures' could have crippled him, but instead, he consistently approached potentially stressful situations as a challenge, rather than a threat. He chose to focus on how he could overcome challenges, improve his tool – the car – and his skills, to perform at the highest level. Eventually, he achieved his goal and won two consecutive World Championships.

Experiencing stress is a normal part of being alive, but we can change our 'stress mindset' and even improve our performance in response to stress. Change takes effort; it makes demands of us, but stress is simply the human response when we experience any form of challenge or demand.

Whether the stress is physical or psychological, our heart rate, breathing rate and blood pressure increase and our mental alertness is enhanced. It would actually be counterproductive to remove all stress from our lives. 'Positive stress' can motivate us, focus our energy, and get us excited about improving performance, but only if we feel that the demands being made of us are within our coping abilities.

Problems arise when we perceive challenges as being beyond our capabilities. This can lead to 'negative stress,' anxiety or concern, unpleasant feelings and impaired performance.

HOW CAN WE LEARN TO MANAGE STRESS?

It can be tempting to focus our attention on trying to avoid stress. However, it's impossible to eliminate all stress from our lives, and many of the techniques we use to 'de-stress', such as trying to distract ourselves with digital technology, may actually increase stress, as we discussed before. So I would encourage you to consider stress in a more positive light and look for ways to work with it.

In many ways, sport is the ultimate testing ground for 'stress management.' Every training session and competition is a 'stressor' and even the most successful athletes will lose many more times than they win, resulting in continuous 'micro-doses of failure.'

In the immediate aftermath of stress, performance is decreased but, provided sufficient resources are available, the body recovers and performance bounces back. We often talk about this 'bouncing back' as the key characteristic of resilient individuals. However, it's possible for humans to adapt to stress and achieve levels of performance even higher than before.

It appears that, even in the most demanding situations, individuals with a clear sense of purpose, who feel engaged and present in their daily life, enjoy what they do, have meaningful relationships and find a sense of measurable accomplishment in their work, can achieve this 'super-compensation' in response to stress [10].

In fact, in a military context, researchers have identified that it's possible for soldiers who exhibit these characteristics to experience 'post-traumatic growth' following even the most stressful experiences [11]. Resilience and our capacity to recover, and even grow, in response to stressful situations can be trained and improved.

CHANGE YOUR STRESS MINDSET

Stress can result in very negative outcomes, but the enhancing nature of stress exists and is often ignored [12]. People who have a more positive view of stress are more likely to respond positively to it.

Shortly after my colleague, Juha Äkräs, became a Vice President for Nokia in the APAC region (all Asian and Pacific countries except China), there was a huge currency crisis. This caused a significant decline in the telecom market, including the mobile networking business, which had been growing well up until that point.

> "Environments change," says Juha. "You can't do anything about it. The question is: 'do you see it as a challenge or a threat?' I claim that our competitors saw it as a threat. Kari Ahola, our Senior Vice President, shared his vision that this was an opportunity. There was a disruption in the market that we could utilise. It was an attitude decision."

Juha and the APAC team responded by concentrating on two things:

1) **House cleaning:** Their business had grown so quickly in recent years that some aspects of the operation had become chaotic. This needed to be addressed and they could use the time during the downturn to do this. Also, Juha's team had 400 people, not including subcontractors, but due to the downturn, they only needed 250. Despite this, they only laid off six people. The rest were sent to other regions that were still growing, so they could continue to learn, and be ready to bring that learning back, when APAC began to grow again.

2) **They decided to win every deal:** At that time, Nokia only had 20% of the market share in the region. Four new mobile network operator licenses were to be offered. They won three out of four.

"South Asia Pacific became one of our most successful markets. We could have seen it as a tough time for a couple of years, lost market share, laid off hundreds of people, and not been ready when the market started to grow again. Instead we used the crisis to double our market share."

There is more than just anecdotal evidence to support the perspective that mindset can have a significant impact on performance in stressful circumstances. In 2013, researchers conducted a three-part study [13] looking at how people perceived stress. First, the researchers validated a test designed to help them understand different stress mindsets. The researchers identified two:

1) *Stress-is-enhancing:* People who believe that stress has a positive effect on performance.

2) *Stress-is-debilitating:* People who believe that stress has a negative effect on performance.

In the second part of the study, the researchers presented the subjects with factual information, defining the nature of stress in one of the two ways: stress-is-enhancing or stress-is-debilitating. They achieved this using short, multimedia film clips.

The results demonstrated that:

a) It was possible to influence and change the subject's stress mindset, simply by asking them to watch short educational film clips.

b) In a public speaking exercise, subjects who believed that stress is performance-enhancing exhibited moderate cortisol reactivity, relative to those who perceived stress to be debilitating, suggesting that our beliefs about stress can have a physiological impact.

c) Those who believed in performance-enhancing stress were more likely to seek detailed feedback after their performance, which can significantly enhance learning and improvement.

The three parts of the study illustrate that perceiving stress as a challenge, rather than a threat, is more likely to result in physiological responses that widen attention, improve thinking, decision making and cause less physical damage. Our stress mindset can be changed relatively quickly and it can enhance both our wellbeing and our performance.

Resilience and our capacity to recover, and even grow, in response to stressful situations can be trained and improved, and this can happen quickly such as in the video example, shown to the study participants. Investing in relationships with people who can support and help us grow through stressful experiences can significantly enhance our response to stress.

I encourage you to experiment with reframing a stressful experience as a challenge and learning experience. This is a mental skill that can be developed and next time you experience stress, remind yourself that it's a normal part of being human!

PART 4: SISU

I recently had a chat with one of our clients, who'd been trying to implement new techniques into some of the stressful, competitive situations in his life. He felt like he was failing to apply them successfully.

"I seem to get it 'right' a few times," he said, "but then I slip back again." The client had only recently started experimenting with these new approaches, but he was frustrated, so I posed the following question:

"Imagine that you've never trained for running in your life. If I asked you to run a marathon tomorrow, how do you think you would you get on?"

He laughed. The answer was obvious. It would be impossible. We're familiar and comfortable with the notion of progression in physical training. No one expects to be able to run a marathon without any preparation. It takes effort, planning and time, as the body adapts to increasing training loads. For some reason, when we think about cognitive performance and behaviour change, we expect to be able to turn it on and off, like a tap, but this means that we can become disheartened when the changes don't occur as quickly as we hoped. Change takes time. It happens in small steps.

"No one needs to be perfect, but everyone can be a little better today than yesterday."
Aki Hintsa

Sisu is a Finnish word, but it doesn't really have a direct English translation. We could describe it as a concept encompassing characteristics such as strength of will, bravery, resilience, hardiness and determination. If you decide to take a course of action, then stick to it in the face of adversity, you need 'Sisu'.

The conclusions of a recently published five-year study, among a group of international track and field athletes, determined that the percentage of successful completed training sessions was one of the strongest determinants of performance [14]. If we want to achieve real change, showing up and doing the work is one of the most significant influencers of success.

Perseverance – continuing along a path in the face of adversity – is a fundamental component in growth and change, but willpower alone is often not enough. We need to keep trying, but that motivation needs to come from a deeper source. What kept the Ethiopian entrepreneur digging holes for his coffee plants, day after day, and buying up his comrades land, even though the harvest was still years away? Angela Duckworth calls it 'Grit.'

Grit is a combination of perseverance and passion. It's not just a nice idea, it's a measurable strength, and it's a strong predictor of success in numerous fields[16].

A year-long study, among 755 people, compared 10 personality strengths and found that grit was the most reliable predictor of who would achieve their goals [16].

So how do we develop this 'gritty' approach to life? We need to draw our attention to our identity: our characteristics and strengths, our purpose: the bigger picture we are living for, but we also need to consider how our mindset influences our sense of control.

Research in this area is still in its early stages, but it appears that a 'growth mindset' is fundamental to persevering with passion. Ideally, we should approach our goals with the view that our ability is fluid, and that we can improve with effort. We should remind ourselves that failure is temporary, and keep running with determination and direction, at marathon pace.

CONTROL AND ACTIVE DECISIONS

Aki has consistently reinforced the importance of 'active decisions.' We can build a vision for the future when we reflect on our identity and our purpose and this influences our perception of the world and the way we act. But in the gap between perception and action, we have to make a decision. Our active decisions are the gearbox that helps us take control.

STRATEGY

It can be helpful to take a step back, and look at our lives in a broader context, considering multiple factors. It's part of widening our field of attention. It's all too easy to launch into a new project, without thinking too deeply about where we want to go and also where we're starting from, and make poor decisions based on automatic thinking and a narrow point of view.

I was speaking with Juha about this recently.

> "The world is so complex. When we have a vision, we need to consider the future state, then define our current state and describe the gap between the two. We need to describe this gap as simply as possible, and create key strategies to address it. There is no way that we can comprehend all the variables, because no strategy ever turns out exactly as we expect, but if we start with broad attention, then narrow to the specific opportunity, we improve our chance of taking the important things into account."

AGILITY

One of Hintsa's Science Board members, Professor Ralph Braun, likes to use the metaphor of a 'ballistic missile' as a way to consider our journey through life. A ballistic missile is always off course, making constant adjustments, but the missile is able to make these adjustments because it knows exactly where it is going. A strategy should improve our agility and our ability to correct our course, rather than restricting us. The following framework provides a way to broaden your attention, consider where you are now, and where you are heading.

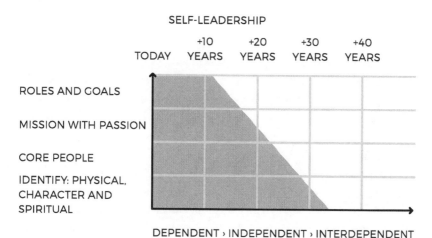

As we mature and journey through life, we should move from dependence, to independence, to interdependence. Our trajectory can be determined by our self-leadership and the active decisions we make each day, week, month and year in the context of our roles and our goals, our mission, passion, core people and our identity. How will the decisions we make today influence the people we want to be, the relationships we want to have, and our mission, in 10 years time?

It's worth taking a moment to reflecting on where you are in this framework now, where you are headed, and think about whether you need to make any adjustments to your trajectory. Define your goals in relation to the four dimensions of the framework, establish milestones so you can check your progress and adjust trajectory, if you need to. We recommend revisiting this framework periodically, to evaluate and review your journey.

> "If you are too stuck with your plan, if things don't go as expected, you may be very disappointed. You can't control everything, but you can choose your attitude. Remind yourself of your goals and take action."
> Juha Äkräs

PROGRESS, NOT PERFECTION

Aki always reminded us that no one is perfect. He was honest about his own journey, his successes and setbacks, and he'd seen familiar patterns in the countless clients he worked with.

I've worked with a lot of competitors in endurance sports, and the most common challenge I've seen is that they work too hard and struggle to give themselves permission to step-back and recover properly. They want to see continual improvement, so they push themselves to the limit in every session. Each week they want to go harder, and longer, but linear improvement is impossible for human beings.

There is a gap between perception and action, but there is also a gap between where people start, and where they would like to be. However, the nature of change and adaptation is that we take a few steps forward, and then a few steps back. If we achieve the appropriate balance between challenge and recovery, we take more steps forward than back, and the general trend is growth, but progress is never linear, or continuous.

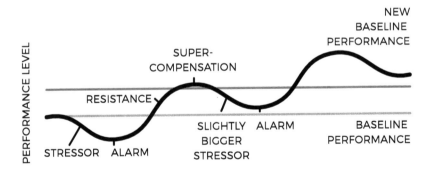

When we work with athletes, or with any client for that matter, we don't try to change or achieve everything at once. Some elements are persistent throughout the year, such as physical activity, but we also break the programme down into chunks, focusing on specific characteristics that the client is trying to develop, at specific times. In sport, this approach is known as periodization. In an athletic context, it reduces the risk of injury and overtraining [17]. It also provides a structure for the periods of work and rest, to facilitate adaption and growth [18], but we apply the principles to a more general population too to provide a framework for the year and make the client's vision more tangible. You can see a sample framework for a programme, in the illustration.

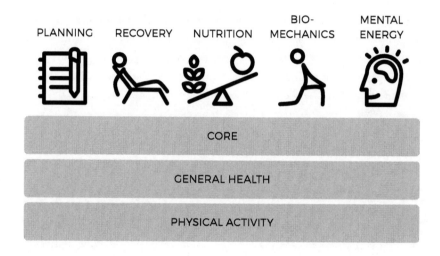

We work logically and in a focused way, but most importantly, we work from the inside out, helping people to imagine a new vision of their future, supporting them step-by-step along the way.

DREAMING IS NOT ENOUGH

It's been a strange experience listening back to the conversation I recorded with Aki last summer. Little phrases stand out and take on new significance. I've been reflecting on one of the things he said, when he told me about the coffee plantation project in Ethiopia:

> "Dreaming is not enough. You have to make your journey step-by-step."

Consider this when you think about what it means to build a better life. Keep your vision of a positive future in mind, describe your goal and think about how you can break it down into achievable steps. You will not get it right every time, sometimes you'll get distracted, but you can choose your path and start walking down it now.

I've watched Aki over the last year and half. He has always been passionate about his mission, but after his diagnosis, his conviction and clarity of purpose served to multiply the impact he had on people.

Your core, your sense of identity, purpose, control, will help to guide your attention and the active decisions you make. Your investment of time and energy is where the rubber hits the road. We can become experts in navigating through life, deciding what to pay attention to, and what we should ignore. We can train and improve our cognitive capabilities. But we are likely only using a fraction of our potential.

> "True success is not a one-off peak achievement. It's about doing small things, consistently well."
> Aki Hintsa

I received a letter from Aki, addressed to the whole team, just a few days before he died. It was just one week before I needed to finish the first draft of this manuscript, so I was working on this chapter. The last words of Aki's letter make a fitting conclusion to this book.

> "I am delighted that you have internalised the Hintsa Philosophy so deeply. I am very proud of you, and I have all the trust in you to take our mission forward exponentially - people need better life."

Aki is someone who ran and finished well. I couldn't have written this book without him. I hope this book has given you the tools and ideas to begin exploring your potential, and that the anecdotes and evidence have inspired you to go beyond what you think is possible.

My conversation with Aki has come to an end, but his mission continues.

Do you know that you are in the right place, and that you are doing the right things? It's never too late to start your own journey to a better life, but the best time to start is today.

ACKNOWLEDGEMENTS

The idea for Exponential emerged in the summer 2015, when Aki set me off on a quest to explore the science of 'knowledge work.' However, the work to transform this idea into reality only began in the latter part of 2016, in a frenzy of deadline-driven activity.

My own executive functioning was tested to the limit, as I squeezed research and writing alongside my day-job, sacrificed sleep, battled fatigue and the inevitable doubts that come with exposing your thoughts to scrutiny in the written word.

I spent many hours alone at my computer, but writing a book is a team effort. Firstly I thank my editor, Laurel Colless, who has been a great source of encouragement and has been invaluable in helping me to clarify my thoughts and shape my writing into a coherent message. Your insight, diligence and willingness to make your own sacrifices to deliver against seemingly impossible deadlines are much appreciated.

Thank-you to Linda Liukas, Mika Häkkinen, Jyrki Törnwall, Jürg Zeltner, Alex Stubb, Geoff Cooke and Ralph Braun for kindly permitting me to share your stories in the book.

This project could never have been realised without the efforts and support of my colleagues at Hintsa Performance; Pauliina Valpas, who reviewed some of the earliest chapters and provided perceptive and incisive comments, which resonated in my mind and guided me through the entire project. Juha Äkräs, for the considerable time and energy he spent in developing my understanding of the challenges and opportunities in the corporate world; for helping me to identify many areas for improvement in the manuscript; and for his logic and clarity of thinking, which were instrumental in crystalising the key messages. Pekka Pohjakallio, for sharing his experiences and helping me learn from his own writing and publishing experiences, and for diligently arranging the many practicalities required to transform a raw document into a printed book. Harri Sundvik, for being an endless source of inspiration and support. You encouraged me to 'go for it' from the very start and continued to cheer me on throughout. I am very grateful. Jussi Raisanen, thank-you for your backing, encouragement, and for saying 'yes' to all my requests for resources to make this project a reality. Pete McKnight, who has provided so much support and uncomplainingly listened to me think out-loud and reflect on my ideas, as the book took shape. Matti Kontsas, for your feedback and thoughtful critique, which challenged me to improve and see things in a different way. Pauliina Soilu, my assistant, who connected the dots and smoothed the path to make sure everything happened when it needed to. Mari Huhtanen and Jyri Öhman at Kilda design; your creativity has brought the text to life and your diligence, flexibility, efficiency and speed is inspirational.

Finally, my highest thanks go to my wife, Anna, for her endless patience and wisdom, for being a calming influence and encouragement through the ups and downs of this project, and for shouldering the burden of looking after our two young sons while I locked myself away with my laptop. You are truly my better half.

REFERENCES

CHAPTER 3 – BEYOND THE POSSIBLE

1. Clarke, A. C. (1962) One: Hazards of Prophecy: The Failure of Imagination. Profiles Of The Future: An Inquiry Into The Limits Of The Possible. London. Orion House.

2. Wittmann, B.C., Bunzeckb, N., Dolana, R.J. Düzelb, E. (2007) Anticipation of novelty recruits reward system and hippocampus while promoting recollection. NeuroImage 38 (1) p. 194–202

3. Tomasello, M. & Rakoczy, H. (2003) What makes human cognition unique? From individual to shared to collective intentionality. Mind & Language. 18 (2) p.121-147

4. De Heinzelin, J. (1962) "Ishango", Scientific American, 206 (6)p. 105--116

5. Gerdes, P. (Retrieved 20/10/2016) On The History of Mathematics in Africa South of the Sahara; http://www.math.buffalo.edu/mad/AMU/amu_chma_09.html#beginnings

6. Brooks, A.S. & Smith, C.C. (1987) Ishango revisited: new age determinations and cultural interpretations. The African Archaeological Review. 5 p. 65-78

7. IBM (Retrieved 19/10/2016) What is big data?; https://www-01.ibm.com/software/data/bigdata/what-is-big-data.html

8. EMC (Retrieved 19/10/2016) The Digital Universe of Opportunities; https://www.emc.com/collateral/analyst-reports/idc-digital-universe-2014.pdf

9. Carman, C. C. & Evans, J. (2014) On the epoch of the Antikythera mechanism and its eclipse predictor. Archive for History of Exact Sciences. 68 (6) p. 693–774

10. Freeth, T. & Jones, A. (2012) (Retrieved 21/10/2016) The Cosmos in the Antikythera Mechanism. Institute for the Study of the Ancient World; http://dlib.nyu.edu/awdl/isaw/isaw-papers/4/

11. Da Cruz, F. (Retrieved 21/10/2016) Herman Hollerith; http://www.columbia.edu/cu/computinghistory/hollerith.html

12. Drucker, P. (1957) Landmarks of Tomorrow: A Report on the New "Post-Modern" World. New York. Harper & Row.

13. Drucker, P. (Retrieved 22/10/2016) The New Society of Organizations; https://hbr.org/1992/09/the-new-society-of-organizations

14. Hamming, R. (1973) Preface. Numerical Methods for Scientists and Engineers. Kogakusha. McGraw-Hill.

15. Eichstaedt, J.C., Hansen, A.S., Kern, M.L., Park, G., Labarthe, D.R., Merchant, R.M., Jha, S., Agrawal, M., Dziurzynski, L.A., Sap, M., Weeg, C. Larson, E.E., Ungar, L.H. Seligman, M.E.P. (2015) Psycho-

logical Language on Twitter Predicts County-Level Heart Disease Mortality. Psychol Sci. 2015 Feb; 26(2): 159–169.

16.   World Health Organization (Retrieved 23/10/2016) The top 10 causes of death; http://www.who.int/mediacentre/factsheets/fs310/en/

17.   World Health Organization (Retrieved 23/10/2016) Cancer. http://www.who.int/cancer/en/

18.   IBM (Retrieved 23/10/2016)Watson provides clinicians with evidence-based treatment options based on expert training by MSK physicians; http://www.ibm.com/watson/health/oncology/

19.   Otake, T. (Retrieved 23/10/2016) IBM big data used for rapid diagnosis of rare leukemia case in Japan; http://www.japantimes.co.jp/news/2016/08/11/national/science-health/ibm-big-data-used-for-rapid-diagnosis-of-rare-leukemia-case-in-japan/#.WAyGU5N97F0

20.   Mordvintsev, A., Olah, C. & Tyka, M. (Retrieved 21/10/2016) Inceptionism: Going Deeper into Neural Networks; https://research.googleblog.com/2015/06/inceptionism-going-deeper-into-neural.html

21.   Copland, M. (Retrieved 23/10/2016) What's the Difference Between Artificial Intelligence, Machine Learning, and Deep Learning? https://blogs.nvidia.com/blog/2016/07/29/whats-difference-artificial-intelligence-machine-learning-deep-learning-ai/

22.   Levy, S. (Retrieved 23/10/2016) An exclusive inside look at how artificial intelligence and machine learning work at Apple; https://backchannel.com/an-exclusive-look-at-how-ai-and-machine-learning-work-at-apple-8dbfb131932b#.fsfskcs6q

23.   Wikipedia (Retrieved 23/10/2016) Skynet (Terminator); https://en.wikipedia.org/wiki/Skynet_(Terminator)

24.   Frey, C.B. & Osborne, M.A. (Retrieved 16/05/2016) The future of employment: How susceptible of jobs to computerisation?; http://www.oxfordmartin.ox.ac.uk/downloads/academic/The_Future_of_Employment.pdf

25.   Dadich, S. (Retrieved 23/10/2016) Barack Obama, Neural Nets, Self-Driving Cars, And The Future Of The World. https://www.wired.com/2016/10/president-obama-mit-joi-ito-interview/

26.   Schwab, K. (2016) The Fourth Industrial Revolution. Cologny. World Economic Forum.

27.   Badishkanian, G.R., Bazinet, J.B., Chang, A., Fordham, T.M., Lai, A., Lehto, T., McShane, K., Pritchard, W.H., Shirvaikar, A., Wightman, F., Wong, K., Rogers, S. (Retrieved 24/10/2016) TECHNOLOGY AT WORK v2.0 ; http://www.oxfordmartin.ox.ac.uk/downloads/reports/Citi_GPS_Technology_Work_2.pdf

28.   Gunawardene, N. (Retrieved 19/10/2016) Humanity will survive information deluge; http://www.arthurcclarke.net/?interview=12

CHAPTER 4 - HIGH-PERFORMANCE BODY & BRAIN

1. Bouchard, C., Dionne, F.T., Simoneau, J.A., Boulay, M.R. (1992) Genetics of aerobic and anaerobic performances. Exercise and Sport Sciences Reviews. 20 p.27-58

2. Pollock, M.L. (1973) Quantification of endurance training programs. Exercise and Sport Sciences Reviews. 1 p.155-188

3. Seiler, K.S. & Kjerland, G.Ø. (2006) Quantifying training intensity distribution in elite endurance athletes: is there evidence for an "optimal" distribution? 16(1) p. 49-56

4. Tønnessen, E., Øystein Sylta, T.A., Haugen, Hem, E., Svendsen, I.S., Seiler, S. (2014) The Road to Gold: Training and Peaking Characteristics in the Year Prior to a Gold Medal Endurance Performance. Public Library of Science; http://dx.doi.org/10.1371/journal.pone.0101796

5. Craig, M.N. et al. (2013) Six weeks of a polarized training-intensity distribution leads to greater physiological and performance adaptations than a threshold model in trained cyclists. Journal of Applied Physiology. 114 p. 461–471

6. Chwalbinska-Moneta, J., Kaciuba-Uscilko, H., Krysztofiak, H., Ziemba, A., Krzeminski, K., Kruk, B., et al. (1998). Relationship between EMG, blood lactate, and plasma catecholamine tresholds during graded exercise in men. J. Physiol. Phyrmacol. 49, 433–441.

7. Londeree, B. R. (1997). Effect of training on lactate/ventilatory thresholds: a meta-analysis. Med. Sci. Sports Exerc. 29, 837–843

8. Stöggl, T. & Sperlich, B. (2014) Polarized training has greater impact on key endurance variables than threshold, high intensity, or high volume training. Frontiers in physiology. 5 (33). doi: 10.3389/fphys.2014.00033

9. Seiler, S., Haugen, O. & Kuffel, E. (2007) Autonomic Recovery after Exercise in Trained Athletes: Intensity and Duration Effects. Medicine & Science in Sport & Exercise 39(8)p. 1366-1373

10. Goel, V.; Dolan, R. (2003) "Explaining modulation of reasoning by belief". Cognition. 87 (1) B11–B22

11. Tsujii, T.; Watanabe, S. (2009) "Neural correlates of dual-task effect on belief-bias syllogistic reasoning: a near-infrared spectroscopy study". Brain Research. 1287 p.118–125

12. Cowan, N. (2001) The magical number 4 in short-term memory: A reconsideration of mental storage capacity. Behavioral and Brain Sciences. 24 p. 87–185

13. Nader, K. (2003) Memory traces unbound. Trends in Neurosciences. 26. p. 65-72

14. Brown, T.E. (2005) Attention Deficit Disorder: The Unfocused Mind in Children and Adults. Yale. Yale University Press.

15. McCabe, D.P., Roediger, H.L., McDaniel, M.A., Balota, D.A. & Hambrick, D.Z. (2010) The Relationship Between Working Memory Capacity and Executive Functioning: Evidence for a Common Executive Attention Construct. Neuropsychology 24(2)p. 222–243

16. O'Jilea, J.R.,Ryan, L.M., Betz, B., Parks-Levy, J., Hilsabecke, R.C., Rhudy, J.L., Gouvier, W.D. (2006)

Information processing following mild head injury. Archives of Clinical Neuropsychology. 21 (4) p. 293–296

17.   Gazzaley, A. & Rosen, L.D. (2016) The Distracted Mind: Ancient Brains in a High Tech World. Boston. MIT Press.

18.   Seligman, M.P., Railton, P., Baumeister, R.F., Chandra, S. (2016) Homo Prospectus. New York. Oxford University Press.

19.   Kahneman, D. (2011) Thinking, fast and slow. Farrar, Straus and Giroux. New York.

20.   Quartz, S. (2009) Reason, emotion and decision-making: risk and reward calculation with feeling. Trends in Cognitive Sciences. 13. p.209-215

21.   Seligman, M.P. Two. Intuitive Guidance: Emotion, Information, and Experience in Seligman, M.P., Railton, P., Baumeister, R.F., Chandra, S. (2016) Homo Prospectus. New York. Oxford University Press.

22.   Behrans, T.E.J., Woolrich, M.W., Walton, M.W., & Rushworth, M.F.S. (2007) Learning the value of information in an uncertain world. Nature Neuroscience. 10. p.1214-1221.

23.   Pleskac, T.J., & Hertwig, R. (2014) Ecologically rational choice and the structure of the environment. Journal of Experimental Psychology: General. 143 p.2000-2019

24.   Schmidt, L. , Lebreton, M., Cléry-Melin, M.L., Daunizeau, J., Pessiglione, M. (2012) Neural Mechanisms Underlying Motivation of Mental Versus Physical Effort. PLOS. http://dx.doi.org/10.1371/journal.pbio.1001266

25.   Massar, S.A.A., Lim, J., Sasmita, K., Chee, M.W.L. (2016) Rewards boost sustained attention through higher effort: A value-based decision making approach. Biological Psychology. 120. p.21–27

26.   Wykowska, A. Anderl, C., Schubö, A. & Hommel, B. (2013) Motivation Modulates Visual Attention: Evidence from Pupillometry. Frontiers in Psychology. 4 (59) doi: 10.3389/fpsyg.2013.00059

CHAPTER 5 – HUMAN INTELLIGENCE

1.   Daniel Kahneman (Retrieved 13/10/2016) Daniel Kahneman – Biographical; http://www.nobelprize.org/nobel_prizes/economic-sciences/laureates/2002/kahneman-bio.html

2.   Paas, F. & Tuovinen, J.E. (2003) Cognitive Load Measurement as a Means to Advance Cognitive Load Theory. Educational Psychologist. 38 p. 63 – 71

3.   Ophir, E., Nass, C.I. & Wagner, A.D. (2009) Cognitive control in media multitaskers. Articles from Proceedings of the National Academy of Sciences of the USA. 106 p. 15583–15587

4.   Budnik, F. (Retrieved 07/10/2016) THE SPEED WITH WHICH WE GET TO MARS; http://blogs.esa.int/rocketscience/2016/03/18/the-speed-with-which-we-get-to-mars/

5.   European Space Agency. (Retrieved 07/10/2016) esa's participation in Mars500; http://www.esa.int/Our_Activities/Human_Spaceflight/Mars500

6.   European Space Agency. (Retrieved 07/10/2016) esa's participation in Mars500; http://www.esa.int/Our_Activities/Human_Spaceflight/Mars500

7.   Cohen, I. et al. (2016) Work content influences on cognitive task load, emotional state and performance during a simulated 520-days' Mars mission. Computers in Human Behavior 55 p. 642–652

8.   IDC Custom Solutions (Retrieved 14/10/2016) Always Connected for Facebook Case Study; https://www.idc.com/prodserv/custom_solutions/download/case_studies/PLAN-BB_Always_Connected_for_Facebook.pdf

9.   Naragon, K. (Retrieved 14/10/2016) Subject: E-mail, We Just Can't Get Enough; https://blogs.adobe.com/conversations/2015/08/email.html

10.   FuzeBox (Retrieved 19/11/2016) FuzeBox Survey Reveals U.S. Workforce Hampered by Multitasking and Disengagement; 2,000 respondents were randomly selected and are a representative national sample of information workers in the U.S. http://www.prnewswire.com/news-releases/fuzebox-survey-reveals-us-workforce-hampered-by-multitasking-and-disengagement-242217771.html

11.   Olmstead, K. (2014) Social Media and the Workplace. Pew Research Center.

12.   Ridley, L. (Retrieved 04/11/2016) People swap devices 21 times an hour, says OMD; http://www.campaignlive.co.uk/article/people-swap-devices-21-times-hour-says-omd/1225960?src_site=brandrepublic

13.   Relic, D. (Retrieved 14/10/2016) Tomi Ahonen: Average users looks at their phone 150 times a day!; http://www.intomobile.com/2012/02/09/tomi-ahonen-average-users-looks-their-phone-150-times-day/

14.   Figueiro M.G., Wood, B., Plitnick, B. & Rea, M.S. (2011) The impact of light from computer monitors on melatonin levels in college students. Neuro Endocrinology Letters. 32(2) p.158-63

15.   Chui, Michael et al. (2012) "The Social Economy: Unlocking Value and Productivity Through Social Technologies. McKinsey Global Institute.

16.   Gouveia, A. (Retrieved 08/10/2016) Workers Are Wasting More Time Than Ever in 2014. 2014 Wasting Time at Work Survey; http://www.salary.com/2014-wasting-time-at-work/slide/2/

17.   KPCB (Retrieved 08/10/2016) 2013 Internet trends; http://www.kpcb.com/blog/2013-internet-trends

18.   Senna (2010). [DVD] United Kingdom: Universal Pictures.

19.   1: Life On The Limit. (2013). [DVD] USA: Exclusive Media

20.   Wittmann, B.C., Bunzeckb, N., Dolana, R.J. Düzelb, E. (2007) Anticipation of novelty recruits reward system and hippocampus while promoting recollection. NeuroImage 38 (1) p. 194–202

21.   Baumeister, R. F. (2005) The cultural animal: Human nature, meaning, and social life. New York. Oxford University Press.

22.   Gazzaley, A. & Rosen, L.D. (2016) The Distracted Mind: Ancient Brains in a High Tech World. Boston. MIT Press.

23.   Oken, B.S., Salinsky, M.C., Elsasa, S,M. (2006) Vigilance, alertness, or sustained attention: physio-

logical basis and measurement. Clinical Neurophysiology 117 (9) p. 1885-1901

24.   Ericsson, K. A. Peak: Secrets from the New Science of Expertise. London. The Bodley Head.

25.   Hofmann, W., Baumeister, R.F., Förster, G., Vohs, K.D., (2012) Everyday temptations: an experience sampling study of desire, conflict, and self-control. Journal of Personality & Social Psychology. 102 (6) p.1318-1335

26.   Eyal, N. (2014) Hooked: How to Build Habit-Forming Products. New York: Penguin

27.   Montague P.R, Dayan P, Sejnowski T.J. (1996) A framework for mesencephalic dopamine systems based on predictive Hebbian learning. Journal of Neurosciences. 16 p.1936–1947

CHAPTER 6 – ATTENTION PARADOX

1.   Cowan, N. (2001) The magical number 4 in short-term memory: A reconsideration of mental storage capacity. Behavioral and Brain Sciences. 24 p. 87–185

2.   Luck, S.J. & Vogel, E.K. (1997) The capacity of visual working memory for features and conjunctions. Nature. 390 p. 279-281

3.   Schmidt, J. (Retrieved 18/10/2016) Always practise safe text: the German traffic light for smartphone zombies; https://www.theguardian.com/cities/2016/apr/29/always-practise-safe-text-the-german-traffic-light-for-smartphone-zombies

4.   Ophir, E., Nass, C.I. & Wagner, A.D. (2009) Cognitive control in media multitaskers. Articles from Proceedings of the National Academy of Sciences of the USA. 106 p. 15583–15587

5.   Trafton, J. et al. (2003) Preparing to resume an interrupted task: effects of prospective goal encoding and retrospective rehearsal. Int J Hum Comput Stud 2003;58:583–603

6.   Deb, A. (2015) Phantom vibration and phantom ringing among mobile phone users: A systematic review of literature. Asia-Pacific Psychiatry. 7 (3) p. 231-239

7.   Mark, G., Gudith, D. Klocke, U. (2008) The cost of interrupted work: more speed and stress. CHI '08 Proceedings of the SIGCHI Conference on Human Factors in Computing Systems. p. 107-110

8.   Pessoa L. (2010). Emergent processes in cognitive-emotional interactions. Dialogues Clin. Neurosci. 12, 433–448

9.   Pessoa L. (2010). Emergent processes in cognitive-emotional interactions. Dialogues Clin. Neurosci. 12, 433–448

10.   Chui, M., Manyika, J., Miremadi, M. (Retrieved 16/05/2016) Four fundamentals of workplace automation; http://www.mckinsey.com/business-functions/business-technology/our-insights/four-fundamentals-of-workplace-automation

11.   Sweller, J., Ayres, P. & Kalyuga, S. (2011) Cognitive Load Theory. Explorations in the Learning Sciences, Instructional Systems and Performance Technologies 1. p. 129-140

12.   Scott, R. (1982) Blade Runner. Warner Bros.

13.	OFCOM (Retrieved 14/10/2016) Communications Market Report 2014; https://stakeholders.ofcom. org.uk/market-data-research/market-data/communications-market-reports/cmr14/uk

14.	Lenhart, A. (Retrieved 14/10/2016) Cell phones and American adults; http://www.pewinternet. org/2010/09/02/cell-phones-and-american-adults/

15.	Frier, S. (Retrieved 14/10/2016) Facebook $22 Billion WhatsApp Deal Buys $10 Million in Sales; https://www.bloomberg.com/news/articles/2014-10-28/facebook-s-22-billion-whatsapp-deal-buys-10-million-in-sales

16.	Olmstead, K. (Retrieved 19/11/2016) Social Media and the Workplace. Pew Research Center; http://www.pewinternet.org/2016/06/22/social-media-and-the-workplace/

17.	Smallwood, J., Obonsawin, M., & Heim, D. (2003) Task unrelated thought: The role of distributed processing. Consciousness and Cognition. 12 p. 169–189

18.	Yang, M.H., Christodoulou, J.A. & Singh, V. (2012) Rest Is Not Idleness: Implications of the Brain's Default Mode for Human Development and Education. Perspectives on Psychological Science.7 (4) p. 352-364

19.	Lee, Y., Chang, C., Lin, Y. & Cheng, Z. (2014) The dark side of smartphone usage: Psychological traits, compulsive behavior and technostress. Computers in Human Behaviour. 31 p. 373–383

20.	Smiler, S., Haugen, O. & Kuffel, E. (2007) Autonomic Recovery after Exercise in Trained Athletes: Intensity and Duration Effects. Medicine & Science in Sport & Exercise 39(8)p. 1366-1373

21.	Mizuno, K., Tanaka, M., Yamaguti, K., Kajimoto, O. Kuratsune, H. & Watanabe, Y. (2011) Mental fatigue caused by prolonged cognitive load associated with sympathetic hyperactivity. Behavioral and Brain Functions. DOI: 10.1186/1744-9081-7-17

22.	Relic, D. (Retrieved 14/10/2016) Tomi Ahonen: Average users looks at their phone 150 times a day!; http://www.intomobile.com/2012/02/09/tomi-ahonen-average-users-looks-their-phone-150-times-day/

23.	Naragon, K. (Retrieved 14/10/2016) Subject: E-mail, We Just Can't Get Enough; https://blogs.adobe.com/conversations/2015/08/email.html

24.	Kaplan, S. (1995) The Restorative Benefits of Nature: Toward an Integrative Framework. Journal of Environmental Psychology 15 p.169-182

25.	Berman, M.G., Jonides, J. & Kaplan, S. (2008) The Cognitive Benefits of Interacting With Nature. Psychological Science. 19 (12) p.1207–1212

26.	Centers for Disease Control and Prevention (Retrieved 17/10/2016) Insufficient Sleep Is a Public Health Problem; http://www.cdc.gov/features/dssleep/)

27.	Dawson, D. & Reid, K. (1997) Fatigue, alcohol and performance impairment. Nature. 388 p.235-237

28.	Lockley, S. & Foster, R.G. (2012) Sleep: A Very Short Introduction. Oxford. Oxford University Press.

29.	Alhola, P. & Polo-Kantola, P. (2007) Sleep deprivation: Impact on cognitive performance. Journal of Neuropsychiatric Disease and Treatment. 3(5) p. 553–567

30. Van Dongen H.P., Maislin, G., Mullington, J.M., Dinges, D.F.(2003)The cumulative cost of additional wakefulness: dose-response effects on neurobehavioral functions and sleep physiology from chronic sleep restriction and total sleep deprivation. Sleep. 26(2) p.117-126

31. Newport, C. (2016) Introduction. Deep Work: Rules for Focused Success in a Distracted World. p.4

32. Csikszentmihaly, M. (2008) Introduction. Flow: The Psychology of Optimal Experience. New York. Harper Perennial Modern Classics. p.3

33. Frey, C.B. & Osborne, M.A. (Retrieved 16/05/2016) The future of employment: How susceptible of jobs to computerisation?; http://www.oxfordmartin.ox.ac.uk/downloads/academic/The_Future_of_Employment.pdf

CHAPTER 7 – EFFICIENT & EFFECTIVE

1. Automobile Club de France (Retrieved 14/11/2016) History of the club; https://www.automobile-clubdefrance.fr/history-of-the-club

2. Grand Prix History (Retrieved 14/11/2016) The Story of the Grand Prix; http://www.grandprixhistory.org/story_a.htm

3. Wikipedia (Retrieved 14/11/2016) Renault Grand Prix; https://en.wikipedia.org/wiki/Renault_Grand_Prix).

4. Glover, J.A., Ronning, R.R., Reynolds, C. (1989) Perspectives on Individual Differences: Handbook of creativity. New York. Plenum Press

5. Levitin, D. (2014) Chapter 5: 'Organizing our time' in The Organized Mind: Thinking Straight in the Age of Information Overload. p.171

6. US National Library of Medicine (Retrieved 23/11/2016) COMT gene; https://ghr.nlm.nih.gov/gene/COMT

7. Schultz, W. (2015) Neuronal reward and decision signals: from theories to data. Physiological Reviews 95 (3) p. 853–951

8. Seligman, M.P. Eleven. Creativity and Aging: What We Can Make With What We Have Left, in Seligman, M.P., Railton, P., Baumeister, R.F., Chandra, S. (2016) Homo Prospectus. New York. Oxford University Press.

9. Amabile, T.M, Mueller, J.S., Simpson, W.B., Hadley, C.N, Kramer, S.J., Fleming, L. (Retrieved 02/11/2016) Time Pressure and Creativity in Organizations: A Longitudinal Field Study; http://www.hbs.edu/faculty/Publication%20Files/02-073_03f1ecea-789d-4ce1-b594-e74aa4057e22.pdf

10. Shikauchi, Y. & Ishii, S. (2016) Robust encoding of scene anticipation during human spatial navigation. Scientific Report. 22;6:37599

11. Duhigg, C. (2016) Smarter, Faster, Better. London. William Heinemann.

12. Allen, J. (Retrieved 14/11/2016) Behind the scenes with Red Bull: How to make an F1 Car Part 1;

https://www.jamesallenonf1.com/2013/09/behind-the-scenes-with-red-bull-how-to-make-an-f1-car-part-one/)

13.   Yang, M.H., Christodoulou, J.A. & Singh, V. (2012) Rest Is Not Idleness: Implications of the Brain's Default Mode for Human Development and Education. Perspectives on Psychological Science.7 (4) p. 352-364

14.   Buckner, R. L.; Andrews-Hanna, J. R.; Schacter, D. L. (2008) "The Brain's Default Network: Anatomy, Function, and Relevance to Disease". Annals of the New York Academy of Sciences. 1124 (1): 1–38. doi:10.1196/annals.1440.011. PMID 18400922.

15.   Kühn, S., Ritter, S.M., Müller, B.C.N, Dijksterhuis, A. (2014) The importance of the default mode network in creativity: A structural MRI study. The Journal of Creative Behaviour. 48 (2) p.152-163

16.   Vaughan, D. (Retrieved 14/11/2016) Mercedes Benz 120HP; http://www.conceptcarz.com/vehicle/z15320/Mercedes-Benz-120-HP.aspx

17.   Mercedes AMG Petronas Formula One Team. (Retrieved 14/11/2016) PU106C; https://www.mercedesamgf1.com/en/mercedes-amg-f1/amg-f1-car/pu106c-hybrid/

18.   Dweck, C. (2006) Mindset: The New Psychology of Success. New York. Random House.

19.   Baumeister, R (2002) Ego Depletion and Self-Control Failure: An Energy Model of the Self's Executive Function. Self and Identity. 1 (2). p. 129-136.

20.   Inzlicht, M & Schmeichel, B (2012) What Is Ego Depletion? Toward a Mechanistic Revision of the Resource Model of Self-Control. Perspectives on Psychological Science, 7 (5). p. 450–463

21.   Bernecker, K. & Job, V. (2015) Beliefs about willpower moderate the effect of previous day demands on next day's expectations and effective goal striving. Frontiers in Psychology. http://dx.doi.org/10.3389/fpsyg.2015.01496

22.   Ganguly K., Poo, M.M. (2013) Activity-dependent neural plasticity from bench to bedside. Neuron. 80 (3) p. 729–741

23.   Ishibashi, T. et. al. (2006) Astrocytes Promote Myelination in Response to Electrical Impulses. Neuron. 49(6) p.823–832

24.   Gazzaley, A. & Rosen, L.D. (2016) The Distracted Mind: Ancient Brains in a High Tech World. Boston. MIT Press.

25.   Kuhn, D. & Pease, M. (2006) Do Children and Adults Learn Differently? Journal of Cognition and Development, 7(3) p.279–293

26.   Diamond, A., Barnett, W.S., Thomas, J. & Munro, S. (2007) Preschool Program Improves Cognitive Control. Science. 318 (5855) p. 1387–1388.

27.   McCabe, D.P., Roediger, H.L., McDaniel, M.A., Balota, D.A. & Hambrick, D.Z. (2010) The Relationship Between Working Memory Capacity and Executive Functioning: Evidence for a Common Executive Attention Construct. Neuropsychology

28.   Guiney H. & Machado, L. (2013) Benefits of regular aerobic exercise for executive functioning in

healthy populations. Psychonomic Bulletin and Review. 20(1) p. 73-86

29.   Themanson, J.R., Pontifex, M.B. & Hillman, C.H. (2008) Fitness and action monitoring: evidence for improved cognitive flexibility in young adults. Neuroscience. 157(2) p.319–328

30.   Colcombe, S. & Kramer. A.F. (2003) Fitness effects on the cognitive function of older adults: a meta-analytic study. Psychological Science. 14 (2) p.125-130

31.   Mikulas, W. L. & Vodanovich, S. J. (1993) The essence of boredom. Psychological Record. 43. p.3-12

32.   IDC Custom Solutions (Retrieved 14/10/2016) Always Connected for Facebook Case Study; https://www.idc.com/prodserv/custom_solutions/download/case_studies/PLAN-BB_Always_Connected_for_Facebook.pdf

33.   Nielsen. (Retrieved 04/11/2016) Tech Or Treat: Consumers Are Sweet On Mobile Apps; http://www.nielsen.com/us/en/insights/news/2014/tech-or-treat-consumers-are-sweet-on-mobile-apps.html

34.   Ridley, L. (Retrieved 04/11/2016) People swap devices 21 times an hour, says OMD; http://www.campaignlive.co.uk/article/people-swap-devices-21-times-hour-says-omd/1225960?src_site=brandrepublic

35.   Levitin, D. (2014) Chapter 5: 'Organising our time' in The Organized Mind: Thinking Straight in the Age of Information Overload. London. Penguin. p.169

36.   Kushlev, K. & Dunn, E.W. (2015) Checking e-mail less frequently reduces stress. Computers in Human Behaviour. 43 p. 220-228

37.   Perlow, L.A. & Porter, J.L. (Retrieved 04/11/2016) Making Time Off Predictable—and Required; https://hbr.org/2009/10/making-time-off-predictable-and-required

38.   Ferriss, T. (Retrieved 14/11/2016) The Art of Letting Bad Things Happen (and Weapons of Mass Distraction); http://fourhourworkweek.com/2007/10/25/weapons-of-mass-distractions-and-the-art-of-letting-bad-things-happen/

39.   World Economic Forum (Retrieved 25/10/2016) The Future of Jobs; https://www.weforum.org/reports/the-future-of-jobs

CHAPTER 8 – ON A NEW TRAJECTORY

1.   Lomborg, B. (2001) The Skeptical Environmentalist. Measuring The Real State Of The World. Cambridge. Cambridge University Press.

2.   Descartes, R., Cottingham, J., Stoothoff, R. Murdoch, D. (1985) The Philosophical Writings of Descartes. Cambridge. Cambridge University Press.

3.   Lakoff, G. & Johnson, M. (1980) Metaphors We Live By. Chicago. University of Chicago Press.

4.   Davidson, R.J., Ekman, P., Saron, C.D., Senulis, J.A, Friesen, W.V. (1990) Approach-withdrawal and cerebral asymmetry: emotional expression and brain physiology. Journal of Personality & Social Psychology. 58(2) p. 330-341

5. Schmidt, L. , Lebreton, M., Cléry-Melin, M.L., Daunizeau, J., Pessiglione, M. (2012) Neural Mechanisms Underlying Motivation of Mental Versus Physical Effort. PLOS. http://dx.doi.org/10.1371/journal.pbio.1001266

6. University of Leeds Science News. (Retrieved 09/11/2016) Nature's Batteries' May Have Helped Power Early Lifeforms; https://www.leeds.ac.uk/news/article/817/natures_batteries_may_have_helped_power_early_lifeforms

7. Törnroth-Horsefield S & Neutze R (2008) Opening and closing the metabolite gate". Proc. Natl. Acad. Sci. U.S.A. 105 (50) p. 19565–19566

8. Wykowska, A. Anderl, C., Schubö, A. & Hommel, B. (2013) Motivation Modulates Visual Attention: Evidence from Pupillometry. Frontiers in Psychology. 4 (59) doi: 10.3389/fpsyg.2013.00059

9. Smil, V. (2006) Transforming the Twentieth Century: Technical Innovations and Their Consequences. Oxford. Oxford University Press.

10. Roser, M. (2016) (Retrieved 08/11/2016) Life expectancy; https://ourworldindata.org/life-expectancy/

11. Shkolnikov, V., Barbieri, M., Wilmoth, J. (Retrieved 09/11/2016) The Human Mortality Database; http://www.mortality.org/

12. Wood, L. (Retrieved 09/11/2016) Antiaging Products and Services Report 2016: The Global Market to 2020 for the $300+ Billion Industry - Research and Markets; http://www.businesswire.com/news/home/20160318005285/en/Antiaging-Products-Services-Report-2016-Global-Market

13. World Health Organization (Retrieved 23/10/2016) The top 10 causes of death; http://www.who.int/mediacentre/factsheets/fs310/en/

14. Booth, F.W., Roberts, C.K., Laye, M.J (2012) Lack of Exercise is a Major Cause of Chronic Disease. Compr Pysiol. 2 p. 1143-1211

15. Morris, J.N., Heady, J.A., Raffle, P.A., Roberts, C.G, Parks, J.W (1953) Coronary heart-disease and physical activity of work. Lancet. 265 (6795) p. 1053–1057

16. Morris, J.N., Crawford, M.D (1958) Coronary Heart Disease and Physical Activity of Work. BMJ. 2 (5111) p. 1485–1496.

17. Basset DR & Howley ET (2000). Limiting factors for maximum oxygen uptake and determinants of endurance performance. Med & Sci Sports & Exerc 32. p. 70 – 84

18. Lazarus, N.R. & Harridge, S.D. (2010) Exercise, physiological function, and the selection of participants for aging research. Journals of Gerontology Biological Sciences and Medical Sciences. 65(8) p.854-857

19. Tanaka, H. & Seals, D.R. (2003) Invited Review: Dynamic exercise performance in Masters athletes: insight into the effects of primary human aging on physiological functional capacity. Journal of Applied Physiology. 95(5):2152-2162

20. Hawkins, S. & Wiswell, R. (2003) Rate and mechanism of maximal oxygen consumption decline with

aging: implications for exercise training. Sports Medicine. 33(12) p.877-888

21. Lazarus, N.R. & Harridge, S.D.R. (2007) Inherent ageing in humans: the case for studying master athletes. Scandinavian Journal of Medicine & Science in Sports. p. 17 (5) p. 461–463

22. World Masters Athletics (Retrieved 13/11/2016) Index of records; http://www.world-masters-athletics.org/records/

23. Cadore, E.L., Casas-Herrero, A., Zambom-Ferraresi, F., Idoate, F., Millor, N., Gómez, M., Rodriguez-Mañas, L., Izquierdo, M.(2014) Multicomponent exercises including muscle power training enhance muscle mass, power output, and functional outcomes in institutionalized frail nonagenarians. Age. 36(2) p.773-785

24. Vidoni, E. et. al. (2015). Dose-Response of Aerobic Exercise on Cognition: A Community-Based, Pilot Randomized Controlled Trial. PLoS One: e0131647

25. Berman, M. et. al. (2008) The Cognitive Benefits of Interacting With Nature. Psychological Science. 19 (12): p. 1207-1212

26. Stathopoulos, N. et al. (2013) Epigenetic regulation on gene expression induced by physical exercise. Journal of musculoskeletal & neuronal interactions. 13 (2) p.133-146

27. Wattles, M. & Harris, C. (2003) The relationship between fitness levels and employee's perceived productivity, job satisfaction and absenteeism. Journal of Exercise Physiology. 6 (1) p. 24-32

28. Conn, V.S. et al. (2009) Meta-analysis of quality-of-life outcomes from physical activity interventions. Nurs Res. 58 (3) p. 175-183

29. Morbidity and Mortality Weekly Report (Retrieved 13/11/2016) Trends in leisure-time physical activity by age , sex, and race/ethnicity—United States 1994–2004; https://www.cdc.gov/mmwr/preview/mmwrhtml/mm5439a5.htm

30. Patel, A.V., Bernstein, L., Deka, A., Feigelson, H.S, Campbell, P.T, Gapstur, S.M, Colditz, G.A, Thun, M.J. (2010) Leisure time spent sitting in relation to total mortality in a prospective cohort of US adults. American Journal of Epidemiology. 172(4) p.419-429

31. Office of Disease Prevention and Health Promotion. (Retrieved 11/11/2016) Chapter 2: Physical Activity Has Many Health Benefits; https://health.gov/paguidelines/guidelines/chapter2.aspx

32. Owen, N., Healy, G. N., Matthres, C.E. & Dunstan, D.W. (2012) Too Much Sitting: The Population-Health Science of Sedentary Behavior. Exerc Sport Sci Rev. 38(3) p. 105–113

33. Katzmarzyk, P.T., Church, T.S., Craig, C.L, Bouchard, C. (2009) Sitting time and mortality from all causes, cardiovascular disease, and cancer. Medicine and Science in Sports and Exercise. 41(5) p.998-1005

34. Van der Ploeg, H.P., Chey, T., Korda, R.J., Banks, E., Bauman, A. (2012) Sitting time and all-cause mortality risk in 222 497 Australian adults. Archives of Internal Medicine. 172(6) p.494-500

35. Morgan, A.L., Tobar, D.A., Snyder, L. (2010) Walking toward a new me: the impact of prescribed walking 10,000 steps/day on physical and psychological well-being. Journal of Physical Activity &

Health. 7(3) p. 299-307.

36.   Choi, B.C., Pak, A.W., Choi, J.C., Choi, E.C. (2007) Daily step goal of 10,000 steps: a literature review. Clinical and Investigative Medicine. 30(3) p.146-151

37.   ACSM (Retrieved 13/11/2016) High Intensity Interval Training; http://www.acsm.org/docs/brochures/high-intensity-interval-training.pdf

38.   Yin, F., Sancheti, H., Liu, Z., Cadenas, E. (2016) Mitochondrial function in ageing: coordination with signalling and transcriptional pathways. The Journal of Physiology. 594(8) p. 2025-2042

39.   Stöggl, T. & Sperlich, B. (2014) Polarized training has greater impact on key endurance variables than threshold, high intensity, or high volume training. Frontiers in physiology. 4.

40.   Gibala, M.J. & McGee, S.L. (2008) Metabolic adaptations to short-term high-intensity interval training: a little pain for a lot of gain? Exercise and Sport Sciences Reviews 36(2)p. 58-63

41.   Kilpatrick, M., Jung, M.E., Little, J.P. (2013) High-intensity interval training: A review of physiological and psychological responses. ACSM Health & Fitness Journal 18(5) p.11-16

42.   Jung, M. & Little, J. Taking a HIIT for physical activity: is interval training viable for improving health. Paper presented at the American College of Sports Medicine Annual Meeting: Indianapolis (IN). American College of Sports Medicine.

43.   Milanović, Z., Sporiš, G., Weston, M. (2015) Effectiveness of High-Intensity Interval Training (HIT) and Continuous Endurance Training for VO_2max Improvements: A Systematic Review and Meta-Analysis of Controlled Trials. Sports Medicine. 45(10) p.1469-1481

44.   Metcalfe, R. S. et al. (2012) Towards the minimal amount of exercise for improving metabolic health: beneficial effects of reduced-exertion high-intensity interval training. European Journal of Applied Physiology. 112(7) p. 2767-2775

45.   National Aeronautics & Space Administration (NASA) (Retrieved 13/11/2016) Effect of Prolonged Space Flight on Human Skeletal Muscle (Biopsy) - 07.14.16; http://www.nasa.gov/mission_pages/station/research/experiments/245.html

46.   Karsten, K. & Martin, E. (2013) Strength and muscle mass loss with aging process. Age and strength loss. Muscles Ligaments and Tendons Journal. 3(4) p.346–350

47.   Power et al. (2012) Motor unit survival in lifelong runners is muscle dependent. Med Sci Sports Exerc.; 44(7):1235-42

48.   Artero, E.G., Lee, D., Lavie, C.J., España-Romero, V., Sui, X., Church, T.S., Blair, S.N. (2013) Effects of Muscular Strength on Cardiovascular Risk Factors and Prognosis. Journal of Cardiopulmonary Rehabilitation and Prevention. 32 (6) p. 351–358

49.   Srikanthan & Karlamangla (2014) Muscle mass index as a predictor of longevity in older adults. Am J Med.; 127(6):547-53

50.   Reid, K.F. & Fielding, R.A. (2012) Skeletal Muscle Power: A Critical Determinant of Physical Functioning In Older Adults. Exercise and Sport Sciences Reviews. 40(1) p. 4–12

51.   Peterson, M.D., Sen, A., Gordon, P.M. (2012) Influence of Resistance Exercise on Lean Body Mass in Aging Adults: A Meta-Analysis. Medicine & Science in Sport & Exercise. 43(2) p.249–258

52.   Chafkin, M. (Retrieved 24/10/2016) Yahoo's Marissa Mayer on Selling a Company While Trying to Turn It Around; https://www.bloomberg.com/features/2016-marissa-mayer-interview-issue/

53.   Knutson, K.L., Spiegel, K., Penev, P., Van Cauter, E. (2007) The Metabolic Consequences of Sleep Deprivation. Sleep Medicine Reviews. 11(3) p.163–178

54.   Havekes, R., Park, A.J., Tudor, J.C. Luczak, V.G., Hansen, R.T., Ferri, S.L., Bruinenberg, V.M., Poplawski, S.G., Day, J.P., Aton, S.J., Radwańska, K. Meerlo. P., Houslay, M.D., Baillie, G.S. & Abel, T. (2016) Sleep deprivation causes memory deficits by negatively impacting neuronal connectivity in hippocampal area CA1. eLife 5:e13424

55.   Mazza, S., Gerbier, E., Gustin, M.P., Kasikci, Z., Koenig, O., Toppino, T.C., Magnin, M. (2016) Re-learn Faster and Retain Longer Along With Practice, Sleep Makes Perfect. Psychological Science. 27 (10) p.1321-1330

56.   Immordino-Yang, M.H., Christodoulou, J.A. & Singh, V. (2014) Rest Is Not Idleness: Implications of the Brain's Default Mode for Human Development and Education. Perspectives on Psychological Science. 7 (4) p. 352-364

57.   Nedeltcheva, A.V. & Scheer, F.A. (2014) Metabolic effects of sleep disruption, links to obesity and diabetes. Current Opinion in Endocrinology, Diabetes and Obesity. 21(4) p.293-298

58.   Mesarwi, O., Polak, J., Jun, J. & Polotsky, V.Y. (2013) Sleep disorders and the development of insulin resistance and obesity. Endocrinology Metabolism Clinics of North America. 42(3) p.617–634

59.   Blask, D.E. (2009) Melatonin, sleep disturbance and cancer risk. Sleep Medicine Reviews. 13 p. 257–264

60.   Nelesen, R. PhD, Dar, Y., Thomas, K., Dimsdale, J.E. (2008) The Relationship Between Fatigue and Cardiac Functioning. Archives of Internal Medicine. 168(9) p.943–949

61.   Thompson, W.R. (2016). Worldwide survey of fitness trends for 2017: 10th anniversary edition. ACSM Health Fitness Journal. 20 (6) p. 8–17

62.   Dempsey, W., Liao, P. Klasnja, P., Nahum-Shani, I., Murphy, S.A. (2015) Randomised trials for the Fitbit generation. Significance. 12 (6) p. 20–23

63.   Patel, M.S., Asch, D.A., Volpp, K.G. (2015) Viewpoint: Wearable Devices as Facilitators, Not Drivers, of Health Behavior Change. Journal of the American Medical Assoication. 313(5) p. 459-460

64.   Figueiro M.G., Wood, B., Plitnick, B. & Rea, M.S. (2011) The impact of light from computer monitors on melatonin levels in college students. Neuro Endocrinology Letters. 32(2) p.158-63

65.   Van de Borne, P. Mark, A.L., Montano, N., Mion, D., Somers, V.K. (1997) Effects of Alcohol on Sympathetic Activity, Hemodynamics, and Chemoreflex Sensitivity. Hypertension. 29 (6) p. 1278-1283

66.   Rainmaker, DC (Retrieved 26/11/2016) Basis B1 Watch In-Depth Review; https://www.dcrainmaker.com/2013/07/basis-b1-review.html

67.   LeWine, H. (Retrieved 26/11/2016) Increase in resting heart rate is a signal worth watching; http://www.health.harvard.edu/blog/increase-in-resting-heart-rate-is-a-signal-worth-watching-201112214013

68.   Jensen, M.T, Suadicani, P., Hein, H.O., Gyntelberg, F. (2013) Elevated resting heart rate, physical fitness and all-cause mortality: a 16-year follow-up in the Copenhagen Male Study. Heart. 99(12) p.882-887

69.   Souto Barreto, P., Cesari, M., Andrieu, S., Vellas, B., Rolland, Y. (2016) Physical Activity and Incident Chronic Diseases: A Longitudinal Observational Study in 16 European Countries. American Journal of Preventive Medicine. doi: 10.1016/j.amepre.2016.08.028

CHAPTER 9 – INSPIRED & IN CONTROL

1.   Newsom, J.T., Huguet, N., Ramage-Morin, P.L., McCarthy, M.J. Bernier, J. Kaplan, M.S. & McFarland, B.H. (2012) Health behaviour changes after diagnosis of chronic illness among Canadians aged 50 or older. Health Reports. 23(4) p. 49–53

2.   Jack, A.I., Boyatzis, R.E, Khawaja, M.S., Passarelli, A.M, Leckie, R.L. (2013) Visioning in the brain: an fMRI study of inspirational coaching and mentoring. Social Neuroscience. 8(4) p.369-384

3.   Goleman, D. (2013) Focus: The Hidden Driver Of Excellence. London. Bloomsbury.

4.   Goleman, D. (2009) Emotional Intelligence. London. Bloomsbury.

5.   Salovey, P. & Mayer, J.D. (1990) Emotional Intelligence. Imagination, Cognition and Personality. 9 (3) p.185-211

6.   World Economic Forum (Retrieved 25/10/2016) The Future of Jobs; https://www.weforum.org/reports/the-future-of-jobs

7.   Pessoa L., Ungerleider LG. (2004) Neuroimaging studies of attention and the processing of emotion-laden stimuli. Prog Brain Res. 144 p.171–182

8.   Goldstein M., Brendel G., Tuescher O., et al. (2007) Neural substrates of the interaction of emotional stimulus processing and motor inhibitory control: an emotional linguistic go/no-go fMRI study. Neuroimage. 36 p. 1026–1040.

9.   Verbruggen F., De Houwer J. (2007) Do emotional stimuli interfere with response inhibition? Evidence from the stop signal paradigm. Cogn Emotion. 21 p.391–403.

10.   Bar-On, R., Tranel, D., Denburg, N.L., Bechara, A. (2003) Exploring the neurological substrate of emotional and social intelligence. Brain. 126(8) p. 1790-1800

11.   Isaacson, W. (2011) Steve Jobs. New York. Simon & Schuster.

12.   Horwitch, M. & Whipple, M. (Retrieved 31/10/2016) Leaders Who Inspire: A 21st-Century Approach to Developing Your Talent; http://www.bain.com/publications/articles/leaders-who-inspire.aspx

13. Cherniss, C. (Retrieved 06/11/2016) The Business Case for Emotional Intelligence; http://www.ei-consortium.org/reports/business_case_for_ei.html

14. Pearce, C.L., & Manz, C.C.(Retrieved 03/11/2016) The New Silver Bullets of Leadership: The Importance of Self- and Shared Leadership in Knowledge Work". Management Department Faculty Publications; http://digitalcommons.unl.edu/cgi/viewcontent.cgi?article=1074&context=managementfacpub

15. Gander, F., Proyer, R.T., Ruch, W. & Wyss, T. (2013) Strength-based positive interventions: further evidence for their potential in enhancing well-being and alleviating depression. Journal of Happiness Studies. 14 (4) p. 1241-1259

16. Proyer, R. T., Gander, F., Wellenzohn, S., & Ruch, W. (2014) Positive psychology interventions in people aged 50–79 years: long-term effects of placebo-controlled online interventions on well-being and depression. Aging & Mental Health, 18(8) p. 997-1005.

17. Peterson, C. & Seligman, M. (2004) Character Strengths & Virtues: A Handbook and Classification. Oxford. Oxford University Press.

18. Wu, C., Odden, M.C., Fisher, G.G., Stawsk, R.S. (2016) Association of retirement age with mortality: a population-based longitudinal study among older adults in the USA. Journal of Epidemiology and Community Health. doi:10.1136/jech-2015-207097

19. Steffens, N.K. Cruwys, T., Haslam, C., Jetten, J., Haslam, S.A. (2016) Social group memberships in retirement are associated with reduced risk of premature death: evidence from a longitudinal cohort study. British Medical Journal Open. doi:10.1136/bmjopen-2015-010164

20. Barraza, J.A. & Zak, P.J. (2009) Empathy toward strangers triggers oxytocin release and subsequent generosity. Annals of the New York Academy of Sciences. 1167 p. 182-189

21. Gouin, J.P., Carter, C.S, Pournajafi-Nazarloo, H., Glaser, R., Malarkey, W.B, Loving. T.J, Stowell, J., Kiecolt-Glaser, J.K. (2010) Marital behavior, oxytocin, vasopressin, and wound healing. Psychoneuroendocrinology. 35(7) p.1082–1090

22. Kellogg, R. (1999). An Analysis of Meaning Making. The Psychology of Writing. New York. Oxford University Press.

23. Oleynick, V.C., Thrash, T.M., LeFew, M.C. Moldovan, E.G. & Kieffaber, P.D. (2014) The scientific study of inspiration in the creative process: challenges and opportunities. Frontiers In Human Neuroscience. 8: 436

24. Horwitch, M. & Callahan, M.W. (Retrieved 06/11/2016) How Leaders Inspire: Cracking the Code; http://www.bain.com/publications/articles/how-leaders-inspire-cracking-the-code.aspx

25. Garton, E. & Mankins, M.C. (Retrieved 06/11/2016) Engaging Your Employees Is Good, but Don't Stop There; https://hbr.org/2015/12/engaging-your-employees-is-good-but-dont-stop-there

26. Wenger, J. & Folkman, J. (2009) The Extraordinary Leader: Turning Good Managers into Great Leaders, 2nd Ed. New York. McGraw-Hill Education.

27.   Buckner, R. L.; Andrews-Hanna, J. R.; Schacter, D. L. (2008). "The Brain's Default Network: Anatomy, Function, and Relevance to Disease". Annals of the New York Academy of Sciences. 1124 (1): 1–38. doi:10.1196/annals.1440.011. PMID 18400922.

28.   Immordino-Yang, M.H., Christodoulou, J.A. & Singh, V. (2014) Rest Is Not Idleness: Implications of the Brain's Default Mode for Human Development and Education. Perspectives on Psychological Science. 7 (4) p. 352-364

29.   Schlegel, R.J. Hicks, J.A., Arndt, J. & King, L.A. (2009) Thine Own Self: True Self-Concept Accessibility and Meaning in Life. Journal of Personality and Social Psychology. 96(2) p. 473–490

30.   Schmidt, L. , Lebreton, M., Cléry-Melin, M.L., Daunizeau, J., Pessiglione, M. (2012) Neural Mechanisms Underlying Motivation of Mental Versus Physical Effort. PLOS. http://dx.doi.org/10.1371/journal.pbio.1001266

31.   Wykowska, A. Anderl, C., Schubö, A. & Hommel, B. (2013) Motivation Modulates Visual Attention: Evidence from Pupillometry. Frontiers in Psychology. 4 (59) doi: 10.3389/fpsyg.2013.00059

32.   Massar, S.A.A., Lim, J., Sasmita, K., Chee, M.W.L. (2016) Rewards boost sustained attention through higher effort: A value-based decision making approach. Biological Psychology. 120. p.21–27

CHAPTER 10 – RUN & FINISH WELL

1.   Seligman, M.P. Afterword. In Seligman, M.P., Railton, P., Baumeister, R.F., Chandra, S. (2016) Homo Prospectus.

2.   Abell, D.F. (1993) Managing with dual strategies: Mastering the present, preempting the future. New York. The Free Press.

3.   Seligman, M. E. P (Retrieved 18/11/2016) Flourish: Positive Psychology and Positive Interventions. The Tanner Lectures on Human Values; http://tannerlectures.utah.edu/_documents/a-to-z/s/Seligman_10.pdf

4.   Wood, A.M. et al. (2009) Gratitude Uniquely Predicts Satisfaction with Life: Incremental Validity Above the Domains and Facets of the Five Factor Model. Personality and Individual Differences. 45(1) p. 49-54

5.   Jack, A.I., Boyatzis, R.E, Khawaja, M.S., Passarelli, A.M, Leckie, R.L. (2013) Visioning in the brain: an fMRI study of inspirational coaching and mentoring. Social Neuroscience. 8(4) p.369-384

6.   Carstensen, L.L. & Mikels, J.A. (2005) At the Intersection of Emotion and Cognition Aging and the Positivity Effect. Current Directions in Psychological Science. 14(3) p. 117-121

7.   Brickman, P., Coates, D., Janoff-Bulman, R. (1978) Lottery winners and accident victims: Is happiness relative? Journal of Personality and Social Psychology. 36. p. 917-927

8.   Diener, E., Lucas, R.E., & Scollon, C.N. (2006) Beyond the hedonic treadmill. American Psychologist. 6. p. 305-314.

9.   Aristotle, Brown, L. & Ross, D. (2009) The Nicomachean Ethics. Oxford. Oxford University Press.

10.   Srivastava, K. (2011) Positive mental health and its relationship with resilience. Ind Psychiatry J. 20(2). p. 75–76.

11.   Reivich KJ, Seligman ME, McBride S. (2011) Master resilience training in the U.S. Army. Am Psychol. 66. p. 25–34.

12.   Crum A.J, Salovey P, Achor S. (2013) Rethinking stress: the role of mindsets in determining the stress response. Journal of Personality and Social Psychology. p. 716-733

13.   Crum A.J, Salovey P, Achor S. (2013) Rethinking stress: the role of mindsets in determining the stress response. Journal of Personality and Social Psychology. p. 716-733

14.   Raysmith, B.P. & Drew, M.K. (2016) Performance success or failure is influenced by weeks lost to injury and illness in elite Australian track and field athletes: A 5-year prospective study. Journal of Science and Medicine in Sport. 19 (10) p.778–783

15.   Duckworth, A. (2016) Grit. London. Vermilion.

16.   Sheldon, K.M., Jose, P.E. Kashdan, T.B. Jarden, A. (2015) Personality, effective goal-striving, and enhanced well-being: comparing 10 candidate personality strengths. Personality & Social Psychology Bulletin 41(4) p. 575-585

17.   Plisk, S. S., & Stone, M. H. (2003) Periodization Strategies. Strength & Conditioning Journal, 25(6), 19-37

18.   Fry, R. W., Morton, A. R., & Keast, D. (1992) Periodisation and the prevention of overtraining. Canadian journal of sport sciences. 17(3) p. 241-248

19.   Deci, E. L., & Ryan, R. M. (1985). Intrinsic motivation and self-determination in human behavior. New York. Plenum.

20.   Deci, E. L., & Ryan, R. M. (2000). The "what" and "why" of goal pursuits: Human needs and the self-determination of behavior. Psychological Inquiry. 11 p. 227-268

21.   Ryan, R. M., & Deci, E. L. (2000). Self-determination theory and the facilitation of intrinsic motivation, social development, and well-being. American Psychologist. 55 p. 68-78

Printed in Great Britain
by Amazon

35859769R00154